THE GOSPEL OF PROGRESSIVISM

THE Gospel OF
PROGRESSIVISM

Moral Reform and Labor War in Colorado, 1900–1930

R. TODD LAUGEN

Foreword by

STEPHEN J. LEONARD

UNIVERSITY PRESS OF COLORADO

© 2010 by the University Press of Colorado

Published by the University Press of Colorado
5589 Arapahoe Avenue, Suite 206C
Boulder, Colorado 80303

 The University Press of Colorado is a proud member of
the Association of American University Presses.

The University Press of Colorado is a cooperative publishing enterprise supported, in part,
by Adams State College, Colorado State University, Fort Lewis College, Mesa State College,
Metropolitan State College of Denver, University of Colorado, University of Northern
Colorado, and Western State College of Colorado.

∞ The paper used in this publication meets the minimum requirements of the American
National Standard for Information Sciences—Permanence of Paper for Printed Library
Materials. ANSI Z39.48-1992

Library of Congress Cataloging-in-Publication Data

Laugen, R. Todd.
  The gospel of progressivism : moral reform and labor war in Colorado, 1900–1930 /
R. Todd Laugen.
    p. cm. — (Timberline books)
  Includes bibliographical references and index.
  ISBN 978-1-60732-052-4 (cloth : alk. paper) — ISBN 978-1-60732-053-1 (e-book) 1.
Colorado—Politics and government—1876–1950. 2. Progressivism (United States
politics)—History—20th century. 3. Labor—Colorado—History—20th century. 4. Labor
laws and legislation—Colorado—History—20th century. 5. Women—Political activity—
Colorado—History—20th century. 6. Political corruption—Colorado—History—20th
century. I. Title.
  F781.L298 2010
  978.8'031—dc22
                              2010037930
Design by Daniel Pratt

19 18 17 16 15 14 13 12 11 10   10 9 8 7 6 5 4 3 2 1

For Zoë

Contents

List of Illustrations ‖ **ix**

Acknowledgments ‖ **xi**

Foreword by Stephen J. Leonard ‖ **xv**

Introduction: The Varieties of Colorado Progressivism ‖ **1**

1. Protestant Progressives and the Denver Party Machine ‖ **11**

2. Public Enemy: Colorado Fuel and Iron or the Saloon? ‖ **41**

3. The Denver Tramway Crisis and the Struggle for
Masculine Citizenship ‖ **65**

4. The Consuming Public and the Industrial Commission ‖ **95**

5. Ben Lindsey and Women Progressives ‖ **125**

6. The Colorado Klan and the Decline of Progressivism ‖ **153**

Epilogue: The Progressive Legacy ‖ **187**

Notes ‖ **193**

Index ‖ **225**

Illustrations

1.1. Denver Breaking His Chains ‖ **16**

1.2. Ready to Grapple ‖ **19**

1.3. Speer Driving Greater Denver ‖ **28**

1.4. Speer Trampling Honest Elections ‖ **29**

2.1. The Missing "Big Stick" Discovered ‖ **48**

2.2. A Shatterer of Idols ‖ **60**

2.3. Double, Double Toil and Trouble ‖ **61**

3.1. Beggars Shouldn't Be Choosers ‖ **72**

3.2. The Thing for Labor to Fight ‖ **80**

3.3. A Bad One to Arouse ‖ **83**

6.1. The New Driver of the Colorado GOP ‖ **166**

6.2. Waiting to See the Doctor ‖ **167**

6.3. Ku Klux Klan — Ladies' Auxiliary ‖ **179**

6.4. Ku Klux Klan Montage ‖ **180**

Acknowledgments

Writing and researching can be lonely endeavors. For this reason, I dearly appreciate the assistance of so many people and groups along the way.

Financial support from various institutions proved invaluable in sustaining an initial vision of this project while I labored frugally as a graduate student. The graduate Distinguished Research Fellowship and the Gloria and Jackson Main Fellowship at the University of Colorado were a lifeline. So too were the Thomas Edwin Devaney Dissertation Fellowship from the Center for Humanities and Arts and the Emerson Humanities Fellowship from the College of Arts and Sciences. The Boulder Historical Society lent a valuable hand with its Thomas Meier Fellowship. The writing prize from the Center of the American West was deeply appreciated. After many years, I remain very grateful to these institutions.

While conducting research, I incurred debts to archivists, librarians, and activists who offered wonderful guidance and insight about sources. I benefited greatly from the help I received from David Hays in the archives at the University of Colorado at Boulder. The professional and patient staff at the Denver Public Library, Western History and Genealogy Department; the Colorado State Archives; the Colorado Historical Society; the Carnegie Library in Boulder; the Kansas Historical Society; and Library of Congress, Manuscript Division, offered tremendous assistance. A past president of the Colorado Federation of Women's Clubs, Helen Johnson, also opened her Denver office and its historical scrapbooks to me.

I deeply appreciate Darrin Pratt's early and consistent encouragement for this project. As director of the University Press of Colorado, he facilitated key revisions that enhanced the big picture and the devilish details. Daniel Pratt, Beth Svinarich, and Caroline Denney have offered able assistance with the production and marketing processes. Laura Furney saved me from some embarrassing errors and enhanced the prose significantly with her careful editing. Maria Montoya, Tom Krainz, and an anonymous reviewer at the University Press of Colorado read the entire manuscript, urging me to refine and clarify my argument. Their careful suggestions and criticisms were of enormous help. Tom also provided steady encouragement throughout the process. As editor of the *Journal of the Gilded Age and Progressive Era*, Alan Lessoff helped me develop an early version of Chapter 4. Elisabeth I. Perry, Karin Shapiro, and T. H. Baughman all read and improved conference papers that informed this manuscript. Robyn Muncy shared her expertise on the life of Josephine Roche. Reading two chapter drafts, Steve Leonard provided great insights into the quirks of Colorado history while sharpening my writing. Of course, I alone bear responsibility for any errors that remain.

Closer to home, other colleagues commented insightfully on portions of this manuscript or helped me confront the challenges of writing while teaching a heavy load. I extend my hearty thanks to a talented and dedicated cohort at Metropolitan State College of Denver: Jim Drake, John Monnett, Kim Klimek, Susan Lanman, Monys Hagen, Tom Altherr, Laura McCall, Tish Richard, Dolph Grundman, Vince C. de Baca, Ellen Slatkin, Tom McInerney, Matt Makley, Andy Muldoon, Paul Sidelko, Brian Weiser, and Justin Stephens. The MUPPETS reading group reviewed a ponderous draft chapter with remarkable forbearance. Members of the Boulder American Studies Reading Group—Mark Pittenger, Martha Gimenez, Erika Doss, and Brian DeLay—offered lively debate about how to write engaging history. At the University of Colorado, graduate colleagues Gerry Ronning, John Enyeart, Carol Byerly, Wendy Keefover-Ring, Nancy Vavra, Steve Dike, and Renee Johnson all enriched my early research on this project with wise advice and critiques. Neighborhood raconteurs Dan Baum and Margaret Knox pushed me to work harder at telling a good story. Finally, Julie Greene inspires me with her remarkable dedication as a scholar, teacher, activist, and parent. I have benefited over many years from her keen intelligence, patient counsel, and impressive example.

Family members have long kept the faith and offered their generous support as I completed this project. Robert and Marilyn Laugen, Annie and Michael Murray, Christian and Misrina Laugen, Heather Cochran and David Allen, Garrett and Janet Cochran, Deirdre Cochran, and Dan Couch all helped to keep me focused on the ultimate goal of publication. I know the process appeared confusing at times, but I dearly appreciate their abiding interest in my work. David Allen helped with an initial design of what became a fantastic cover. My grandmother, Audrey Myers Baker, offered encouragement at the start of this project, although she did not live to see it finished. Evan, Trevor, and Sasha deserve great thanks for their patience. Watching them grow wiser along with this book has been a tremendous joy. Last, Zoë has endured and still championed this project through great obstacles. Her generous spirit and deep loyalty made this book possible in so many ways. She has always served faithfully as critic and reviewer of the first and last resort. Her friendship has buoyed and sustained me throughout. To her, I dedicate this book, at last.

Foreword

Who are these men who . . . are cracking their whips over Republicans and
playing school-master to the Republican party and its conscience and convictions? . . . Some of these worthies masquerade as reformers. Their voca-
tion and ministry is to lament the sins of other people. Their stock in trade
is rancid, canting self-righteousness. They are wolves in sheep's clothing.
Their real object is office and plunder. When Dr. Johnson defined patriotism
as the last refuge of the scoundrel, he was unconscious of the then undevel-
oped capabilities and uses of the word "Reform."

—ROSCOE CONKLING, 1877

R oscoe Conkling, US senator from New York, knew how to oil a political
machine with gobs of patronage. You grease my hand with a postmaster's job or a customhouse post and I'll grease yours with fifty votes,
a hundred, or a thousand. The senator knew what worked and what did not.
"Parties," he declared, "are not built up by deportment, or by ladies' magazines, or gush." Would-be do-gooders, who favored "snivel service" and
other strange political experiments, were, in his opinion, "like grasshoppers
in the corner of the fence [which] sometimes make more noise than the flocks
that graze upon a thousand hills."

Yet for all his realpolitik, Conkling was swimming against the tide of history. He lived until 1889, long enough to see the beginning of the end of the system that created and sustained him. In 1883, Congress initiated a civil service system that in time severely limited congressmen's ability to name their supporters to federal jobs. In 1886 a young upstart, Theodore Roosevelt, gained the Republican nomination in the New York City mayoralty election. He lost, but he did not go away. In 1887 with the passage of the Interstate Commerce Act the federal government took a feeble stab at controlling railroads. Still, when Conkling died, wide-scale reform was still only mist on the horizon.

Conkling's ghost gave thanks that Roscoe did not have to endure the years between 1890 and 1917, when the waters of reform, abetted by ladies' magazines and gush, rose so high that even oligarchs such as J. P. Morgan and John D. Rockefeller had to take notice. In the 1890s, Populists insisted that the "voice of the people is the voice of God." In 1896, voters elected Republican William McKinley to the presidency as men of Conkling's stripe dodged the danger posed by William Jennings Bryan, a "vox populi" Democrat.

McKinley won reelection in 1900. His moneyed backers rejoiced, for they assumed they could control a man belittled for having no more backbone than a chocolate éclair. To their dismay, however, Theodore Roosevelt, reputedly the author of the chocolate éclair crack, became vice president, a position that put him one shot from the presidency. That fateful shot felled McKinley on September 6, 1901, and nine days later Roosevelt was president.

From their corner of the fence, ecstatic, change-sensing grasshoppers mounted a cacophonous din, hoping to sway the new man in the White House. They succeeded in part. TR shook his antitrust stick at a few corporations, vigorously protected the nation's forests and scenic wonders, and pleased reformers in other ways. His successor, William Howard Taft, seen by historians as at least a moderate reformer, lacked Roosevelt's charisma and angered the Roosevelt wing of the Republican Party. In 1912, Roosevelt ran as the Progressive Party candidate for president, Woodrow Wilson as the Democratic candidate, and Taft as a regular Republican. Together, Wilson and Roosevelt garnered more than 10 million votes. Taft, perceived as the least reform-minded, counted fewer than 4 million. Conkling's ghost sobbed.

From the 1890s into the early 1900s, reformers also flourished in Colorado. The Populists appealed to many voters because they wanted the federal government to purchase tons of silver. To Coloradans who mined silver by the ton, silver was gold and so, briefly, were the Populists. The Populist Davis H. Waite, elected governor in 1892, borrowed an image from Revelation 14:20 that terrified moderates and conservatives: "It is better, infinitely better, rather than our liberties be destroyed . . . that we should wade through a sea of blood: yes, blood to the horses' bridles." Many powerful mineowners despised Waite because he refused to help them break labor unions. Ousted in 1894, he fluttered into the wastebasket of history, a reformer inept and before his time.

John F. Shafroth, governor from 1909 to early 1913, did better. Buoyed by a coalition of laborers, moral uplifters, women's and religious groups, as well as by citizens anxious to secure efficient, honest government, he got the stiff-necked General Assembly to pass numerous Progressive measures, including giving citizens the right to initiate laws. In Denver, peppery judge Benjamin B. Lindsey donned the armor of righteousness, in his case a Prince Albert coat, to fight against child labor and for clean government. Lindsey's muckraking serialized exposé of rotten Denver politics, *The Beast*, brought the city's sins to national attention and prompted increasing numbers of Denverites to wage holy war against Mayor Robert W. Speer's corrupt machine.

Between its high-water mark in the 1912–1916 period and 1920, the reform tide ebbed so completely that those schooled in the doings of the dead could easily see the delighted bones of Roscoe Conkling dancing on his grave. Shafroth, elected to the US Senate in 1912, was ousted in 1918 by the multimillionaire Lawrence C. Phipps. Woodrow Wilson's reform ship was torpedoed by World War I. He was succeeded in 1920 by Warren Harding, a man whose commitment to domestic reform was thinner than the thinnest playing card in his slim mental deck. Ben Lindsey survived until the mid-1920s, when a combination of Ku Klux Klan forces and other enemies scuttled his career as a Denver judge.

The ups and downs of reform movements have often attracted scholarly attention. Colorado has been blessed with studies of the Populists and Progressives, most of them focusing on movers and shakers such as Edward P. Costigan, Lindsey, Shafroth, and Waite or on watershed events such as the 1914 Ludlow Massacre. Unfortunately, the habit of looking at the big animals has stolen attention from thousands of lesser creatures—prairie dogs, sparrows, noisy grasshoppers. Although lower on the food chain than mountain lions and bears, those little critters were vital to the Progressive movement.

In *The Gospel of Progressivism: Moral Reform and Labor War in Colorado, 1900–1930*, R. Todd Laugen provides a fresh view. By digging at the roots of Progressivism, by examining its coalitions and crosscurrents and its thousands of unsung supporters, he demonstrates the movement's complexity. He shows the importance of Protestant religious groups, women's clubs, and labor unions in creating the voice of the people that sustained Costigan, Lindsey, Shafroth, and other leaders. Laugen proves Roscoe Conkling wrong. Parties can be partially made of gush, deportment, canting self-righteous people, and ladies' magazines.

Tackling a thirty-year time span, Laugen sifts through layers of Progressivism, demonstrating that it did not abruptly end when Warren Harding walked into the White House. By encouraging Colorado historians to compare the reform impulse in their state with similar efforts in other states, he charts a course leading to an understanding of the complex local issues and political coalitions that undergird the national Progressive movement. In offering a well-researched and sophisticated analysis of Progressivism in one state, he provides a model valuable to scholars across the country.

R. Todd Laugen received his B.A. from the University of Virginia, his M.A. from Stanford, and his Ph.D. in 2005 from the University of Colorado at Boulder. He has taught at the University of Colorado at Boulder and the University of Denver. Since 2005 he has been an assistant professor in the History Department at Metropolitan State College of Denver, where in addition to teaching large classes he labors to educate student teachers. His pains to encourage his colleagues to embrace new teaching methods, his bicycle riding, and his residence near Boulder suggest that he too is a reformer. He is quick to point out, however, that he is not of the self-righteous, sanctimonious tribe that so offended Conkling.

The Gospel of Progressivism, Laugen's first book, provides a well-constructed template for those engaged in writing Colorado political history. His multilayered, grassroots approach gives scholars a nuanced and sophisticated view of the past. As such, it is a worthy addition to the University Press of Colorado's Timberline series, which strives to publish significant and pathbreaking works on Colorado.

STEPHEN J. LEONARD
COEDITOR OF THE TIMBERLINE SERIES

THE GOSPEL OF PROGRESSIVISM

Introduction

The Varieties of Colorado Progressivism

S oon after cofounding a new independent voters group in 1905, Denver attorney Edward Costigan appeared before the South Broadway Christian
Church to appeal for support. Although the church was not yet fifteen
years old, its Romanesque facade suggested centuries of tradition. Standing at
the altar in front of vaulted organ pipes, the Republican attorney condemned
the "evil forces" corrupting local politics. As a young Republican activist,
Costigan bridled at the violations of law and decency he had witnessed in
his brief political career. He lost election to the state Senate a few years earlier when Democrats padded the registration rolls with unqualified voters.
Democratic ward heelers had even ejected Costigan from his post as a watcher
of registration clerks while the police turned a blind eye.

In light of such brazen abuse by party operatives, the attorney insisted
that the church needed to "assert a positive, an affirmative, a practical and a
vigilant resistance." He solicited "the sanction and baptism of the church" on
his nonpartisan voters' group. With city and state representatives little more
than "creatures of certain private and selfish interests" answering ultimately to
party bosses and corporate donors, the Voters' League demanded "honest men

in public office" and "honest and untrammeled legislation in the interests of the public." The league would back candidates from either party who demonstrated independence and integrity. The audience at the South Broadway Christian Church likely shared Costigan's faith in the power of moral zeal and public exposure of political corruption. Located roughly a mile south of the more affluent Capitol Hill neighborhood, the stone church hosted Protestant congregants who did not have the financial resources of the city's elites. Yet Costigan optimistically concluded that with the help of zealous congregations, "decent government" would triumph.[1] His new voters' group helped launch a movement of religiously inspired reformers. These churchgoers would back Costigan when he later campaigned as the Progressive Party candidate for governor.

Soon after Costigan's speech, Denver labor leader H. B. Waters similarly demanded political change. Invoking the Populist tradition, Waters asked, "[S]hall the people rule or be ruled? Shall they own the government or be owned by it?" The labor leader insisted that the tools of direct democracy, the initiative and referendum, would at last enable working people to challenge corporate and party corruption of the political process. With these changes in government, "the power of bribery will be infinitely diluted. . . . The lobby will die; rings and bosses will lose their power."[2] Waters appealed directly to the working class, sharing the urgency of Costigan.

Workers too felt outrage over recent political events. Union campaigns had persuaded state legislators to grant mine workers an eight-hour day in 1899. Yet before the new law could take effect, the Colorado Supreme Court overturned it as an unconstitutional intrusion of lawmaking power. A few years later, mine workers in Cripple Creek confronted private guards and state police in pitched battles over working conditions. The deaths of thirty workers in 1903 offered a painful reminder of the chaos and inequities of economic life in Colorado. Waters believed that the tools of Progressive reform were the remedy workers needed to achieve a measure of justice and influence in government.

A comparable faith in the power of direct legislation animated activist women in Colorado during these years. Advocating these reforms in Denver, women faced "partisan treachery," "insolent and tyrannous" political bosses, and "all the powers that plunder," in the words of a sympathetic observer. Women's club leaders especially urged members to approve the initiative and referendum to counter political corruption. These tools would also enable reforming women to secure a city-owned water utility, ending the manipulations and inefficiency of a privately owned firm. Upon achieving these political changes, organized clubwomen leveled a "disconcerting blow to the . . . bosses" of both parties.[3] By 1912 an influential cohort of women's club leaders championed similar reforms at the statehouse.

These Colorado Progressives appeared to share common enemies. The party boss and the corporate lobbyist undermined honest and responsive government. As political outsiders, these reformers advanced similar solutions: direct primary elections, the initiative, and nonpartisan campaigns. All claimed to speak for the public in defense of the common good against the selfish interests of party and corporate leaders. Their political crusades, in fact, renegotiated what was public and private in social and economic realms.

A final group of Colorado Progressives invoked the public in similar terms, but with different implications. By 1915, self-proclaimed mediation experts emerged who sought to protect the consuming public from the self-interested negotiations of corporate employers and organized labor. Strikes and labor unrest interrupted economic activity in ways that state investigations could prevent, they claimed. Consumers were "the real party in interest in all disputes between employer and employe[e]," insisted one administrative Progressive in the state. They "suffer all the hardships and pay all the bills."[4] These mediation reformers, however, did not organize a movement, nor did they challenge party control over politics. Still, they proposed another Progressive opposition between the people and special interests.

These Progressive groups in Colorado relied on a common language to defend the public against special interests. Their memberships overlapped in many instances. Clubwomen and union workers attended Protestant churches. Some unionists served as mediation experts. But the leadership of each group tended to remain distinct, hoping to mobilize the public along lines of religion, class, sex, or faith in scientific investigation. They determined to root out selfish political action with public exposure.

These leaders differed in their relative influence on the political landscape of Colorado and interacted in uniquely revealing ways. Reformers and journalists relying on the language of Protestant morality successfully reshaped the framework for political debate and motivated a core of activists to advance their version of Progressivism in the state. Costigan was one of many leaders advocating "Christian citizenship." This meant nonpartisan, morally informed voting that challenged party machines and corporate corruption of politics. Its advocates insisted that prohibition and an end to prostitution and public gambling were political goals that would eliminate the rule of the party boss. Nonpartisan office holders could then defy corporate lobbyists, curb patronage-ridden government, lower taxes, and advance efficiency and economy. As one leader of Denver's Ministerial Alliance preached, "We Christians must be interested, not only in so-called moral questions, but in the whole great problem of democratic government." Another insisted that "corporations have no business in politics! They are always a corrupting element." In 1912 this minister urged his congregants to support a Progressive candidate for office and thus to "vote as you pray." Progressivism assumed the urgency of the gospel for such civic leaders.[5]

Religiously motivated political reform, however, did little to temper the dramatic confrontations between workers and corporate leaders in this rapidly industrializing western state. In communities such as Cripple Creek and Huerfano County, as well as on the tramway lines of Denver, workers challenged their bosses for control over their economic and political lives. Workplace disputes easily became violent clashes. Local and state police often proved unable to protect life and preserve order. The "class problem," which so engaged nationally recognized reformers such as Jane Addams, Paul Kellogg, and John Commons, proved particularly intense and intractable in this Rocky Mountain region.

Drawing on Colorado's Populist tradition, labor reformers advocated a more class-conscious vision of Progressivism than the religious activists. Colorado Populism began in the 1890s as a movement of farmers and workers but became increasingly non-agrarian in its focus. The election of Populist governor Davis Waite in 1892 gave workers a brief glimpse of the promise of a sympathetic government. Waite unsuccessfully confronted the depression of 1893 and the plummeting price of silver. Yet his administration defended the right of industrial workers to organize and strike for improved working conditions. With Waite's support, the demand for the eight-hour day for mine workers emerged as a key legacy of Colorado Populists.[6] Industrial laborers backed the Populists in hopes of securing economic legislation to counter and curb the power of mine owners.

Party ties to corporate monopolies, especially within the state legislature, led unionists to champion reforms to restore lost economic and political independence. In 1896, Pueblo unionists called workers together to create the Colorado State Federation of Labor (CSFL) to focus their political activism. The platform demanded the liberation of the General Assembly from "the grip of the Colorado Fuel and Iron Company and other companies who had a stranglehold on . . . the majority of legislators."[7] Monopoly power remained the chief enemy of working-class citizenship. Court injunctions and limits on striking further weakened the economic power of workers. Labor progressives consistently struggled to define the "public interest" in terms that included a living wage for workers.

Unlike Protestant Progressives, labor activists only enjoyed a few key moments of political success. These moments particularly reveal the importance of coalitions and allies within state bureaucracy. Working with women activists around 1910, labor Progressives persuaded legislators to approve the initiative, referendum, and government protections for workers. In 1912 this coalition of labor and women activists used the initiative process to enact new protections for male and female workers as well as mothers and children. World

War I provided a favorable context for the State Bureau of Labor Statistics to improve enforcement of labor law. Repeated waves of violent strikes in the state, however, undermined broad support for labor Progressivism. Even after the massacre at Ludlow in 1914, most Colorado voters demonstrated greater enthusiasm for prohibition than efforts to restrain the "barony of the Colorado Fuel and Iron Company," whose officials dominated the hinterlands of the state.[8] The labor-women's coalition fractured over moral reform.

Clearly, male industrial workers were not the sole concern of Progressive reformers. They also focused their attention on the problems of children and working-class women. Between 1902 and 1914, a number of activist women mobilized the female public to protect wage-earning women and children. They, like Protestant ministers, wanted to rid cities of prostitution and gambling. Women's club leaders joined labor activists in condemning the abusive power that business owners wielded over workers. Again, these problems were linked to party machines.

Women's club leaders appealed to their members in different terms than did labor or Protestant Progressives. The state's first female state senator, Denver clubwoman Helen Ring Robinson, insisted that women should be elected to office because they represented "the maternal in politics."[9] Motherhood suggested both a condition of vulnerability and the potential for improving a broad range of conditions outside the home. Like Chicago women in these years, Denver's women's club activists incorporated notions of maternalism, motherhood, and municipal housekeeping into a vision of a better society. This included social welfare, economic justice, and government responsiveness to citizens.[10] Although some female activists called for political changes that were not strictly maternalist, most achieved their greatest successes and forged the broadest coalitions when appealing to women as mothers.

Because Colorado's cities lacked the extensive settlement house network so important for women's politics in cities like New York and Chicago, women's clubs in Colorado offered the main sites for mobilizing a feminine public in support of Progressive reform. Enfranchised since 1893, Colorado women participated in politics more directly than their sisters in most other states. Women's club leaders made consistent efforts to rally members along feminine rather than party lines. They made journalistic appeals to the "organized women of the state" and launched educational and civic campaigns to focus the political influence of both middle- and working-class women independent of party affiliation. Although parties did offer alternatives to clubs for some activist women, most celebrated nonpartisanship.[11] Women Progressives, both within and outside the parties, secured their major legislative victories in coalitions and with key institutional allies like Denver's juvenile court, the state Board of Charities and Corrections, and the Child Welfare Bureau.

Ultimately women and labor Progressives had less impact on the class problem in Colorado than did administrative Progressives. This latter group insisted that industrial warfare could be scientifically investigated and impartially mediated. Labor peace could prevail, they insisted, without government reforms to alter the balance of power between worker and corporation. Organized labor, in the eyes of state industrial commissioners, appeared an equal competitor with capital, issuing demands based on its own selfish interests. In their view, the public interest meant an uninterrupted supply of consumer goods, even at the expense of a living wage for workers.

For all of these Progressive groups in Colorado the struggle between the people and corrupting special interests was consistently gendered. The contest to represent the public at the state and local levels often involved struggles over the political meaning of manhood and womanhood. Through political cartoons, newspaper photographs, and visual metaphors, Colorado reformers and their partisan opponents sought to represent the public as if it had inescapable implications for male and female citizenship. Protestant reformers insisted that their nonpartisan, Progressive public undergo a renegotiation of masculinity. Confronting the traditional links among party loyalty, civic activism, and male voting, religious reformers sought to replace the centrality of party organizations with nonpartisan associations of morally virtuous male citizenry.

In contrast, union visions of restrained manhood rested on Populist ideals of economic independence and alliances with sympathetic party leaders. Nonpartisanship was less important to working-class men than it was to Protestant activists. The labor ideal of manhood proved less persuasive in these years. Meanwhile, women Progressives in Colorado were often divided by partisanship, with Democrats, Republicans, and Progressive party leaders claiming to defend the mothers and children of the state. Although Progressive feminine citizenship always included suffrage, it suggested different ways of focusing maternal instincts. Administrative Progressives, for their part, assumed a paternalistic duty to protect a feminine consuming public. The weight of their interventions, however, fell much harder on union labor than on corporate elites. The success of religious and administrative Progressivism ultimately undermined class-based and maternalist-inspired reform in the state.

This story of Colorado reformers demands attention to more than a few prominent individuals. Attorneys like Edward Costigan and Judge Ben Lindsey frequently appear as the chief movers in accounts of Progressivism in the state. Yet it was lesser-known women's club and trade union leaders who broadened the scope of reform and who rallied their members in hopes of change.[12]

In rediscovering those voices, this book documents neglected coalitions and negotiations between social groups that are too easily overlooked in the narratives of individual lives. The history of women Progressives is incomplete without a careful consideration of labor and religiously motivated reformers. Although only a few individual leaders remained consistently active in Denver and Colorado politics between 1900 and 1930, the social groups that advocated reform largely endured.

This larger and more inclusive story also highlights the importance of religion, class, and rhetoric for understanding Progressivism in this western state. Scholars of the Progressives have stressed secular motivations (especially social anxieties), organizational imperatives, women's networks, structural limitations, and transnational exchanges of ideas.[13] A largely separate literature on American Protestantism has reconstructed the social gospel movement and growing demands for amelioration and mediation of class conflicts and hardships resulting from industrialization, without paying sufficient attention to the politics of Progressive reform. Although many have noted that "morally ambitious Protestantism" inspired Progressives, few have fully explored the implications of this connection. Michael McGerr has insightfully noted the extent to which Progressives targeted individual behavior as much as institutions.[14] In Colorado, the religious character of the earliest and most influential Progressives gave a moral cast to this style of political activism. They helped define reform more in terms of moral issues like prohibition than economic justice.

Class conflict in Colorado consistently jeopardized the Protestant ideal of social harmony and reconciliation. Religion often fails to appear in histories of Progressivism, but scholars have frequently commented on the middle-class backgrounds of most Progressives. Recently, local studies have also begun to illuminate "petit bourgeois" and working-class support for reform. Demands for public ownership and urban reform in cities like Detroit, Toledo, Cleveland, and San Francisco often stemmed from working-class voters. Workers demonstrated less hostility to the party system per se, allying frequently with partisan reformers to achieve their goals.[15] Colorado offers an important, if neglected, site for understanding the character of labor Progressivism, particularly in the West. Labor Progressives contested the religious character of reform and frequently allied with the Democratic Party in hopes of challenging both Protestant activists and corporate elites. The ultimate success of moral and mediation Progressives generated a suspicion of the coercive power of state interventions among Colorado workers.

If religious and class lenses shed light on the unique aspects of western Progressivism, the rhetoric of reformers reveals the ways in which politics shape social identities. Colorado Progressives typically cast their agenda in the languages of Protestantism, popular republicanism, maternalism, and efficiency. Excessive individual power, especially when sustained by party machines or corporations, threatened corruption and waste. Drawing on these political languages, reformers hoped to frame not only the goals but even the political identities of their respective social groups. An emerging sensational press, both in Denver and on the national level, presented new opportunities for these efforts. In their muckraking exposés and reform newspapers, Progressive leaders often suggested more the appearance than the reality of grassroots mobilization. Their potent collection of oppositions—the public versus the interests, the honest citizen against the boss, the people against the corporation—did not so much reflect material realities as it did structure political debate and define opportunities for political mobilization.

Studies of politics in San Francisco and Boston in these years have similarly highlighted what James Connolly called the "political sources of group identity."[16] Although Progressive leaders shared a common style of public action, they did not mobilize the same "publics." Reform leaders pushed for structural alternatives to political parties that promised to enhance the influence of their respective social groups. Given their unique use of languages of reform, the importance of Protestantism, and frustrated efforts to mobilize voters along class and gender lines, Colorado Progressives have much to tell us about political reform in the early twentieth-century West.

The regional context for these campaigns makes Progressivism in Colorado different than in Chicago, the Northeast, or the South. First, the interactions between Denver and hinterland communities profoundly shaped Progressive reform, as this book demonstrates. The capital city developed relatively quickly from mining camp to entrepôt, facilitating the economic growth of the entire state by 1900. Early political leaders were outspoken boosters, hoping to promote the city and state as a whole. As the site of the state house, Denver witnessed the debates and contests for state leadership firsthand. State campaigns and political party machines often shaded into local city government. Yet middle- and working-class residents of Denver experienced different economic and political conditions than those of workers in mining camps.

The overwhelming importance of extractive industries, especially mining, led to rapid industrialization and urbanization in mountain towns. Silver and gold mining often required significant investments of capital, technical expertise, and machinery. Large corporations brought these to bear on the challenges of extraction and came to dominate the economic landscape. As mining and railroad corporations emerged in Colorado, they encountered a stark and harsh landscape with "little political or social undergirding," noted historian Anne Hyde. Mining camps exploded into "instant cities," which were poorly planned, rootless communities. They tended to fade dramatically during the economy's bust cycles.[17] Mining workers often experienced corporate capitalism in the context of remote company towns. Their hopes for dramatic economic and political reform were vast and often more radical than those of Denver residents. In contrast, Denverites experienced rapid urbanization without large-scale industrialization. Hinterland workers were thus much more likely to find employment in large corporate enterprises than Denver laborers. In order to capture the important interactions between Denver Progressives and those workers beyond the capital city, this book shifts its geographic focus in the chapters that follow.

Second, the varied character of the Colorado electorate is another important regional factor to consider. This electorate included white women voters with limited racial minority representation during the Progressive Era. Euroamerican women were only loosely mobilized within political parties, which remained male-dominated throughout the Progressive Era. Antiparty reforms like direct democracy received strong support from the female electorate. Mexican American and African American residents, however, struggled to maintain a political voice well into the twentieth century, often relying on minimal machine and corporate backing for token minority candidates. Additionally, party loyalties among voters remained weaker in Colorado than in eastern or southern states. Both the Democratic and Republican parties had reform factions in early twentieth-century Colorado. Female and male reformers from each gained more traction when working through nonpartisan associations than within existing parties.

Third, corporate elites in the state proved remarkably resilient and resourceful in their maintenance of party organizations and manipulation of politics. Unlike business leaders in other regions who hoped to rationalize urban politics and replace the party boss with Progressive reforms like expert commissions or city managers, Denver's elites consistently opposed "good government" and antiparty reforms.[18] They preferred to control the party machines, even throwing their support behind the candidates of opposing parties in strategic elections. The managers of the industrial steelmaking and coalmining giant, Colorado Fuel and Iron, also paid much less attention to the creation and operation of new administrative bureaucracies like the Colorado Industrial Commission than they did to their bipartisan political machines. Consequently, good-government crusades in Colorado were linked with corporate critiques more often than in Chicago, Boston, or New York.

Finally, Colorado Progressivism differs from reform projects in many other states because of its connections to the Ku Klux Klan in the 1920s. The Klan initially grew when its leaders drew on the rhetoric of Protestant Progressives and co-opted reform tools like the direct primary. Creating an aggressively masculine political machine, Klan leaders captured control of the governorship and state House in November 1924. Both the Klan and Progressive organizations drew members from the ranks of Protestant churchgoers, and both championed moral renewal and prohibition.

The Colorado Klan, however, did not back Progressive reform with much sincerity. It sought to expand Progressive state agencies, but only as a means of strengthening its own political machine. Once in power, Klan legislators launched an attack on the leaders of women's and labor agencies within the state government in order to bring them under Klan control. Klan politics particularly discredited the effort to define the interests of "the public" in terms of Protestant morality.[19] Understanding Colorado Progressivism thus requires a more careful examination of state politics in the 1920s. Although many scholars mark the end of the Progressive movement with the disruptions and disappointments of World War I, Colorado reformers persevered through that conflict only to face their greatest challenge in the 1920s.

This book chronicles the negotiations of competing Progressive groups and the obstacles that constrained them through the early years of the Great Depression. It is also a story of promising alliances that were never fully realized, of zealous crusaders who resisted compromise, and of reforms that had unexpected consequences. Seen from the capital city and hinterlands, from the different perspectives of middle-class attorneys, Protestant ministers, union workers, club women, and expert administrators, Colorado Progressivism acquires the richness and complexity it deserves.

One

Protestant Progressives and the Denver Party Machine

In his second year as Denver's juvenile court judge, Benjamin Barr Lindsey invited police commissioners to his courtroom. Judge Lindsey had just begun a series of innovative reforms to help delinquent children. However, urban temptations continually led his charges astray. Gambling halls, saloons, and brothels operating chiefly in downtown Denver mixed closely with working-class homes. Numerous boys and girls had come before the judge to relate stories of easy access to alcohol, drunken children as young as four, and friends lured into prostitution. After a series of fruitless appeals to the district attorney and police to uphold city ordinances regulating closing hours and barring entry to children, Lindsey could no longer contain his frustration. When the police leadership appeared on that Saturday morning in May 1902, they were met by a crowd of boys, a handful of reporters, and the bantamweight Lindsey raring for a fight.

The kid's judge wasted little time on pleasantries. He insisted that crime was forced on poor children in the city when police so consistently refused to regulate the saloons and "gambling hells" in the downtown district. "If the surroundings of children are tainted with the foul and pestilential vapors of the evils," how could the commissioners expect his juvenile court to save them? Lindsey begged the commissioners to "war upon these places" and break the spell that the "devil's agents" had over them. Only then would the officers have the respect and goodwill of decent people of the city.[1]

Lindsey's public shaming of the Democratic police leadership was vividly reported in the newspapers. The event launched his career as a muckraker, exposing the ills of urban, industrial life in moral terms familiar especially to church-going readers. He inspired a number of clergymen to back his criticism. Although educated at Notre Dame's preparatory academy, Lindsey would not openly champion any particular faith. He celebrated the "church element" in Denver for its fight against saloons, gambling houses, and brothels on behalf of children of the city. It was "good Christian people who conquered . . . the political supporters of protected vice."[2] Like his good friend Edward Costigan, the judge increasingly recognized the political potential of Protestant voters in the city. In his first decades on the bench, he would frame his crusades for child welfare in terms that appealed to Denver's Protestant public.

For Lindsey as for many churchgoers in Denver, political corruption was linked to various sins. As a leader of the city's Progressives, Lindsey helped to define a gendered opposition between honorable, independent manly citizenship and a morally corrupting party system. Progressive reformers launched a variety of associations designed to curb voting fraud and police corruption. They demanded an end to party reliance on private utilities, saloon owners, gamblers, and prostitutes. Even the municipal ownership of utilities assumed the character of a religious reform in Denver, given perceptions of an insidious network linking Mayor Speer's administration with saloon and utility owners. Temperance advocates also exerted a strong influence within Denver's Protestant crusade, advancing local option along with structural reforms to end the reign of the party machine. Local option would have allowed voters to ban saloons within their designated neighborhoods.

The main target of Protestant reformers in early twentieth-century Denver was Mayor Robert Walter Speer's Democratic Party machine. These reformers worked to link Speer with all the evils of urban life, particularly highlighting those that threatened moral purity. Speer had only recently ended his service on the Fire and Police Board when Lindsey leveled his accusations against law enforcement officials. Control over the police was crucial to party-machine success. Progressive leaders and their Protestant allies insisted that decency, transparency, and Christian morality guide city government. Yet Mayor Speer offered a different vision for the municipal public, one stressing the compromise of competing group interests and the need for coalition building. A booster at heart, Speer sought to expand urban infrastructure and create the City Beautiful by enlisting the support of Denver's elite and employing a significant section of its working class. Between 1902 and 1912,

Progressive reformers and their Protestant supporters battled Boss Speer for control of Denver.

PARTY AND CORPORATE ALLIANCES IN NINETEENTH-CENTURY COLORADO

In 1900, Speer's party machine was hardly unique on the political landscape. Parties and corporations had developed in mutually beneficial ways in late nineteenth-century Colorado. Along with other western states, Coloradans created political institutions in the heated context of rapid industrialization and consolidating corporate capitalism. After 1865 the Republican Party devoted the resources of a recently unified federal government to support the Euroamerican settlement of the state. Republicans dominated Colorado's politics from its territorial days through the 1890s.[3]

Denver grew rapidly from the 1880s through 1910 because of mining expansion in the Rockies. A transcontinental rail link in the 1870s helped transform Denver into a financial and commercial center to serve previously isolated mining camps. Denver became primarily a distribution and collection point and never developed substantial heavy industry, although mining corporations opened smelters in the city. Its manufacturing was diversified and oriented toward regional markets. Stockyards and meatpacking plants processed growing numbers of livestock raised in the state. Yet city boosters relied chiefly on the fortunes of mining and railroad owners to build urban infrastructure and fund party campaigns while keeping tax rates low.

Because of these developments, political parties functioned differently in this western state than in the East or South. First, party organizations remained weaker and yet more dependent on corporate backing in Colorado than in the northeast. Bipartisan corporate funding limited interparty competition across much of the state. Additionally, Colorado voters were more likely to split tickets and switch parties on the basis of short-term issues. Ethno-cultural divisions proved less salient here than in the East, at least until the Progressive Era.[4]

By 1900 both the Republican and Democratic parties had developed political machines with ties to utilities in Denver. Controlling the downtown precincts with election monitors and sympathetic police support was only one tactic. Denver reformer George Creel insisted that the "tramway company, the water company, the telephone company, the coal companies, the smelters—all operating as a unit—controlled both parties and named both tickets in every election."[5] Parties also falsified voter registration records and cast ballots for the dead. Judge Lindsey gave a name to this network of party activists, saloonkeepers, and utility sponsors in early twentieth-century Denver— "the Beast."

Party and corporate dominance over politics in the city had generated potent nineteenth-century opposition. The Populist campaigns of the 1890s offered a broad critique of corporate consolidation in industry in hopes of revitalizing democracy. A Farmers' Alliance organizer in Colorado insisted in 1890 that "the toilers of the earth have become the mere vassals of the railway potentates, and the victims of the political leaders of both parties who . . . serve them." Mobilizing behind gubernatorial candidate Davis Waite in 1892, farmers and laborers elected the entire Populist state ticket that year. Governor Waite railed against a "ruthless plutocracy" and briefly challenged Republican dominance. Populist electoral success inspired the hope that, in the words of one zealous supporter, "Colorado, at last, has been lifted up out of the political cess-pools of degenerated filth."[6] Confronting the devastating depression of 1893 with a tenuous coalition, however, Populists achieved few of their reform goals save the passage of a measure granting women full suffrage in 1893. Governor Waite did earn the enduring gratitude of workers and opprobrium of corporate owners for his defense of striking miners at Cripple Creek in 1894. His defiance of mine-owner power shaped Populism as a radical movement, appealing chiefly to foreign-born workers.

In the mid-1890s, Denver reformers challenged utility and party dominance through a range of civic associations. A reform mayor in 1895 endorsed the program of the Taxpayers' Reform Association. This association called for a separation between city hall and the utilities, hoping to reduce taxes and curb corruption. Several Denver clubwomen joined together in these years to form the Civic Federation, modeled on the Chicago organization of the same name, to promote honest elections, nonpartisan city administration, and municipal ownership of utilities. Protestant activists in the Anti-Saloon League and Denver's Ministerial Alliance endorsed these campaigns. Reform mayors Platt Rodgers (1891–1893) and Thomas McMurray (1895–1899) had drawn on discontent in the new suburbs to challenge the saloon–party machine network. Yet in 1899, McMurray lost to a Democratic candidate with ties to the tramway utility.[7] Progressives in the twentieth century would expand on these crusades.

HOME RULE FOR DENVER

The struggle over home rule for Denver between 1899 and 1904 led Protestant reformers to mobilize politically in hopes of remaking city politics. Responding to growing calls for a city government independent of the governor and his partisan loyalists, Denver attorney John Rush introduced Senate Bill 2 in 1901. The Rush bill proposed a separate City and County of Denver with elected, not governor-appointed, officials. As passed that spring, the Rush Act called for voters to ratify a new article to the state constitution. Rush created the

Municipal League to advocate for passage, assuring voters home rule would lower property taxes and ensure efficient administration. After voters overwhelmingly approved home rule in 1902, religiously motivated reformers began to mobilize.

The first charter convention met over the summer of 1903 and reformers dominated the proceedings. Members included the director of the recently formed Honest Elections League, journalist Ed Keating at the *Rocky Mountain News*, Denver Woman's Club members such as Ellis Meredith, and several from the Women's Christian Temperance Union. Wealthy flour miller and temperance advocate John K. Mullen was a Catholic participant. Although some Catholics and even a few Jewish leaders shared the crusading zeal of many Protestant Progressives, they were typically underrepresented among reformers. Behind the leadership of John Rush, convention members drafted a charter that called for tight regulation of utilities, civil service requirements for city boards, and at-large elections for councilmen. The proposal included provisions to close "disreputable" saloons and abolish gambling.[8] Hopes for moral renewal were joined with calls for efficiency and lower taxes.

Protestant activists quickly took up the campaign for this moral charter. The campaign sparked Protestants to create new political organizations across the city. Foremost among these was the Denver Christian Citizenship Union, a group led by Protestant ministers in affluent neighborhoods. The director was Harry Fisher, who advocated a host of Progressive reforms in early twentieth-century Denver, especially in partnership with Judge Ben Lindsey. In September 1903, Fisher insisted that "Christian people are awake" and would "rally to the standard of good citizenship" and "public spirit" to vote for the charter. The Christian Citizenship Union held numerous pro-charter rallies in churches across Denver in the weeks leading up to the citywide vote.[9]

Democratic senator Thomas Patterson also threw the full weight of his newspaper, *The Rocky Mountain News*, behind the effort. The moral charter campaign initiated a discursive contest to define the character of masculine citizenship in Denver. A front-page cartoon in support of the moral charter depicted a brawny but shackled male "Denver" breaking the fetters of "Corporation Rule," "Bossism," the "Gang Machine," "Election Frauds," and not least "High Taxes!" by means of this reform charter (Figure 1.1).

The challenge to boss and corporate rule would require the muscle and determination of a physical struggle. The cartoon projected an assertion of masculine strength by the Christian activists. The illustration projected the views of the paper's political editor, charter convention member Ed Keating, in prominent terms. Initially a Democratic activist, Keating became a leading spokesperson for the moral charter on behalf of religious Progressives. With their moral charter campaign, reformers like Keating defined their muscular Christian ideal for urban government. His Catholicism did not interfere with

BREAKING THE FETTERS—A FORECAST FOR TUESDAY.

1.1. DENVER BREAKING HIS CHAINS (*ROCKY MOUNTAIN NEWS*, OCTOBER 20, 1903)

his partnership with the otherwise Protestant Christian Citizenship Union. They shared a desire to enact civil service rules to undermine party machines and liberate the enslaved male citizen, temperance to curb the influence of the saloon, and regulations to curtail lobbying and campaign spending by utility corporations.

Several prominent women's club leaders backed the moral charter, appealing to women voters with less masculine and more maternal rhetoric. Julia Welles stumped for the charter at Christian Union meetings in Protestant churches throughout the city. She particularly stressed its poor relief provisions. For Welles, the charter deserved support largely because the enemies it had generated—utility and saloon owners, the city Democratic Party machine—threatened feminine virtue. The women's executive committee of the Denver County Democratic Party even endorsed the moral charter over the objection of the Democratic men. One member argued that it stood "for a broader morality" and "protection for the young." The activist also noted that the moral charter should result "in a lower rate of taxation by cutting down the expenses of city government, and that as the bulk of taxes upon small homes are paid by women . . . they should all be in favor."[10] Again moral appeals were combined with hopes for fiscal restraint. Yet the Denver Christian Citizenship Union relied more on its male leadership, as supportive women tended to assume secondary roles in the struggle for the home rule charter.

ROBERT SPEER AND THE DEMOCRATIC MACHINE

As religious Progressives appealed for charter support on the eve of the election, they noted the opposition of both party organizations along with the "liquor interest, the breweries, and the liberal element." These opponents feared that the moral charter would destroy party organizations and constrain saloons and gambling.[11] Coordinating this opposition was the head of Denver's Board of Public Works and the city's Democratic machine, Robert Speer. Many urban workers formed a significant base of support for Speer, having already forged ties to his Democratic machine.

Born in 1855, Speer moved from Pennsylvania to Colorado in 1878, hoping the dry air would aid his recovery from tuberculosis. Once cured, he turned his attention to real estate. Speer became an inaugural member of the Denver Fire and Police Board in 1891. Later appointed by the governor to the Board of Public Works, Speer supervised street construction and park projects from 1901 to 1904. Utilities worked directly with him to gain permission to string electrical wires and lay water pipes and rail lines. In his years building the Democratic Party machine, Speer also cultivated ties to downtown saloon owners, their patrons, and diverse urban workers in the heart of the city. His association with gambling and burlesque-hall owners Edward Chase and Vaso Chucovitch was particularly galling to reformers. In 1900, Speer created a modest poor-relief program, instructing police to distribute coupons to unemployed residents that could be redeemed for cash to purchase food. Workers increasingly looked to the Democratic Party and Boss Speer for support in their efforts to secure union recognition and the eight-hour day on city jobs.[12]

In Denver, private utility owners forged close ties to leaders of both parties. Denver Union Water Company head Walter Cheeseman and Denver Tramway president William Gray Evans worked closely with railroad executive David Moffat to promote candidates within the Republican Party. Yet the Republican Evans also became a close ally of the Democratic Speer. Evans ran the Denver Tramway Company from 1902 to 1913 and provided Speer with access to the boardrooms and parlors of Denver's elite. The two men shared a vision of the "City Beautiful" with Evans facilitating the funding and Speer providing the administrative leadership. Speer also helped fend off demands for lower tramway fares, increased regulation, and municipal ownership. Evans in return helped sustain the party machinery of Speer's Democrats, earning him the dubious title "Boss of the Boss" among Progressives. Reformer Clyde King was not far off the mark when he wrote that it was "through party machinery that the public service corporations [exerted] their control over city officials. . . . [I]n the agents of franchise-holding and franchise-seeking companies . . . the professional politicians have found . . . their principal allies and sources of supply."[13]

With such backing, Speer's machine followers turned out the vote against the moral charter in September 1903 and defeated it by nearly 7,000 votes of the 36,000 cast. Religious muckrakers like Keating were quick to cry foul. The election was a "carnival for the united election thieves of both parties," which resorted to "fist fights and clubs" to "clear the polling places of charter watchers," he complained in the *Rocky Mountain News*. The editor further contended that the "money supplied by the gambler, breweries and water and tramway companies flowed with a lavish hand, more money being spent than ever before" to distort a city election. The "honest protests" of Protestant Progressives were met with laughter from partisan "thugs." The "most disgraceful scenes," reported Keating, were those in which drunken prostitutes were bribed to vote against the charter. Keating used the *News* as a platform to publicize election frauds, claiming that as many as 10,000 illegal votes had ensured defeat of the charter.[14]

Progressivism in Denver assumed the character of a religiously inspired exposé of party and even moral corruption in urban life. Yet the Protestants initially failed in their battle with Speer's Democratic machine. A second charter proposal passed in spring 1904 with strong support from Democrats, utility corporations, saloon owners, and the working-class wards in central Denver. It lacked all previous provisions that threatened party patronage, utility lobbying, gambling, and alcohol.

When Speer launched his campaign for mayor later that spring, Progressives resumed their opposition, casting it again in terms of manly, moral citizenship. "Vote against the Speer Machine . . . and Deliver Denver from Conspiracy to Rob Its People," ran the Democratic *News* headline during the

1.2. Ready to Grapple (*ROCKY MOUNTAIN NEWS*, MAY 17, 1904)

spring campaign. A front-page cartoon insisted that the "HONEST CITIZEN,"
a lean, energetic, and honorably unarmed man with his sleeves rolled up, was
"READY TO GRAPPLE" with "THE MACHINE," a corpulent masculine figure in checkered pants with bulbous nose wielding a club of "FRAUD" (Figure
1.2). The fattened ward heeler appeared against a darkened background in
contrast to the determined "citizen." Electoral politics again assumed the
character of a literal fight among men.

In the capital city and many mountain mining towns, political campaigns
routinely became aggressively physical contests. Elections often generated
street brawls over ballot-box stuffing. Fistfights and assaults at times resolved
deadlocked party conventions. Even Lincoln Steffens, the experienced muckraker of urban party corruption, was surprised by the unusually audacious
abuses of city party leaders.[15] Machine activists, most from the working class,
earned the opprobrium of moral reformers as the masters of rough street tactics. Labeled "savages," these party workers enjoyed both notoriety and a
measure of admiration for their defiant determination and physical courage.[16]
Male middle-class reformers countered by insisting on their own masculine
fortitude and stamina in the face of hostility from the boss and his savages.

BEN LINDSEY, THE FIGHTING PROGRESSIVE

In his confrontations with the Speer machine, juvenile court judge Ben Lindsey struggled to define an alternate reform masculinity to replace that based on exclusive party loyalty, ritual, and patronage. Lindsey's effort closely resembled that of his hero, President Theodore Roosevelt, who also sought to legitimate the project of Progressive reform for men by asserting a virile and virtuous masculinity.[17] Born in Tennessee in 1869, Lindsey moved to Denver with his family as a child. When Lindsey was eighteen, his father committed suicide. Thereafter Lindsey and his younger brother assumed primary responsibility for the family's economic survival.

A year after his father's death, Lindsey came close to taking his own life. Weighed down with the economic responsibilities of supporting his family and fearing his prospects were limited, Lindsey placed a revolver to his temple in a moment of despair and pulled the trigger. When the cartridge failed to explode, Lindsey felt a wave of "horror and revulsion" sweep over him: "I realized my folly, my weakness; and I went back to my life with something of a man's determination to crush the circumstances that had almost crushed me." He studied law, passed the Colorado bar in 1894, established a small law practice, and campaigned for the Democrats before becoming judge in 1900.[18]

In his numerous campaigns for reelection as a city judge, Lindsey shifted party affiliations, received multiple party nominations for the same election, ran independently, and consistently attacked what he considered corrupt and unfair practices in both major parties. He also organized several nonpartisan reform organizations to mobilize Protestants and curb the allegedly emasculating influence of the party machines. His charges of corruption provoked an ongoing renegotiation of masculinity and its political meanings for middle-class male reformers struggling to mobilize a constituency against machine corruption.

First among these challenges was Lindsey's attempt to break the traditional link between party loyalty and masculinity. Political parties had served as the central route for male political socialization, as even Jane Addams admitted: "All the social life of the voter from the time he was a little boy . . . has been founded on this sense of loyalty and of standing in with his friends. Now that he is a man, he likes the sense of being inside a political organization, of being trusted with political gossip, of belonging to a set of fellows who understand things, and whose interests are being cared for by a strong friend in the city council itself."[19] Cultivated and rewarded by political machines, party loyalty offered an affirming connection among men.

Lindsey, however, highlighted the contradictions within this association. Machine politics corrupted masculine loyalty. Parties functioned as deviant gangs for adult men, argued Lindsey. What most outraged Lindsey were those party bosses who manipulated their working-class "savages" to ensure that these party loyalists took the blame for any illegal activity. Party-machine conditions had apparently corrupted these "savages," men whom Lindsey asserted otherwise possessed "daring loyalty and unselfishness." The party bosses lacked reciprocal loyalty to their ward heelers, sacrificing them when necessary to ensure their own survival. Political machines thus created an unnatural relationship among men, undermining male loyalties.[20] Lincoln Steffens offered a similar view. In his extended interview with Lindsey, Steffens acknowledged a natural group instinct among men. Problems occurred when gangs "absorb[ed] all the loyalty of the members, turning them from and often against home, the Law, and the State." Speer's machine, like Tammany Hall, appeared as "a gang which, absorbing the loyalty of its members, turns it, for the good of the gang, against the welfare of the city." Steffens continued, "Political parties, founded to establish principles for the strengthening of the State and its citizenship, betray principles and manhood and the State for the 'good of the party.'"[21]

In May 1904, Lindsey and his "honest citizen" allies were again disappointed by the mayoral vote as "repeaters held full sway and carried the election" for the machine and its corporate backers. "It was an election whose results were influenced almost entirely by money," insisted Keating at the *News*. "Not less than $100,000 was spent by the [utility] corporations to elect the Speer ticket." Yet the *News* editor had to concede that Speer had received significant support from organized labor.[22] Workers remained largely unmoved by Lindsey's effort to make Protestant reform masculine. Fears of debauchery, prostitution, and betrayed loyalties did not resonate among working-class voters as they did among Lindsey and other middle-class Protestant men.

Although moral appeals gained little traction with working-class voters, some Denver union activists had expressed concern about the role of the saloon in politics. In the 1880s, union leaders forged an alliance with the Prohibition Party to challenge the corrupting influence of the saloon and its ties to Republican Party machinery. Knights of Labor organizers in Denver sought to remake saloons as recreational sites with their own meeting rooms, libraries, and social activities for working men and women. In 1891 the Denver Trades Assembly called for the nationalization of the U.S. liquor industry in hopes of undermining local corruption. While union leaders supported temperance, the brief alliance with the Prohibition Party ultimately proved divisive for nineteenth-century Denver labor.[23]

LABOR WAR AND EARLY PROGRESSIVES

By the early twentieth century, temperance had largely faded from working-class discussions of politics. Far more prominent were the confrontations between industrial workers and corporate owners. As the Protestant Progressives began to confer about a new charter in 1903, class warfare emerged in Cripple Creek between the Western Federation of Miners (WFM) and the statewide Mine Owners' Association. WFM leaders railed against mine-owner manipulations of politics in mining camps and the oppressive conditions faced by smelter workers. Appeals for moral reform of Denver's city government assumed far less importance among these WFM unionists.

For most workers, Governor James Peabody and his Citizens' Alliance allies became the leading political concern. In 1903, WFM unionists confronted metal mine and smelter owners across the state in hopes of securing an eight-hour day through direct action. Governor Peabody used the state militia to back mine owners in an open-shop drive to crush the WFM. Mine union leaders were harassed, jailed, and even deported from the state without due process. Militia men and private guards burned union halls and destroyed printing presses owned by labor-friend editors. Mine owners intimidated and forced the resignation of public officials sympathetic to the WFM in mining communities.[24]

At a mass rally organized by the Colorado State Federation of Labor, speakers condemned "gubernatorial Czarism" across the state. "[M]ilitary might rides rampant over the Constitution and law. The laborers' home . . . is no longer sacred. The hearthstone, the family fireside, is invaded and desecrated by military outlaws, and citizenship subjected to all the indignation, humiliation, and reproach which corporate cunning and power can suggest and devise. . . . Civil authority has been strangled."[25] Here was a rhetorical challenge to corporate manipulation and political corruption that matched in intensity that of the Protestant Progressives.

Yet Denver's Protestant reformers remained largely silent on such abuses in this dramatic class conflict. In these years they continued to focus exclusively on Denver voting frauds, utility corporations, and the city's Democratic machine. Worse still, Catholic bishop Nichols Matz openly championed Governor Peabody and mine owners from his church on Logan Avenue in Denver. As the spiritual leader of Colorado's largest single denomination, representing nearly half of the state's churchgoers, Matz stridently opposed the WFM in a series of published sermons beginning in May 1903. The bishop insisted that Catholic workers had to choose between their church and the socialistic WFM. Governor Peabody, Matz insisted, "merited the praise of every honest citizen and lover of order in Colorado" for his assaults on the WFM.[26] For Matz a defense of the political and economic status quo was the paramount order of the day.

As Matz attacked the WFM, the newly formed Denver Citizens' Alliance launched its own open-shop drive and openly backed Governor Peabody. Some Progressive charter activists supported the new employer's union.

Banker James Temple was both an Honest Elections League activist and a leader of the Denver Citizens' Alliance. Mattress factory owner George Kindel helped create the anti-union organization while also backing calls for honest government. In 1903, Denver Citizens' Alliance members defeated strikes by butchers, cooks, waiters, bakers, brewery workers, mattress workers, and smeltermen, bolstering the open-shop drive of the state's mine owners.[27] As Denver voters considered the merits of a new moral charter, union workers across the city experienced a series of defeats.

In response to such attacks, the Denver labor movement struggled with internal divisions. Although WFM leaders and supporters pushed the city labor federation toward syndicalism and a break with the American Federation of Labor (AFL), many skilled workers dissented. The city federation had split in 1902 between industrial unionists and what an opponent called the "old-times trades-union organizations." The latter, in fact, represented the large majority of Denver workers. In these years more than 80 percent of Denver's workers found employment in firms with fewer than twenty-five employees. Printers, book binders, pressmen, cigar makers, machinists, plumbers, and bartenders were among the influential members of the city labor federation. Corporate capitalism had not shaped their work lives nearly as extensively as it had smelter workers or miners.[28] Although WFM leaders urged a citywide general strike in 1903, the AFL-style craft unions resisted.

By the time Democratic candidate Robert Speer ran for mayor in the spring of 1904, the WFM and industrial unions in Denver were on the brink of collapse. Under intense pressure from state officials and employers, WFM affiliates disbanded across the state in 1904 and skilled craft unionists increasingly came to dominate the state and city federations of labor. Governor Peabody and the Citizens' Alliances across the state worked to purge the Denver labor movement of its most radical voices.

In this period of intense labor conflict, the appeals of the Protestant Progressives persuaded few union workers. For most Colorado workers in these trying years, religion shaped political action in ways different from that of middle-class Progressives. In the elections of 1904 and 1906, Catholic, foreign-born miners and millworkers tended to vote the Democratic or Socialist ticket. These voters had formerly supported Populist candidates in the early 1890s. In 1904, protesting Peabody and the Republican Party was among their chief concerns. The Populist legacy in Colorado, supported especially by radical foreign-born miners, did not translate into support for Protestant Progressivism. Many AFL-affiliated unionists in Denver also backed Democratic candidates, including Speer.[29] In early Progressive campaigns, the manipulations of mine owners in hinterland communities were of far less concern to Denver Protestants. Speer and his Democratic machine remained their overriding concern.

MAYOR SPEER'S COALITION

Once in office, Speer refined his vision of urban politics, limiting the zeal of the moral reformers and rejecting the urgency of their masculine renegotiation. In a 1907 speech, the mayor declared that ideal city government "should be Progressive along conservative lines—push needed improvements and add the ornamental at the lowest possible cost. Refuse to be puritanical or used in spasms of reform, yet earnestly strive for betterment year by year along moral lines." Speer committed his administration to an ambitious urban renewal program to create the City Beautiful, which drew increasing praise from elites, clubwomen, and unionists. Among the many projects that Speer promoted were a public bathhouse for the urban poor, railway viaducts at dangerous intersections, and a municipal auditorium hosting free Sunday concerts. His grand vision was a civic center near the state capitol building comprising a central park surrounded by museums, a library, and various government buildings. Speer urged residents to help him make Denver the "Paris of America."[30] He strategically adopted a milder version of the Protestant emphasis on uplift and civic improvement. Under his rule, Denver would have few regulations of utility corporations and gambling halls, saloons, and brothels.

Ultimately, Mayor Speer brokered a coalition of elite businessmen and urban workers, club women and madams, Democrats and Republicans. Commercial elites did not support calls for reform of urban government but rather preferred to work with Speer. The mayor brought significant predictability and stability to city politics long marked by disorder and uncertainty. Speer's broker politics enabled private utility corporations to secure predictable franchise renewals without the need to persuade a wary voting public. Business leaders appreciated this consistency.[31] In fact, as Speer's reelection campaign began in spring 1908, elite members of Denver's Chamber of Commerce organized a Denver Business Men's League to back Speer. While cities like Boston, Chicago, and New York witnessed broad business opposition to party machines and support for structural reforms of city government, Denver's elite Republicans remained steady advocates of the city's Democratic machine and strong-mayor system under the city's 1904 charter.[32]

Elite businessmen favored Speer for his sympathetic handling of utility issues, and their wives praised the mayor for his civic vision and beautification projects. The Women's Auxiliary to the Business Men's League worked to mobilize "Republican and society" women into the Speer camp.[33] Among the chief promoters of this effort was the *Denver Post*. The *Post* created the impression of newly politicized elite women rallying to the Speer coalition: "For the first time in the history of woman suffrage in Colorado, the society women of Denver are taking an active interest in a political campaign. They have forsaken bridge, pink teas and other social diversions to plunge into the mysteries of the game of politics and incidentally to re-elect Robert W. Speer mayor." Moreover, "of all women," insisted the *Post*, "they stand for Denver's moral welfare," which they believe "is safe in the hands of Mayor Speer." Speer's City Beautiful campaign offered its own "ethical influence" and uplift, argued Speer's Republican women backers.[34]

A number of clubwomen, impressed by Speer's street improvement projects, public bathhouse program, and auditorium, joined with formerly Republican voters to back the mayor. Addressing a rally at the Denver Woman's Club auditorium, one Republican activist announced her defection to the Democratic Party with praise for Speer, who "always . . . had time to look after the comfort of the children." Democratic activist Mary Bradford, having recently served two terms as president of the Colorado Federation of Women's Clubs, declared that Speer had made Denver clean and safe for its children. With his playground construction, Speer fostered "well-regulated and protected play" and thus deserved the title of "children's mayor."[35] Although these women maintained a "nonpartisan" lobby under the auspices of their city club and state federation, they also identified themselves publicly with Speer and the Democratic Party. Both clubwomen, in fact, came in for censure from Ben Lindsey, who considered them party hacks who lacked independence and did "the work of the . . . corporation machine."[36]

Additionally, many labor activists maintained their support for Denver's Democratic Party and Mayor Speer in 1908. Following the lead of the Building Trades Council, many craft unionists in the city backed the mayor in his reelection bid. Several members of the building trades ran in 1908 for city council on Speer's Democratic ticket, including Denver Trades and Labor Assembly (DTLA) president and Building Trades Council agent George McLachlan. Speer had previously appointed McLachlan to fill a vacancy on the city council. He along with other building trades unionists had benefited directly from Speer's ambitious urban improvement projects and his mediation of disputes in the face of Citizens' Alliance union-busting efforts. The Colorado State Federation of Labor created a political committee, composed chiefly of building trades unionists, which endorsed Speer's candidacy along with unionists running on the Democratic ticket. Committee spokesmen noted that Speer had raised wages and shortened hours for city workers as well as reduced taxes. Mayor Speer received credit for creating "beautiful boulevards," parks, and public baths. The unionists, remarkably, praised the Business Men's Democratic ticket: "Once again the business man and the laboring man, realizing that their interests are identical, have joined hands for the greater upbuilding of Denver." African American workers frequently supported the Speer machine, citing his employment of increasing numbers of black residents within the city administration, some even in positions of authority. The mayor also relied on the support of a number of saloon-owning aldermen to guide his projects through the city council. Nine of Denver's sixteen council-men were saloonkeepers in the early twentieth century.[37] The integrity of this latter group faced regular challenges from Costigan's State Voters' League.

ALCOHOL AND PROTESTANT PROGRESSIVES

To counter Mayor Speer's coalition, Protestant reformers leaned increasingly on temperance groups such as the Anti-Saloon League and Women's Christian Temperance Union in an effort to rally a broad moral coalition. Created in 1898, the Colorado Anti-Saloon League had busily investigated saloon ties to the Denver Democratic Party machine from the start. Judge Ben Lindsey won the support of prohibitionists in 1901 when he broke with the Democratic ma-chine over a court decision by a machine judge who overturned a law barring women from saloons.[38] As a consistent supporter of the dry cause, Lindsey was hardly unique among Protestant reformers. Edward Costigan worked as chief counsel to the Anti-Saloon League. He also served on the board of the Denver Law Enforcement League, an organization of Protestants devoted to upholding saloon regulations. Costigan implored Denver voters to unseat the liquor boss who sought to impose "on us some other government than our own and to hand us over to the mercies of the political boss." Denver's utili-ties, Costigan insisted in the 1908 campaign, were "cooperating with a syn-dicate of gamblers and brewers' associations controlling the saloons, and all of the worst elements of the city." *News* editor Ed Keating also supported the dry cause.[39]

In 1908, prohibitionists led the moral charge against Boss Speer. Protestant ministers and saloon opponents assailed Speer for "winking at crime" and protecting gambling and liquor interests. In response to those who praised Speer's City Beautiful improvements, Presbyterian minister Robert Coyle in-sisted, "There is no asset of a city to be compared with its morals." Coyle in-sisted that "manhood values" should weigh more heavily in urban politics than "money values." Reverend David Fouse of the First Reformed Church, referring to Speer's loose regulation of Denver's red-light district, insisted that "Market street has no more right to have a voice in our government than the baser passions of a man have a right to dominate him. Appetite and greed, the two elements which make up every saloon, should no more rule in our city than in our personal life." Again, moral reformers argued for parallels between the project to remake individual men and to transform city politics. "Ours is a representative government," Fouse insisted, "yet we Christian peo-ple are not represented."[40] The Progressive challenge to Speer reflected the Protestant effort to transform male citizenship as well as city government.

Unfortunately for the reformers, opposition to moral corruption was not so easily mobilized. They found it difficult to rally support for the anti-Speer reform candidate, Republican Horace Phelps. Although Phelps won the endorsement of the Anti-Saloon League for his support of local option, he possessed little administrative experience beyond his small law practice. Yet Lindsey and Costigan worried that he was too much a tool of the Republican machine and its corporate backers.[41] His earlier support of Governor Peabody earned Phelps the enmity of union voters. Protestant women's club leaders appealed to female voters, given Phelps's pledge to regulate prostitution and gambling. Democratic women Sarah Platt Decker, Helen Ring Robinson, and Ellis Meredith; independent Helen Wixon; along with Republican women such as Minnie T. Love formed the Women's Nonpartisan Association to oppose Speer. Rather than simply joining the Republican campaign, these club leaders stressed their independence from party machinery. A *Rocky Mountain News* reporter wrote sympathetically of the inaugural meeting of this association that "women who understand politics, women who play politics, women of all political parties, joined with women who know nothing of politics" to demand clean city government. Speakers denounced Speer's ties to breweries, saloons, and gambling houses. His civic improvement projects were "merely graft at the expense of the taxpayers." Speer was the "worst mayor Denver has ever had" in terms of protecting "children from vice."[42]

Some Denver Woman's Club leaders as well as Judge Lindsey further resented Speer's tendency to co-opt their own City Beautiful initiatives, such as playground construction, street clean-up efforts, and the city bathhouse. Speer rarely credited clubwomen or Lindsey for launching these projects. Sarah Decker resented the competition that Speer's party machine posed to women's club initiatives.[43] The anti-Speer women's association thus revealed a significant division among club women along the lines of Protestant Progressivism. Women's club members were divided over Speer and the appeal of the religious Progressives.

The press sought to define the moral issues of the campaign again in gendered terms, relying on different conceptions of corruption. The *Post* cast the do-gooder Phelps in terms of a childish innocent, not grown man enough for the job of managing an expanding city government. As one Speer supporter put it, "This is a contest between a strong, experienced man and a little boy in knee pants."[44] Speer supporters stressed his fatherly restraint and reassuring command of complex urban affairs. *Post* cartoonist Wilbur Steele cast Speer as a chivalrous chauffeur escorting "Miss Denver" along urban streets while "Baby Phelps" begged for a turn behind the wheel (Figure 1.3). Speer supporters viewed the city in feminine terms, in need of reassuring, paternal guidance.

In reply, the *News* reprinted a Steele cartoon from the previous election, depicting Boss Speer, in the checkered suit of the machine politician, trampling on the prostrate young female image of "Honest Elections," as his party

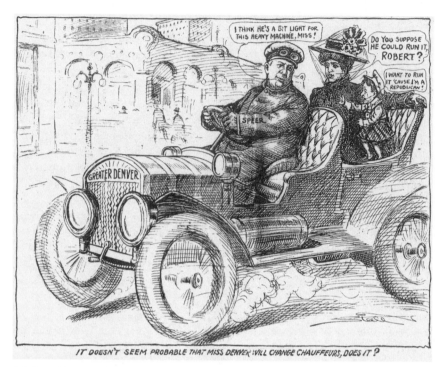

1.3. SPEER DRIVING GREATER DENVER (*DENVER POST*, APRIL 28, 1908)

henchmen held smoking guns (Figure 1.4). *Post* cartoonist Steele demonstrated the inconsistency of the paper's editorial position.

While highlighting the switch by the *Post* owners from opposition to support for Speer, Keating also hoped to advance his Protestant vision of politics. The aggressive and morally corrupt Speer, alleged Progressive reformers, would continue a pattern of disregard for law, decency, and feminine purity.

News editor Keating attempted to rally working-class voters behind the moral-reform cause. The editor insisted that the state labor federation endorsement of Speer reflected only the views of a few "professional" labor leaders and Speer's patronage recipients. Keating asked, "Do the labor unions of this city want to be sold out to the 'interests'?" He saw a fake labor committee maneuvering to deliver the working-class vote to Speer, "to the liquor interests against local option, and to the water monopoly."[45] The state labor political committee was little better than the labor arm of the Speer machine, argued the journalist.

The May 19 election proved a major victory for Speer and a minor one for the Protestant reformers. Speer carried the city by nearly 3,000 votes out of 58,000 cast.[46] The City Beautiful advocate won impressive gains in elite

1.4. Speer Trampling Honest Elections (*ROCKY MOUNTAIN NEWS*, MAY 19, 1908)

and middle-class neighborhoods, which in 1904 had voted overwhelmingly Republican. Working-class precincts again voted for Speer along with most of the union candidates for city council on the Democratic ticket. An editorial in the Denver *Republican* noted that "[t]he people . . . voted for what they believed to be the best interests of the city as a corporation" despite the appeals of moral reformers.[47]

Although their candidate lost, Protestant reformers took solace in a relatively clean election. In the downtown wards that had long served as Speer's base of machine support, many fewer votes were cast in 1908 than in 1904, even though the population had increased slightly. Growing numbers of poll watch-ers associated with the Anti-Saloon League thwarted the efforts of repeaters and fraudulent voters. Some ballot watchers even threatened to evict Speer's police observers from one polling place if they attempted to force through fraudulent votes. Speer's chief machine operatives remained relatively quiet on Election Day. One reporter described an immigrant precinct with a repu-tation for rough electioneering tactics as resembling "a Sunday school."[48] The election signaled growing middle-class support for Speer the city manager even as Protestant Progressives advanced their vision of honest elections.

Religious reformers had particularly energized middle-class women vot-ers with the question of local option. The *Post* was not alone in its percep-tion that a feminine political awakening had occurred. Catholic leader Father O'Ryan had also argued that this was the first campaign in Colorado where the suffrage question had been put to the test. A *News* observer of the voting in affluent wards around Capitol Hill witnessed a "keen, almost feverish in-terest" in the election among women. "There were women on every hand, sometimes more women than men; and they were always active." One female voter stated, "It is the biggest election we have ever had here on the hill."[49] She referred less to Speer's candidacy than to the question of local option. While Speer won a majority in many residential middle-class wards, local option also passed, even in neighborhoods that lacked a saloon. Protestant reform-ers failed to convince many middle-class women of the corrupting power of Speer's Democratic machine, but they had shaped perceptions of the saloon.

In these early years of the twentieth century, Protestant reformers popu-larized rhetorical opposition central to Progressivism in Denver. The corrupt-ing influence of party machines with their ties to utilities, saloons, and gam-bling houses required a countermobilization of independent Protestant voters. The upright, honest male citizen had to fight the debauched, drunken ward heeler for control. Clubwomen remained largely divided by the Protestant crusades, with Speer opponents and supporters both drawing on mater-nal rhetoric to bolster their respective positions. By publicizing the electoral abuses of the Speer machine and continually stressing its corrupt ties to util-ity corporations, the religious reformers did generate growing pressure for structural change in city government. When the water utility franchise came up for renewal in 1910, moral reformers found their years of agitation begin-ning to pay off.

PROGRESSIVES AND MUNICIPAL OWNERSHIP OF UTILITIES

In debates about the water utility, Protestant Progressive activists came to champion municipal ownership. This was not the first call for the public own-ership of natural monopolies. The Populists of course had advocated the government ownership of the railroads, in addition to telephone and telegraph networks. In 1895 the middle-class Denver Civic Federation promoted city-owned utilities. In 1897 the state labor platform, shaped especially by Western Federation of Miners members, demanded state control over mines and the municipal ownership of utilities. The 1890s saw a range of reformers advocating public control and administration of natural monopolies.

Yet in the early twentieth century, middle-class Protestant reformers led the campaign for city-owned utilities. The reform promised more efficient and lower-cost service as well as honest administration. Protestant Progressives rarely called for municipal ownership in the name of economic justice or fair treatment for utility workers. Instead, the drive for city-owned utilities in Denver became a moral reform to limit public spending, reduce taxes, and establish honest administration. Consider two key utility franchise elections: one for gas and electric service in 1906 and one for water in 1910.

In 1906 voters would decide the fate of the Gas and Electric Company franchise. Protestant Progressives led the campaign to oppose renewal of a franchise they deemed unfair to city residents. Unable to stand on its own merits, the franchise needed the corrupt manipulations of Speer's Democratic machine, they insisted. Ed Costigan and Ben Lindsey joined forces with Keating and Patterson at the *Rocky Mountain News* in an effort to convince voters of Speer's corrupt ties to the utilities. A May 1 front-page cartoon featured a sycophantic image of Speer accepting orders from Denver Tramway Company head and GOP party chief Evans in collusion to "PUT THIS FRANCHISE THROUGH." The water and electric utilities heads agree upon Speer's slavish dedication and unscrupulous tactics.[50] Costigan's Voters' League reported that several of Democratic candidates for city council had ties to utilities, gambling hall owners, and breweries.

Protestant reformers in response created a Municipal Ownership League endorsing an independent slate of city council candidates committed to a rejection of utility franchises and the support of public purchase of the facilities. This was to be nonpartisan political mobilization of Denver voters. Home-rule champion John Rush chaired this league, and Christian Citizenship Union advisor John Gabriel served as secretary. The People's Sunday Alliance, representing Denver's small African American, middle-class community, and the Christian Citizenship Union endorsed its efforts. Women's clubs were also supportive. The *Rocky Mountain News*, through Ed Keating's editorials, assured Denver voters that municipal ownership of utilities, not unlike public control over education, was not inherently socialistic. City control would reduce costs, lower property taxes, and enhance the climate for new business, insisted the *News*.[51]

Union leaders supported the drive for city ownership but remained wary of the moralistic zeal that characterized Voters' League activities. Cigarmaker

George Le Roy served as an advisor on the governing board, and the DTLA endorsed league goals. Yet unionists devoted little attention to the election. Many in the building trades remained loyal to Speer and worked to renew the utility franchise on Election Day. The Municipal Ownership League remained largely a middle-class organization staffed and supported mainly by Protestant activists. Still, *News* editor Keating appealed to labor voters as the election neared: "Do you want the corporations to own this city as they have for years? If you do, vote the machine ticket," he challenged.[52]

Without broad working-class support, the challenge to utility influence was lost, although narrowly. The gas and electric franchise was renewed by only 685 votes, and all but two of Speer's sixteen allies on the city council were elected. In a modest show of success, Municipal Ownership League candidates did win two seats on the city council. Soon after the election, the good-government reformers uncovered convincing evidence of voter fraud. The *Rocky Mountain News* reported that Gas and Electric Company employees and Democratic Party activists had forged 2,000 tax receipts in order to qualify illegal votes. The paper paired a photo of members of the League of Honest Elections inspecting the illegal records with a cartoon in which the torchlight of "Publicity" was cast upon a group of four men, corporate elites and gang politicians, forging the documents.[53] The league members presented the tax records along with confessions from utility forgers to a city judge who launched an investigation. Yet utility appeals to the Colorado Supreme Court presented by the city attorney secured a writ of prohibition against the city judge, forcing him to halt his investigation and heed the order of the Election Commission declaring the franchises passed. Keating expressed the collective outrage of his fellow reformers when he argued that the city attorney was "paid THE PEOPLE'S MONEY to defend . . . the corporations that are endeavoring to steal from THE PEOPLE."[54] Protestant Progressives had damning evidence of utility corruption of the electoral process. But the campaign for city-owned gas and electric service had failed.

In spring 1910, these reformers again campaigned against a utility franchise renewal and corporate influence in City Hall. The Denver Union Water Company, a private corporation, had provided the city water for decades under a franchise that required popular renewal that year. Long frustrated with Speer's lenient handling of utility franchises, reformers saw a new opportunity to rebuke the Democratic boss and reject the water franchise. High water prices and poor service did not endear the utility to Denver voters. Reformers decided to launch a Citizens' Party to promote public ownership of this utility. Significantly, clubwomen enjoyed a new prominence in this crusade. The 1910 campaign for a city-owned water system was joined with calls for the initiative and referendum in city government.

The contest generated a passionate debate among clubwomen and trade unionists about Mayor Robert Speer, his Democratic Party machine, and utility influence in municipal politics. Clubwomen such as Sarah Decker and Ellis Meredith joined the crusade against renewal of the water franchise. Long an advocate of women's independence from party loyalty, Decker nonetheless displayed a preference for reform Democrats like William Jennings Bryan. At the turn of the century, Decker served on a state civil service board that possessed only advisory powers, but nonetheless she insisted that "Civil Service is not politics; it is religion." Like Jane Addams, to whom Decker was compared, the Colorado leader resented the competition between clubwomen and Speer's machine in addressing the problems of Denver's poor neighborhoods.[55] Meredith had helped draft the anti-patronage moral charter proposal in 1903. She also reported for Patterson's *Rocky Mountain News* and used her columns to lend support to the crusades of the Protestant moralists. Unlike women such as Alma Lafferty and Mary Bradford, who sought to advance the women's club agenda from within political parties, Decker and Meredith insisted on women's political activism without party association.

Their 1910 Public Service League revived and expanded upon the Women's Nonpartisan Association, created in 1908 to oppose Speer's reelection. After voters defeated the Speer-backed franchise, Meredith claimed victory "for the people of Denver" against "monopoly domination" through the party boss. The "corporations in Denver have given the public lessons in both graft and petty larceny," Meredith argued. "They have openly robbed the city and lowered public morality." The private water company "suffered for the sins" of other utilities, which had "manufactured taxpayers and stuffed ballot boxes" during the campaign in 1906. Meredith also noted that temperance forces backed the drive to secure the initiative and referendum for city voters. "Every one elected on the Citizens' ticket owes a great debt" to temperance activists.[56] As Meredith's analysis indicates, support for direct democracy at the city level reflected an intermingling of moral crusading, good government reform, and critique of corporate wrongdoing.

Given such links, it is not surprising that union support again remained tenuous. Labor leaders expressed consistent interest in publicly owned utilities but were divided about moral crusading. Some labor activists, like printer Otto Thum, were sympathetic.[57] Yet the water issue split unionists over Speer's machine. In 1909 the city's labor federation appointed a committee of unionists to investigate and propose options for a city-owned water system. Headed by printers George Eisler and Sidney Eastwood and a cigarmaker, the committee condemned recent city valuations of the private utility as excessive and unfair. Charging that Speer would block attempts to purchase the monopoly for a lower price, Eisler insisted that city voters also needed to secure the initiative and referendum. The printer had already joined forces with Lindsey stumping for the Direct Legislation League. Workers attended neighborhood Ward Water Users' Clubs across the city to advocate the labor plan.

Veterans of the Municipal Ownership League soon joined the DTLA in calling for charter amendments to achieve city ownership of this key utility. Labor Progressives effectively launched the campaign for this reform.[58]

Yet in January 1910, divisions between the Protestant Progressives and labor activists emerged over the role unionists would play on a proposed water commission. The labor committee hoped for a broad commission to regulate all urban utilities with union power to appoint one commissioner. Attorneys John Rush and John Gabriel opposed the union candidates that the DTLA put forward and favored a more modest water commission to regulate this single utility. Further complicating union political efforts, Speer loyalists within the building trades increasingly dominated the DTLA's water committee. This newly composed labor committee urged support for Mayor Speer's confusing proposal to merely investigate prospects for municipal ownership. Building trades committee members particularly resented the presence of former Citizens' Alliance leader George Kindel among the Progressive reformers. Nonetheless, some union activists like Eisler and Thum, who spoke the language of the Protestant Progressives, increasingly abandoned the labor committee's efforts and worked instead with Kindel as well as Rush, Lindsey, and Costigan.[59] The city's leading Progressives would increasingly turn to the Christian Citizenship Union, Protestant churches, and women's clubs for their municipal ownership campaign. By spring, labor's water committee was increasingly isolated.

Delegates to the city labor federation grew increasingly frustrated. Eisler encouraged them to back the municipal ownership campaign, but Speer allies within the DTLA continued to press for the mayor's alternative plan. In April, loyalties to Speer's machine created a crisis for Denver unionists. Cigarmakers and printers denounced building trades delegates with ties to Speer. Painters and carpenters were divided over influence of the Democratic machine within their ranks. Printer and *Labor Bulletin* editor James Conkle urged federation members to support the initiative and referendum as well as the plan for municipal ownership. Yet even the DTLA president campaigned against another unionist who was a Citizens' Party candidate. The campaign for municipal ownership of the water system appeared more a moral than a socialist reform. And the Speer machine still had some strong defenders among the working-class voters of Denver.[60]

The May election saw voters narrowly approve the municipal-ownership plan for the water utility and direct democracy provisions. Despite divisions among union workers, Keating at the *News* saw a growing tide of support for religious Progressivism. Just two years after Speer's reelection, Protestant reformers now had the momentum. "It looks now as if the effect of the recent city election," Keating contended in 1910, "will be to bring together into a compact vigilant body those voters who believe in a better Colorado, one where the people [not parties] shall choose their own officials and shall have a voice in their own laws."[61] By 1910 then, Protestant reformers in Denver had achieved some successes. They popularized a potent opposition between virtuous citizens and the morally corrupting Democratic Party machine. City voters could now make their own laws via the initiative. The vote in favor of city ownership of the water utility appeared to empower "the People" and rebuke corporate interests. Progressive reformers had rallied Protestant churchgoers and temperance activists into an influential movement. Unionists, however, remained divided about the promise of Protestant Progressivism.

THE DEFEAT OF BOSS SPEER

Following the approval of a city-owned water utility in 1910, Protestant Progressives launched a major drive to replace Speer with commission government. Progressive activists Ed Costigan, John Rush, and John Gabriel created the Non-Partisan Charter League in 1911 to advance this change. The league gathered signatures, especially in middle-class Presbyterian and Methodist churches, to submit a plan for commission government to city voters. Open-shop champion and former Chamber of Commerce president Allison Stocker was among the leading supporters. In early 1912, Mayor Speer's attorneys delayed a vote on the commission proposal with various court appeals. Yet Protestant Progressives continued to advocate this reform, rallying support in churches throughout the year. Before they could secure a city vote on the proposal however, Mayor Speer generated a new and more pressing controversy with his ouster of county assessor Henry Arnold. Again, Boss Speer found himself confronting the anger of Protestant Progressives.

Arnold had won election as Denver County assessor in 1910 as a Speer Democrat. Formerly an insurance broker and real estate speculator in southwestern Colorado, Arnold forged connections to the city's real estate brokers and later Speer's machine after he moved to Denver in 1902. Yet once in office, Arnold antagonized Speer by equalizing assessments of county property. He reduced taxes on small homeowners while increasing those of some downtown developers. For these efforts, Arnold earned the support of reformers hoping to reduce the cost of city government. By 1911, he was speaking before church audiences organized by the Christian Citizenship Union about reducing the cost of government and limiting saloon and gambling operations.[62]

Speer's City Beautiful projects had dramatically increased city spending. Reformers regularly linked their calls for moral, honest administration with those for less costly government. The costs of building new streets, gutters, and sewers in 1910 exceeded the entire city budget in 1902. The daily administration of city services also increased significantly in these years. By 1910, Denver residents paid higher per capita property taxes than citizens of any other city of comparable size.[63] In this context, Arnold's tax reduction efforts for homeowners generated a great deal of enthusiasm.

When Speer attempted to replace Arnold as assessor in December 1911, he handed his opponents a perfect political opportunity. Speer had hoped to use a recent state Supreme Court decision that combined the city and county governments of Denver to his advantage. Although elected as county assessor, Arnold vowed to stay on, since he had no counterpart within the city administration. Speer balked. He steered a replacement appointment through the city council on the evening of December 14 and then secured a police escort for the new assessor, who hoped to physically occupy Arnold's courthouse-square office. Getting word of Speer's plan, Arnold abruptly left a meeting of the CCU and raced to his office just in time for a tense confrontation, which the *Denver Republican* called "the battle of courthouse square." After barricading his office door for a two-hour standoff, Arnold eventually yielded around midnight given the prospect of a forced removal by police loyal to Speer.[64]

Progressive activists quickly rallied to Arnold's defense. Organizing a protest on a Sunday afternoon on the steps of the capitol, reformers tore into Speer as a despot and "Cossack." With tens of thousands assembling to hear Speer's chief critics, Ben Lindsey insisted that the "day marks the baptism of Denver's civic regeneration." Creel assured the crowd they were the "priests of the religion of democracy." He wrote the next day that "there was Christianity in that vast gathering—the Christianity of him who cried out against 'burdens too grievous to be borne' and who preached equality of justice."[65] The Sunday rally became an open-air revival for Progressivism with Arnold the man of the hour. Ed Keating pledged that if Speer blocked commission government, "then we will elect Arnold mayor of Denver next May and we will have such a housecleaning as will live in the history of this beautiful city."[66]

Arnold's campaign for mayor effectively began with that rally. Although Progressives hoped foremost to establish commission government, the mayoral election rapidly approached. With petitions for a structural change to city government tied up in court, reformers decided to focus on electing a replacement for Speer in May 1912. Arnold's Progressive credentials were thin, but Speer had made him a martyr for the reform cause. He became the Progressive's "Galahad," wrote Creel.[67] Arnold's pledge to work for commission government helped to win him additional support from the Progressive public. Reform leaders like Costigan and Patterson revived the Citizens' Party with Arnold heading its ticket.

As with earlier Progressive campaigns in Denver, middle-class churchgoers would play a prominent role. Just after Arnold's removal as assessor, the Christian Citizenship Union urged Denver pastors to open their churches for political reform meetings. Pledging support for Costigan's Non-Partisan Charter League, the CCU urged Protestants to work for commission government. The CCU hoped to "impress churches with their responsibilities in civic affairs." This included holding nonpartisan reform gatherings, for which the CCU supplied speakers and publicity. Although initially cool to Arnold, the CCU eventually endorsed him. In a letter sent to churches across the city, CCU leader Harry Fisher urged backing for the Citizens' Party candidate because he pledged "himself to strict and unbiased enforcement of law if elected mayor."[68]

A number of Protestant ministers responded favorably to CCU appeals. Reverend Orrin Auman, pastor of the Grant Avenue Methodist Church, preached that "the commission form of government would make it easier for us to get hold of the [prostitution] problem and conquer it." Reverend Clark of the Park Hill Methodist Church challenged his congregation on the eve of the mayoral election: "If you want clean politics, make it impossible for dirty politicians to serve a second term. . . . When Mayor Speer crowbarred Mr. Arnold out of office, he invited violence and insurrection. So you are not to stay out of politics because they are dirty. Let us make them clean on Tuesday by aiding Mr. Arnold." Arnold's candidacy assumed the character of a moral crusade for Denver's Protestant leaders.[69]

In the face of growing support for Protestant Progressivism and Citizens' candidate Arnold, Mayor Speer chose not to run for reelection. Although still guiding his Democratic machine, Speer tapped city engineer John B. Hunter to challenge Arnold in the May election. Hunter had supervised a range of Speer's City Beautiful projects and would be "indispensable to Denver's march of progress," insisted the mayor. Hunter had also endorsed good-government campaigns during the 1890s, although he had remained distant from early twentieth-century Progressives in Denver. His wife, tellingly, was active in women's Democratic Party politics rather than female nonpartisan, Progressive organizations. As one historian has aptly noted, Speer's Democratic machine would face reformers "with the shadow, not the substance."[70] Progressive prospects for success had rarely looked better.

With the campaign drawing to a close, Progressives cast the election in familiar terms. The editor of the *Express*, for instance, claimed that the main issue was "whether the city of Denver shall be governed by the people . . . or whether it shall be run by tools of the corporations who tax every enterprise for their own benefit." The CCU appealed to the "good women of Denver to exercise their right to vote."[71] Progressives saw the contest as one of moral, nonpartisan citizens advocating fiscal restraint against corrupt, self-interested partisans who would bring on extravagance and depravity. Although challenging corporate manipulations of politics, Protestant Progressives had forged no official alliances with the working-class "public."

The May 1912 election was a sweeping victory for Arnold and Protestant Progressives. The Citizens' Party carried every ward in the city with Arnold winning 58 percent of the popular vote in a three-way contest. Progressive candidate Ben Lindsey successfully challenged the machine in its most entrenched downtown wards, advancing not only his own but other Citizens' candidate victories. Protestant Progressives had also stamped out the electioneering abuses of the Speer machine. Lindsey boasted of the aggressive tactics of his civic Progressives, who broke into polling places amid flying glass in machine-dominated wards to ensure Honest Elections League poll watchers could monitor the balloting. Creel characteristically chose religious metaphors to claim the election meant "Glory for all" Progressives who contributed to a "harmonious movement" of disaffected Democrats and Republicans working with the Women's Public Service League, the Christian Citizenship Union, and the Direct Legislation League. The "Citizens' victory puts an end to the Reign of Terror that has kept clean men OUT of politics," he celebrated.[72]

The election also signaled a triumph for feminine Progressive citizenship. The *Rocky Mountain News* featured a story on the "last gasping, creaking groans of the machine" as it drove prostitutes to the polls. "A most pitiful sight it was," wrote a reporter, "to see these women victims of the unjust social system being utilized to help make the last fight for the machine that has held them in sway for so many years." In striking contrast, the journalist noted that "farther uptown in the resident districts . . . women of another and more happy strata of life" flocked voluntarily to the polls. These potent political symbols—the extorted prostitute and the virtuous middle-class feminine Progressive—highlighted the election issues in bold relief. The balloting "marked the passing of . . . old organizations and the rise of a new power which means cleanliness and decency," insisted the *News*.[73] Progressive reformers, it appeared, had at last defeated the morally corrupting party machine in Denver.

Among the new mayor's initial appointments was George Creel as commissioner of police. Creel had asked for the job in hopes of tackling the moral evils he had so long crusaded against. Moving to Denver from Kansas City in 1909, Creel had quickly joined the reformers in attacking Boss Speer. Writing editorials for the *Denver Post* and then for the *Rocky Mountain News*, Creel worked to create the impression of an outraged moral public that demanded change. As police commissioner, Creel insisted that the police uphold liquor laws and regulations on closing times. He took nightsticks away from patrolmen to limit beatings of suspects. Protestant leaders initially applauded the reforming zeal of the former newspaperman.

Creel in turn tapped social worker Josephine Roche to become the new inspector of amusements in October 1912. This new post was created at the request of Mothers' Congress and women's club members. The daughter of a coal-mining executive, Roche had worked for Judge Lindsey on the juvenile court after completing her master's degree in social work at Columbia.

On the Denver police force, she was responsible for enforcing curfew regulations for children and, more significantly, restricting their access to alcohol, saloons, and dance halls. Creel and Roche were committed to eliminating prostitution but also feared driving it underground into new districts within the city. In early 1913 both Creel and Roche publicized the lack of police enforcement of regulations on brothels, dance halls, and saloons.[74] Lindsey's tradition endured.

Yet soon after these condemnations of the police, Mayor Arnold fired first Creel and then Roche. Protestant leaders and women Progressives were outraged, especially over the dismissal of Roche. At a protest rally the day after her dismissal in April 1913, women's club leaders insisted that the "vice question was the greatest problem before the city today." A few days later, 600 club members and church congregants met at the Central Presbyterian Church to hear Costigan and state senator Helen Robinson denounce the new mayor and his corrupt police force. Robinson insisted that Roche's firing was an insult to the women of Denver.[75] Arnold appeared increasingly similar to Speer. The need for commission government assumed new urgency in light of Roche's dismissal. Mayor Arnold had failed to address the moral evils that Protestant Progressives had so long protested. Only structural change to city government, it seemed, could address the problem of moral corruption in urban life.

Progressive support for Arnold faded quickly after his dismissal of Josephine Roche. Yet the victory over Speer in 1912 revealed the importance of Progressives on Denver's political landscape. Reformers mobilized and guided a nonpartisan public chiefly composed of Protestant congregants in their repeated battles against Mayor Speer and corporate corruption of politics. Moral crusades against the saloon, gambling, and prostitution occupied a central place on reform platforms. Activist women frequently joined with male Protestant leaders in targeting these urban ills. In 1913, commission government promised both efficiency and honesty in city hall as well as a new tool to combat prostitution. With Speer out of power at last, Creel and other Progressives looked beyond Denver as the new stage for their reforming crusades. "A redeemed Denver," wrote Creel, will lead to "a redeemed Colorado."[76] Yet Creel's religious vision of Progressivism was not the only viable one at the statehouse.

Two

Public Enemy: Colorado Fuel and Iron or the Saloon?

In July 1908, Denver hosted the Democratic National Convention. William Jennings Bryan received the presidential nomination on the first ballot with few dissenting votes. Colorado voters had overwhelmingly supported Bryan in his previous presidential bids, and 1908 would prove no exception. His pro-silver stance was only partly the reason. When he came to Denver, Bryan had developed a reputation as a leading Progressive Democrat. Behind his 1908 campaign slogan "Shall the People Rule?" Bryan decried corporate manipulations of politics. His party platform included a plank to limit the use of injunctions against organized labor and another in support of woman suffrage. Pooling resources with the American Federation of Labor in the campaign, Bryan actively courted the labor vote. In November many Colorado workers gave it to him.

Yet Bryan's appeal in Colorado also reflected his ability to blend radical politics and Protestant Christianity. His Social Gospel faith inspired many listeners with the hope that religion could reform and uplift politics and social conditions alike. Denver Progressives had already drawn on the language and moral vision of Protestant Christianity in their crusades against the Speer Democratic machine. Now, it seemed, Bryan would give even traditional Republican voters in the state a moral reason to vote Democratic. After Denver pastor Christian Reisner concluded his celebration of Bryan as a "Christian citizen" on the convention's third day, one delegate quipped, "That's a d—n good prayer . . . and if the Lawd was really listenin' it ought to make Him a good Democrat." Bryan's Social Gospel appealed as well to many clubwomen in the state. Behind the leadership of Denver's Sarah Platt Decker, some Republican activists openly endorsed the Woman's Bryan Club. As one noted, the reform "spirit of the Republican Party had passed" to the Democrats.[1]

Bryan's campaign in turn generated new momentum for women's club and labor reform projects at the Colorado statehouse between 1909 and 1913. Their Progressive campaigns rested, like Bryan's, on ethical visions of public life. For clubwomen, feminine virtue was the remedy that promised to eradicate party corruption. For union leaders, Jefferson more than Jesus offered an ethical model for politics. Popular republicanism highlighted for many workers the dangers of corporate concentrations of economic and political power in the state. Both clubwomen and union activists came to embrace Progressive reforms to enhance civic independence, protect vulnerable workers, and promote social justice.

DIRECT LEGISLATION AND THE EIGHT-HOUR DAY

Among the leading demands of women and labor Progressives at the state capitol was direct governance. The initiative, referendum, and recall offered promising tools to bypass the corporate lobby in the General Assembly, promote active and deliberative politics, and enact laws on behalf of the people. Both women's clubs and labor unions had campaigned for these reforms in the 1890s. The Colorado Federation of Women's Clubs regularly endorsed direct legislation. At their founding convention in 1896, state labor federation delegates called for the adoption of the initiative and referendum in their first resolution. Women's club and union leaders shared their enthusiasm with reformers like Ben Lindsey in the early 1900s. Several union printers actively promoted direct legislation along with Lindsey, who served as chair of the Colorado chapter of the Direct Democracy League.[2] Although some Denver workers might prefer to trust in Speer and party politics, at the state level unionists had no such friendly ally. There the initiative and referendum promised to revolutionize the political system by circumventing parties and elected officials and to enhance civic engagement.[3]

In practical terms, direct democracy appeared important because of the repeated failure of the legislature to enact effective laws for protecting workers and children and because of court hostility to those laws that did pass.

Protective labor laws were essential if workers were to secure a measure of economic independence in the state. As in other Mountain West states, the nonpartisan drive for protective labor legislation focused first on *male*—not female—workers.[4] Between 1894 and 1904, the Western Federation of Miners (WFM) waged intense and at times violent campaigns for the eight-hour day on behalf of metal miners and smelter workers in the state. In these same years, WFM and Colorado State Federation of Labor (CSFL) leaders repeatedly lobbied for an hours law in the legislature. Unionization *and* protective labor laws were twin goals for the state's miners.

The public had an ethical interest in extending the state's police power to regulate hours in such dangerous work, unionists insisted. They convinced Colorado legislators to pass an eight-hour bill in spring 1899. It was based on the Utah statute recently upheld by the US Supreme Court. The Colorado law was in effect less than a month before state Supreme Court justices with ties to the state Republican machine struck it down. Anticipating the US Supreme Court's *Lochner v. New York* decision by six years, Colorado justices held that a health risk to individual male workers was not sufficient to justify such a limitation of workers' or owners' private rights. Such limits threatened the masculine independence of mine workers, the court suggested. Mining and smelting were purely private businesses and not "affected with a public interest or devoted to a public use." The hours law was not a legitimate exercise of the state's police power authority to protect public health.[5]

Securing protective labor laws would thus require a renegotiation of the public interest in industries like mining. Labor leaders and clubwomen shared a broad view of the public interest tradition in US law. This identified the public authority assumed by private business and advocated a degree of popular sovereignty over marketplace activity.[6] The Colorado Supreme Court, like that in other states, narrowed the public interest in market relations and constricted the government's power to regulate working conditions and wages. Protective labor legislation in particular highlighted the ongoing debate in the courts over the meaning of public interest and its implications for state police power.[7]

Clubwomen and labor reformers in Colorado agreed that the public interest in economic activities demanded an ethical consideration of what benefited the community. In this effort the Populist goals of male unionists dovetailed nicely with the feminine vision of clubwomen. Labor leaders defined citizenship with reference to work and gendered notions of public and private spheres.[8] Threats to male independence in the workplace, such as the overwhelming power of mine operators, undermined the promise of working men's civic participation. State interventions on behalf of male miners could begin to equalize power relations in the workplace and thus in politics, not just protect life and limb. In terms of female citizenship, male workers often romanticized motherhood and domestic femininity while at times backing female workplace activism.

Clubwomen began from a different starting point but reached similar conclusions. Informed especially by maternalist concerns, most Colorado clubwomen endorsed the male breadwinning ideal and sought labor protections for working-class women given their potential roles as mothers. While Colorado Federation of Women's Club (CFWC) leaders acknowledged financial need as a legitimate reason for women to seek wage work, most nonetheless considered homemaking and motherhood "the highest calling on earth."[9] Motherhood remained the ideal aspect of femininity for most clubwomen. Labor and women's Progressivism thus linked the promise of nonpartisan activism and direct democracy with popular republican and maternal conceptions of citizenship.

This labor Progressive vision emerged during the miner's struggle for an eight-hour day. In 1900, CSFL unionists organized a "nonpartisan" Industrial League, which successfully rallied the electorate to approve, by overwhelming majority, a constitutional amendment authorizing an hours law for male miners and smelter workers. These reformers hoped that the constitutional amendment defined the state's police power to protect the public health in ways that the courts could not contest. Both Democratic and Republican candidates campaigned in the fall 1902 election on promises to enact such a law once in office. In spring 1903, the CSFL again mobilized popular pressure on state lawmakers in hopes of at last obtaining an hours law. Yet the mining and smelter owners effectively lobbied the legislature that spring to defeat the proposal.

As muckraking journalist Ray Stannard Baker railed, "It was nothing to them that the people of Colorado had declared such a law to be their will by an immense majority; it interfered with their business interests!" Baker continued, "Rarely, indeed, has there been . . . a more brazen, conscienceless defeat of the will of the people, plainly expressed."[10] Although some frustrated unionists turned bitterly away from legislative lobbying to direct-action campaigns, the CSFL and Denver Trades and Labor Assembly (DTLA) retained faith in politics and renewed calls for direct democracy at the state level. And unlike the national AFL leadership, Colorado's union federations endorsed both protective legislation and unionization for endangered male workers.

PROTECTING LAUNDRY WORKERS

A cross-class campaign to secure state protection for vulnerable female workers began a few years later on behalf of women in laundries. In summer 1906 a Denver printer and Democratic Party activist led an organizing drive among the women laundry workers of Denver. Building on successful campaigns by some unionists to achieve the eight-hour day, the Denver Trades and Labor Assembly hoped to organize these women workers in order to achieve a similar goal where the state government had failed. In 1903 the Colorado legislature had passed an eight-hour law regulating the work of women and children in any industry deemed "unhealthful and dangerous."[11] Laundry owners, however, insisted that their work sites were healthy and ventilated. They ignored the Women and Children Act of 1903 as irrelevant to their operations. Unorganized laundry workers appealed to the city's union federation for help.[12]

The Progressive Era struggle to shorten the workday for women laundry workers became the focus for reformers nationwide. The famous test case began in Portland, Oregon. In 1905, laundry owner Curt Muller challenged the legality of Oregon's recent law limiting women to a ten-hour day. Three years later, the US Supreme Court upheld the Oregon law. In *Muller v. Oregon,* the court accepted arguments about women's physical limitations as mothers and prospective mothers. Gender-specific dangers of overwork justified their protection. While generations of scholars applauded the *Muller* decision as a break with the court's traditional laissez-faire hostility to protective labor law, recent historians are much less sanguine. Several have stressed the economic and personal costs associated with protective labor legislation under *Muller,* noting that the decision gave judicial sanction to assumptions about women's biological weaknesses and essentialized notions of female domesticity.[13] The case of Denver laundry workers proceeded alongside that of Muller's employees. Yet protective legislation worked indirectly to enhance unionization among women in Denver.

The organizing drive among Denver laundry workers initially benefited from Colorado's women's hours law. Organizers pointed to laundry owner defiance of the law as a reason for the women to unionize. In 1906 and 1907, Denver's Laundry Workers Local no. 22 dramatically expanded its membership. By summer 1907, more than ten of the city's laundries had signed working agreements with the union, limiting hours in accordance with the state law. Gendered assumptions guided the union efforts. Union leaders distributed flyers throughout the city that asked, "Would you like your mother to work or iron steadily for ten hours?" Another challenged Denver men specifically: "IF YOU ARE A MAN you will not care to be responsible for making A WOMAN work longer than she can without inhuman cruelty." The CSFL organized a boycott campaign against non-union laundries in defiance of the state's recently passed anti-boycott law.[14] Union workers were not the only ones to take part.

By the summer of 1907, Denver clubwomen openly called for their members to support the union boycott and back unionization for laundry women. Mabel Costigan, secretary of the Denver Woman's Club and wife of reformer Edward, argued that the city's clubwomen had a "moral responsibility" to patronize laundries that observed the eight-hour day. The Woman's Club especially feared for the "welfare of this class of oppressed womanhood." Ellis Meredith invited laundry unionists to speak at club meetings, urging support for their organization drive. Union leaders happily welcomed the endorsement of Denver's clubwomen and, indirectly, their opposition to the state anti-boycott law. Their support positioned the clubwomen in opposition to the men's Citizens' Alliance, which called for indictments against CSFL leaders for organizing the boycott. Historian Maureen Flanagan has noted similar support from middle-class Chicago women for oppressed working-class women in that city. Yet she found little cooperation between male unionists and the middle-class women.[15]

Non-union employers in Denver rallied together to form the Laundryman's Association, which union leaders strategically labeled the "Laundry Trust." The leader of the employers and president of the Colorado Towel and Supply Company, Frank Burcher, repeatedly defied the women's eight-hour law. One of his employees, Belle Johnson, complained to the state Labor Commission that Burcher required her to work nine- and ten-hour days. State labor commissioner Ed Brake investigated in 1905 and confirmed Johnson's allegations, whereupon the attorney general indicted Burcher for violating the eight-hour law. The Denver District Court found Burcher guilty and ordered him to pay a fine. Burcher appealed to the state Supreme Court. The Denver Citizens' Alliance backed the laundry owner. Burcher's attorneys insisted that the Women and Children Act did not specifically declare laundry work to be dangerous to women's health. Union and women's club leaders saw organized interests challenging the will of the people to oppress working women and prospective mothers.

In early December 1907, the Colorado Supreme Court sided with employers in a six-to-one decision. Although not disputing the legislature's authority to regulate dangerous working conditions in the public interest, the court found that the 1903 law failed to specify what occupations were dangerous for women workers.[16] Without this precondition to validate the regulation, the court considered the law unconstitutional. Unlike US Supreme Court justices in the *Muller* case a few months later, Colorado justices in late 1907 focused on the relative dangers of laundry work rather than on women's bodies per se. The lone dissent came from Chief Justice Robert Steele, whose wife was active in the city's women's club and who himself served as an important bridge between the unions and clubwomen.

Union leaders and clubwomen reacted swiftly to the decision. State Bureau of Labor chief Ed Brake drafted a new bill to address the court's ruling. At a mass meeting on December 15, Brake and union legislator Harvey Garman condemned the court decision. Ellis Meredith pledged the cooperation of the Colorado clubwomen to enact a new law and punish those judges sitting for reelection the next year. Clubwomen reaffirmed their support for the union boycott of non-union laundries as well.[17] The campaign to organize laundry workers helped to spark a remarkable moment of cross-class cooperation between male unionists and clubwomen, who shared ethical expectations of business.

The failure to secure state protections for laundry workers and miners renewed interest in direct democracy. Despite an impressive campaign against the court decision, club and labor leaders were unable to convince the 1909 legislature to approve an hours law for women or the initiative and referendum. These defeats aroused middle-class women and unionists to wage a broad campaign for direct legislation over the next three years.[18] In fall 1910, William U'Ren of Oregon joined Ben Lindsey at rallies of the Direct Legislation League and city labor federation to campaign for the initiative and referendum. U'Ren spoke on the success of direct democracy in Oregon and its promise to counter corporate monopolistic corruption.[19] Labor leaders worked to mend divisions from the spring city election and hoped to present a unified voice in support of direct legislation at the state level.[20]

PROGRESSIVES AND THE DEMOCRATIC PARTY

To achieve direct democracy and protective labor legislation, Progressive union and women's club activists turned increasingly to the state Democratic Party. Bryan's fall 1908 campaign signaled to many in Colorado a new embrace of Progressive reform by the Democrats. Many clubwomen and unionists backed the Democratic ticket as Bryan swept the state and voters elected the Democratic reformer John Shafroth as governor. Shafroth had campaigned for the initiative, referendum, direct primary, and headless ballot. In his inaugural address, he insisted that campaign pledges by legislators to enact direct legislation constituted "a contract between the people" and state officials. The voters of Colorado, "politically the most independent of any in the union," would consign to oblivion those legislators who failed to redeem their pledges.[21] As state leader of the "platform" Democrats, Shafroth ironically sought reforms to weaken party dominance over politics. He cultivated an image of being above the partisan fray, championing the reform masculinity of Lindsey and even former president Teddy Roosevelt. The sympathetic *Rocky Mountain News* pictured Shafroth borrowing Roosevelt's "big stick" in order to pressure anti-reform legislators. Roosevelt appears to give his blessing to Shafroth's "worthy cause—hammer 'em good!" (Figure 2.1).

Ed Keating at the *News* upheld Shafroth as a "real man in the governor's chair."[22] Although not explicitly religious in his reform stance, Shafroth did draw upon the Protestant vision of independent masculinity advanced by Denver reformers.

2.1. *The Missing "Big Stick" Discovered* (*ROCKY MOUNTAIN NEWS*, MARCH 25, 1909)

Sensing the shift in the political winds, Speer Democrats in the legislature, many with union ties, did approve some Progressive protections for workers in 1909. Elected to head the state labor department, Edwin Brake led a campaign, supported by both the labor and women's federations, to create a factory inspection division. The legislature approved Brake's bill, which Shafroth

PUBLIC ENEMY: COLORADO FUEL AND IRON OR THE SALOON?

signed even though it lacked sufficient appropriation to make the law broadly effective. Brake appointed Kathryn Williamson, women's club activist and labor federation member, as factory inspector. She focused attention on conditions of working women in the laundries. Williamson became chair of the state women's club legislative committee in the summer of 1910. She also served on the executive board of the state labor federation.

Williamson often spoke at Denver churches on the importance of women's eight-hour law. Overworked women factory workers, she argued, were a menace to the morals of the city. Williamson urged church women to use their "Christian influence" and work for an eight-hour standard. Here was a reformer poised to ally women, labor, and Protestant Progressives. Williamson nearly secured the Democratic nomination for congressional representative in 1912. Despite her campaigning, however, state legislators rejected bills to limit hours for miners and laundry women. Sympathetic reformer George Creel cast the state legislature in terms of a central Progressive opposition. The division was not "Democratic or Republican, but Corporation and the People."[23] State Democrats would soon surprise him.

Although frustrated in his attempts to secure reform legislation in the 1909 session, Governor Shafroth strategically pressed anti-reform legislators of both parties into backing initiative, referendum, and direct primary measures in a 1910 special session of the General Assembly.[24] Shafroth maintained a delicate balance within the state Democratic Party. Allies of the Speer machine in Denver, including a number of unionists, opposed the governor's anti-partisan zeal. But Speer Democrats also understood electoral realities and realized that Shafroth and his reform supporters had profoundly shaped the terms of the debate on direct legislation. With an election approaching in the fall, their "covenant with the people," as Keating termed it, could not be ignored.[25] Clubwomen and union leaders in the CSFL were delighted that Shafroth had held lawmakers to their campaign pledges.

In November 1910, Shafroth won easy reelection thanks to significant support from clubwomen and organized labor. *Union Labor Bulletin* editor Conkle enthused that workers in Denver should "rejoice over the election of Shafroth."[26] Former Denver labor federation president and Speer ally George McLachlan became speaker of the House with a Democratic majority. McLachlan was a fierce opponent of the Denver Citizens' Alliance, whose members continually hounded him for his open violations of the state's anti-boycotting law. With McLachlan and other Speer Democrats joining forces with Shafroth reformers, the 1911 legislature appeared promising.

When lawmakers adjourned that spring, labor Progressives were delighted with the results of the session.[27] Democratic majorities in both houses approved a Miner's Eight Hour Bill; an Anti-Coercion Bill, to prevent employers from firing workers solely because of union affiliation; a False Advertising

Bill, to prohibit employers from advertising for strikebreakers without acknowledging strike conditions; and an Employers' Liability Bill, among others. Clubwomen and union leaders together pressured lawmakers to pass a bill, drafted by Ben Lindsey, to curtail child labor. Shafroth signed all into law. Both the labor and women's federations rejoiced that so many of their legislative goals were achieved. Democratic Party lawmakers had at last responded favorably to the pressure of labor and women Progressives. This reflected both the intensity of their shared lobby and the waning influence of the Speer machine over the party.

Still, union and club leaders did endure some legislative failures. In light of the investigations by state factory inspectors, the governor had called for laws to protect coal miners and to create a system of workmen's compensation. However, the Senate then so weakened these bills that Shafroth vetoed them at the request of labor leaders.[28] Former labor federation president Harvey Garman introduced a women's eight-hour law in the Senate to a gallery packed with women's club supporters. When the clubwomen hissed a Senate opponent of the bill, he responded: "Snakes and geese are the only animals that hiss. I thought those were ladies [in the gallery] but I see they are club women."[29] Activist women were clearly not without their hostile critics. Although the Senate approved the bill, House members rejected it. Again, the legislature failed to support longstanding demands for hours regulations for women workers. And the new miners' law could not take effect before Colorado Fuel and Iron Company organizers gathered enough signatures to refer the law to the voters on the 1912 ballot.[30] Labor protections for female and male workers continued to elude labor and women Progressives.

THE PROGRESSIVE PARTY CAMPAIGN OF 1912

Although lawmakers in 1909 and 1911 had resisted direct legislation reforms, Shafroth had overseen a coalition of Speer Democrats from Denver with anti-machine Democrats from outside the capital city that enacted significant Progressive reform. Clubwomen and many unionists praised the governor for his economical and honest administration on behalf of the people, not his party. The public interest was rarely so closely aligned with labor and women's club goals as under his administration. At the 1912 state labor convention, president and miner John McLennan claimed that workers "were never in a better position to obtain necessary reforms."[31] Union leaders and clubwomen determined to push their agenda further.

Thus they broadened their campaign in 1912 to make broad use of direct legislation on behalf of the people. In the general election that fall, a record thirty-two measures faced Colorado voters. This was the first opportunity for them to unleash their new lawmaking powers. Progressive reformers like Ben Lindsey and Edward Costigan had each drafted several initiatives. On Election Day, voters overwhelmingly endorsed two reforms advanced by labor and women Progressives: a women's eight-hour law and a mothers' compensation law, both sponsored by Lindsey's Direct Democracy League. By narrow margins, voters also approved a miners' eight-hour law, the headless ballot, civil service regulations, recall, and a provision to subject state Supreme Court decisions to popular referenda.[32] Voters narrowly defeated a measure, drafted by Costigan, to designate mining and smelting as businesses "affected with a public interest," and thus subject to state regulation of working conditions.

Overall, the measures to protect workers and limit court interference benefited from broad support among clubwomen and unionists. Yet partisan divisions emerged in revealing ways. Votes for the labor initiatives of Lindsey's Direct Democracy League correlated most closely with votes for Socialist candidates. Counties that had supported Populists in 1894 tended to support labor Progressives' measures in 1912.[33] Party loyalties were still important for Catholic foreign-born voters, who tended to continue their support of Democrats.

The initiative that generated the greatest interest from voters was for statewide prohibition. Women's Christian Temperance Union (WCTU) leaders had campaigned statewide for the initiative, but Anti-Saloon League activists focused instead on county-level efforts. This division among prohibition advocates helped to ensure the defeat of the statewide initiative in 1912 by more than 40,000 votes. In Denver, opposition was especially strong in working-class neighborhoods. Formerly Populist counties in the mountains overwhelmingly rejected the measure.[34] The failure of this initiative meant an unusual setback for Protestant activists — in a year that saw them oust Boss Speer in Denver no less. The labor-women's coalition, however, had achieved great success.

Additionally, many women's club and union leaders in 1912 had hoped to join forces with farmers to support Ed Costigan for governor on the Progressive Party ticket. Costigan promoted a tenuous alliance of labor, women, and Protestant Progressives within the state Bull Moose Party. When reform Republicans abandoned Taft in the summer of 1912, Costigan emerged as the state leader of this new party. In his campaign for governor, Costigan worked to mute religious issues like prohibition while focusing attention on questions of social and industrial justice. While working as a Denver police officer, Josephine Roche stumped for the state Progressive Party. In 1913 she assumed primary responsibility for organizing women into the new party.

Yet Roche and Costigan had only modest success in the 1912 election. Their party had the support of only one Denver newspaper. And the Democrats could point to their recent legislative record in appealing to union and women activists. Clubwoman and journalist Helen Ring Robinson emerged from the Democratic primary as a candidate for the state Senate. The Democrats also ran more union members for office than the new Progressive Party. The latter party had suffered from poor and late organization during the campaign.

The head of the state Democratic ticket, rancher Elias Ammons, won the nomination as a modest reformer and leading opponent of President Roosevelt's conservation policies. Ammons received the most votes in the general election given the split among traditional Republicans. Costigan did manage to outpoll the Republican candidate to come in a close second behind Ammons. Despite Costigan's appeals to labor, votes for the Progressive Party leader correlated with Protestantism, farming, and traditional Republican loyalties. Progressive Party voters were also the most ardent supporters of the prohibition initiative. Miners particularly rejected Costigan and supported the Democrat for governor. Ammons's victory met with denunciations from Progressive labor editors, who lamented the "mistake" many workers made in voting for the head of the Democratic ticket, especially those in Denver with ties to Speer.[35] But the election demonstrated that Protestant Progressives and farmers continued to stress moral over economic reforms. Costigan could not sufficiently broaden his appeal to working-class voters.

Nonetheless, voters sent a record number of unionists to the state legislature in 1912 along with the first woman to the state Senate. The Democratic governor would enjoy Democratic majorities in both houses of the legislature in 1913. Despite Costigan's defeat, prospects for the labor-women's coalition appeared promising in spring 1913. Senator Helen Robinson and Representative Frances Lee in the House worked closely with women's clubs, female trade unionists in Denver, and the state labor federation to pass a women's minimum wage bill, which the governor signed into law.[36] The legislature also approved a coal mine inspection bill and ratified the miner's eight-hour initiative approved by voters in 1912. The success of the former bill reflected the public investigations by state factory inspectors of the abusive and unsafe conditions miners faced, especially in southern Colorado and the tragic mine disasters at Primero, Starkville, and Delagua in 1910. Miners in Colorado could at least hope for state regulation of their hours.[37]

An American Federation of Labor press release enthused that trade unionists in Colorado had made an "unparalleled" legislative record. The state labor federation praised the women's club members of the state legislature for their support of labor bills.[38] Leaders of labor and women's federations were pleased that Colorado voters at last had the tools of direct democracy and that they had made swift use of them to secure protections for workers. Their ethical view of the public interest decisively shaped the terms of the political debate, which party machines and corporate elites could no longer ignore. Reformers within the Democratic Party seemed in command.

COAL MINERS AND CORPORATE POLITICS

Yet there remained in 1913 one region largely untouched by the promises of Progressive reform. The southern coalfields, under the dominance of the Colorado Fuel and Iron Company (CFI), stood as a world apart. As the largest employer in the state, CFI paid the wages of one of every ten Colorado workers. The industrial giant owned 300,000 acres of bituminous coalfields, primarily in Las Animas and Huerfano counties in order to feed steel production centered in Pueblo. The Rockefeller family controlled 40 percent of the company stock, and CFI's management controlled the lives of its roughly 30,000 employees and the politics of the region in an apt demonstration of "industrial feudalism."[39] In 1913 the United Mine Workers (UMW) organized a defiant challenge to the CFI on behalf of its oppressed workforce. Union efforts sparked confrontations that Progressive reformers could not contain.[40]

The political abuses of the state Republican machine in the coal districts of the state were among the leading complaints of miners. As early as 1903, Ed Keating had agreed that "as the Colorado Fuel and Iron Company goes, so goes the [Republican] party. It has always been the dominating influence in party affairs, for it controls enough votes in the various counties in which it operates to hold the balance of power."[41] The Huerfano County Courthouse was little more than a branch office of the CFI. The local Republican machine boss in the county was Sheriff Jefferson Farr, who looked after both his own saloon interests and those of the coal giant with equal enthusiasm.[42] Although labor reformers had long complained of these abuses of power, they could not arouse a broad movement for state reform in the coal districts.

By the spring of 1913 this had begun to change. In February, reformers in the Colorado Senate held three weeks of hearings to investigate charges of fraud in Las Animas County during the 1912 election. The Senate committee, chaired by railroad unionist Joseph Berry, included several other labor-friendly senators, such as women's club member Helen Ring Robinson. The inquiry focused on specific allegations of corruption against Senator Casimiro Barela, a Republican from Las Animas County and consistent CFI ally. Barela had faced charges of corruption for the last twelve years, but this was the first time senators had undertaken an investigation of one of their own members.

The committee uncovered a range of tactics deployed by the Republican machine in this coal county. These included ballot-box stuffing, buying votes and intimidating voters, and, most salaciously, protection for loyal gamblers and saloon owners while party activists paid prostitutes to back the machine.[43] This list of moral offenses closely resembled the charges against the Speer machine a decade earlier. Senate investigators could hardly have asked for better indictments to arouse the moral indignation of Protestant Progressives. The majority of the witnesses subpoenaed by the Senate committee were saloon owners and bartenders. Democratic senator Helen Robinson concluded from the hearings that industrial conditions in the southern counties were "hopeless, because the political situation appeared to be hopeless." These counties were little better than "a barony or a principality of the Colorado Fuel and Iron Co.," which ruled in collusion with saloon interests.[44] Senate investigators, despite all their work, were unable to muster enough votes to unseat Senator Barela or to condemn officially the coal company abuses that had secured his election.

Meanwhile, conditions for miners in the southern coalfields had become intolerable, not only because of such political corruption by the operators. Company-town conditions, with camp guards and CFI-owned stores and churches, constrained worker freedom, manhood, and opportunity. CFI violations of state labor laws and the refusal to recognize unions gave workers legitimate grounds for protest. The militarization of coal camp perimeters further provoked workers.[45] A two-year-long strike in the northern Colorado coalfields had produced few results. In September, the UMW called southern Colorado workers out on strike, insisting on union recognition and company compliance with existing state labor laws. More than 12,000 miners left their jobs and company houses behind, taking up refuge in tent colonies like the one near the railroad station of Ludlow. In a larger sense, mine workers pressed for an expanded vision of public rights, one informed by republican ideology. They lived in a private world, isolated from representative government and denied civic independence. As *New Republic* editors argued at the time, the situation that precipitated the strike was one in which "a man's employer owns not only the place in which he works but also the store at which he must buy, the house in which he must dwell, the streets upon which he must walk, and the roads leading to and from this privately owned city. The workman is surrounded by private property rights, and all these rights inhere in his employer. . . . The whole life of the worker is one continued trespass upon private property."[46] The strike at last focused attention on the hopes of mine workers to inhabit a public space in which state and even federal laws applied.

INDUSTRIAL WARFARE AND THE MASSACRE AT LUDLOW

In the course of the strike, local government was increasingly unable to maintain order. CFI strikebreakers, supported by armed Baldwin-Felts detectives and company guards, provoked confrontations with union miners. Governor Ammons ordered the National Guard to southern Colorado in October 1913. By December, the state militia escorted strikebreakers from railroad stops to CFI mines in defiance of union pleas. Many contemporary observers agreed with unionists that the operators effectively dominated the state militia and Governor Ammons as they had the local political scene in Huerfano and Las

Animas counties. Mother Jones again appeared in Colorado mining towns to denounce the CFI and Governor Ammons. She soon endured twenty-six days in the Walsenburg County Courthouse Jail for her incendiary speeches in support of the miners. In January 1914 mounted National Guard troops rode down a parade of women who were protesting the incarceration of Mother Jones, injuring many. *New Republic* editors observed that "the police power of the state was captured by one of the parties to a bitter industrial dispute, and it was used ruthlessly not merely to suppress violence, but to terrorize the strikers into submission."[47] The state was unable to uphold its most basic responsibility to enforce its laws, protect citizens against organized violence, and use military power to secure public order.

More damning still, the private power of the operators proved morally corrupting for workmen and their families. Union leaders sought to arouse Protestant and maternal indignation by stressing corporate ties to the saloon. A United Mine Workers official reported in the early months of the strike that he had seen children as young as ten "coming out of the company saloon so drunk they could scarcely walk." He found these saloons and brothels never closed, not even on Sundays. The operators had additionally enlisted into the state militia "saloon bums" from Denver's red-light district, "their faces scarred and the breath strong with whiskey."[48] One militia leader, Major Patrick Hamrock, was in fact a Denver saloon owner. A federal grand jury investigating strike conditions in the fall of 1913 charged the coal companies with responsibility for the "deplorable situation" created by the saloons in the mining camps.[49] Miners argued that the militiamen also attracted prostitutes from local communities, insulted "respectable women," and threatened feminine virtue and working-class motherhood.[50] Protestant leaders in Denver did not immediately react.

In February, Governor Ammons decided that the cost of maintaining the militia in the strike zone was too great. Recalling most of the National Guard troops, Ammons allowed a small detachment composed chiefly of strike-breakers and CFI company guards to remain. After a series of provocations, the small militia company attacked the Ludlow tent colony on the morning of April 20. National Guard troops killed eighteen strikers including their leader, Louis Tikas. Militia commander Karl Linderfeldt first knocked Tikas unconscious with a rifle butt to the head before other militiamen fired shots into his back. The tent camp at Ludlow caught fire, burning alive two women and eleven small children trapped in small pits designed to protect them from gunfire. The "massacre of innocents" led mine union and state labor federation leaders to call striking workers to arms. A guerrilla war ensued, with strikers attacking mine after mine, and National Guard troops flooding back into the counties. Strikers felt keenly the charges that they had failed to protect women and children. A desire to reassert their masculinity fueled the retributive violence that followed in ten days of war. Historian Thomas Andrews estimates that the death toll for the coalfield strike of 1913–1914 may have reached a hundred. State authorities were unable to halt the violence, as armed strikers drilled openly on town streets in what Andrews aptly called a Ten Days' War.[51]

As violence raged after Ludlow, clubwomen and moderate workers alike pleaded with President Wilson for the intervention of federal troops. These Progressives hoped initially for some federal mediation of the conflict. For state senator Helen Robinson, only federal intervention could protect the "ignorant, innocent, terrified wives, daughters, and children of the strikers." More than a thousand women, many from Denver's clubs and some cradling babies, held a sit-in outside the governor's office to demand that he wire the president for help. Robinson, Democratic state representative Alma Lafferty, and a former Populist legislator, all clubwomen, led the Women's Peace Association in a day-long vigil and display of feminine resolve. One reporter commented that "the mothers of the state" had "awakened to their power." The press widely credited the feminine public with exerting sufficient pressure on Governor Ammons to request federal aid.[52] On April 28, President Wilson sent in a small force of US Army soldiers who soon established order in the strike zone.

STRIKING WORKERS AND THE SALOON

When Ammons called the legislature into special session to address the emergency soon after Ludlow, however, the saloon loomed far larger than calls for arbitration or justice. Rejecting proposals to force arbitration of the strike or to declare coal mines public utilities, legislators could only agree on two measures: one approving a bond measure to pay for the costs of the militia and another to grant the governor the authority to close saloons and prohibit the sale of alcohol in the strike zone. President Wilson wired Ammons as the special session neared an end, imploring him to propose some settlement of the strike, but Ammons only professed his powerlessness to influence legislators. Protestant Progressives had again begun to assert the importance of moral renewal through prohibition. Ignoring issues of industrial justice, most legislators worked only to curb the influence of the saloon and compensate militiamen.[53]

In the months immediately following Ludlow, public attention continued to focus on the corrupting influences of the company town and its saloon. In a May 1914 dispatch for *Outlook* magazine, Colorado national guardsman W. T. Davis indicted coal company owners for creating unhealthy, miserable communities and an "atmosphere of decided lawlessness." Invoking the rhetoric of Protestant moralists, he noted that in "every village the company owns at least one building which is used as a saloon. The saloons are farmed out to men who prove in most instances to be the very worst of characters." These saloon owners and gamblers "pander to passion, and vice exists literally in swarms." Thus company saloons created explosive conditions. "Drink-befuddled and maddened by want, these men became perfect firebrands, assigning all their woes to the companies and to society in general." The miners were "essentially as good as the average man, but that they are being debauched and degraded by conditions over which they have no control seems to be only too apparent."[54] The saloon appeared be the spark that ignited the conflict.

Although hostility to the operators remained high in the spring and summer of 1914, a subtle but decisive shift occurred in public debates. Commentators increasingly focused on the role foreign "agitators" and the saloon had played in the strike while questions of coal operators' culpability faded from view. Historian Elliott West has argued that the violence in the coalfields and subsequent investigations "furnished well-publicized examples of many of the dangers drys had tried for years to associate with the liquor trade." Coal owners were among the first who tried to place blame for unrest on independent saloon owners who allegedly incited their foreign-born patrons to violence.[55] By August 1914, prohibition supporters sensed a new momentum emerging as a consequence of Ludlow. At an Anti-Saloon League rally with 500 Denver supporters that summer, the founder of the league argued that alcohol "brought about a condition of unrest and dissatisfaction which resulted in the anarchistic situation in the strike zone."[56]

Coal operators particularly sensed a shift in the political winds. Rockefeller liberally financed the Anti-Saloon League petition drive and campaign on behalf of a statewide prohibition initiative for the 1914 election. CFI president Jesse Welborn publicly embraced the prohibitionist cause in September, reporting that workers in the strike zone had boosted productivity while the saloons were closed. This also translated into an increase in wages, he contended, and thus more money that reached the home rather than the saloon.[57]

The gubernatorial campaign of 1914 particularly revealed the steady erosion of concern with industrial justice, as the promise of prohibition came to reinforce a Republican vision of law and order. This election, like that in 1912, became another three-way race. Progressive party leader Edward Costigan waged a second campaign for governor, backed by the able Josephine Roche. The Republicans nominated Fort Collins district attorney George Carlson, and the Democrats supported former *Rocky Mountain News* owner and longtime Progressive activist Thomas Patterson. Although the popular republican vision of the union miners featured prominently in the campaign, it was gradually overshadowed by prohibition and the saloon.

The Progressive party was particularly divided by prohibition and the coal strike. Having defended striking miners in the courts and before the US

Commission on Industrial Relations, Costigan championed their cause and attempted to focus on the campaign on economic inequalities. Despite his earlier work as an attorney for the state Anti-Saloon League, Costigan resisted appeals to endorse prohibition in the 1914 campaign. The Progressive Party leader hoped to reach a broader audience than his Protestant supporters in Denver and farmers across the state. Costigan came to acknowledge that corporate dominance, rather than the saloon, posed the greater threat to democratic politics in the state. The "cause of exploited men, women, and children" was the primary one in 1914, he wrote a party activist in Colorado Springs, "and the liquor question will distract attention from it and arouse collaterally the passions of the people who should be united" behind it.[58] Yet Costigan's advisers questioned this focus, as Elliot West has perceptively noted. One advisor wrote to the candidate: "I differ from you in thinking that the saloon is as great an exploiter of men, women, and children as the Colorado Fuel and Iron Company or the Denver Union Water Company. . . . There are laboring men that cannot see that the saloon is their enemy just as there are many farmers who cannot see that the Colorado Fuel and Iron Company is striking directly at them when it refuses to treat with the striking miners."[59] Costigan remained unmoved, however, convinced that prohibition forces would not endorse a party ticket but pursue a nonpartisan strategy to secure their fundamental goal.

Over the summer of 1914 Costigan worked tirelessly to focus the campaign on the question of economic justice and invoked the republican critique of monopoly power. His party would champion the "welfare of the whole public," he insisted at a Denver rally. The Republicans "worshipped" property while the Democrats exalted "license," which "permitted the special interests to seize and abuse the privileges of property. Therefore, the Democratic, like the Republican, party has become a party preferring property to the welfare of the whole community."[60] Again the rhetorical style of Progressivism was visible, with selfish partisans threatening the public. But Costigan no longer indicted the liquor boss or saloon owner.

In response to Republican calls for a restoration of law and order in the coalfields, Costigan enlisted the support of national Progressive Party leader Theodore Roosevelt. In August 1914, Roosevelt publicly endorsed the Colorado Progressive program that Costigan had developed. In a letter widely reprinted during the fall campaign, Roosevelt also attacked the Republican and Democratic parties in Colorado for creating conditions of "governmental bankruptcy." He flayed "law-and-order" Republicans who called only for state policing of working men but not corporations responsible for the conditions in the coalfields. Roosevelt explicitly singled out the CFI for its abuse of power and denounced the Colorado custom in which the state "surrendered its right and duty to enforce the law and maintain order" to mining companies in times of labor conflict. Roosevelt backed Costigan's calls to declare coal mining a public utility in Colorado, empowering the state to regulate working conditions. The ex-president also voiced his support for labor's right to collective bargaining.[61] State labor progressives at last had a national champion.

Despite Costigan's best efforts, however, the law-and-order Republicans used prohibition to obscure questions of economic justice as the campaign progressed. The Anti-Saloon League and WCTU mended their differences from the 1912 campaign and forged a more effective approach to advance the dry initiative. With Rockefeller philanthropy, the WCTU circulated initiative petitions and canvassed neighborhoods while the men of the league oversaw advertising and organization.[62] The Republicans worked strategically to ally with prohibition advocates.

United behind thirty-eight-year-old district attorney George Carlson, Republicans projected an image of masculine power and self-assurance. The stocky, blond son of Swedish immigrants had been football captain and heavy-weight boxing champion at the University of Colorado. Carlson cultivated his image as the native-born son of northwest Europeans as a dramatic counter to the southeast European striking coal miner. His reputation in largely rural Larimer County for strict law enforcement helped woo rural voters concerned about bootlegging in dry towns. Although the GOP platform did not officially endorse the prohibition initiative on the November ballot, Carlson made clear in campaign speeches his support for a dry Colorado.[63] With Costigan refusing to back prohibition, Carlson was the only candidate to campaign for the moral initiative. Additionally, many Protestant reformers retained suspicions of saloons and union labor from their battles against the Speer machine in Denver. They lent a sympathetic ear to Republican law-and-order appeals and voted for the GOP.[64]

Labor leaders worked to rally workers to vote in both the Democratic and Progressive party primaries. But union political action remained divided during the campaign between these two parties. Carlson came in for attack for his indictments against striking miners in the northern coalfields where he served as district attorney as well as for his ties to the coal operators. Labor editors considered him the "C. F. & I.'s fair-haired boy." The state labor convention in August that year condemned the prohibition initiative, giving union workers additional reasons to oppose Carlson. To counter Anti-Saloon accusations that brewery workers and bartenders were little better that "tools" and "victims" of "booze corporations," Denver unionists formed Labor's Anti-Prohibition Association. The labor press was among the most insistent voices in the state, calling attention to the financial support that the CFI lent to the prohibition campaign. In late October, the Denver and state labor federations endorsed practically the entire Democratic ticket. Defeating Carlson and prohibition

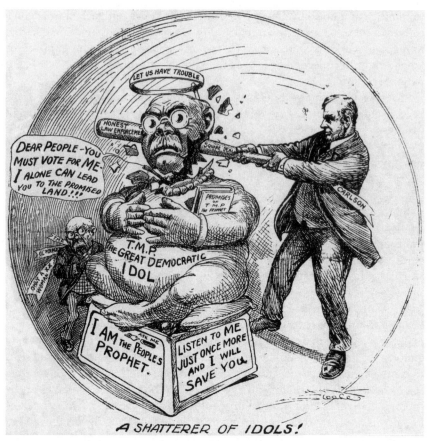

2.2. *A Shatterer of Idols* (DENVER POST, OCTOBER 21, 1914)

remained their paramount goals. Patterson had a more promising chance than Costigan, argued union leaders. As in the 1912, the Progressive Party again would struggle without strong labor backing.[65]

FRACTURES IN THE LABOR-WOMEN'S COALITION

By October the leading papers in the state all but ignored Costigan and the Progressive Party, devoting their attention to the battle between Carlson and Patterson. A series of Wilbur Steele cartoons in the *Denver Post* illustrates the broad outlines of the campaign as Election Day neared. The gendered imagery of Protestant Progressivism proved a useful tool for GOP allies like Steele. On October 21, the cartoonist depicted a strong, lean Carlson swinging a bat representing "honest law enforcement" and a "square deal" to de-

2.3. *Double, Double Toil and Trouble* (DENVER POST, OCTOBER 30, 1914)

molish a fattened idol of Patterson, the people's false "Prophet" (Figure 2.2). Carlson's mighty swing promised to liberate those deceived by the misguided Democrat in his earlier crusades.

Now it was the Republican candidate for governor wielding a "big stick" in political battle. Patterson's counsel to Ammons during the coal wars tainted him with the frustrations and hostility many felt toward the standing Democratic governor. Then just days before the election, Steele cast Patterson, along with state labor chief Ed Brake and a Democratic machine activist, as the witches of *Macbeth*, circling a cauldron and chanting "Double, Double Toil and Trouble" (Figure 2.3).

The adjoining editorial made clear that only the reassuring, muscular Christian Carlson could save the state from such scheming feminine figures.

Republicans alone could protect voters from emasculating party activists and false prophets.

The depiction of labor commissioner Brake as little better than a menacing witch was revealing. Earlier in 1914, Brake had exposed the breadth of political abuses by the CFI before a congressional investigating committee. Under Governor Shafroth he had been a key institutional ally for clubwomen and unionists alike. He had helped draft the miners' and women's eight-hour laws and long pressed for their enforcement. Yet in fall 1914, Brake became the target of women's club reformers bent on ending "party-machine" rule at the statehouse. National suffrage activist and *Post* reporter Frances Wayne led the charge against Brake, who, she insisted, had used his appointment as labor commissioner to expand the operations of the Democratic party machine within the state government. Worse still for Wayne, Brake had assumed control over a free employment bureau that the Denver Woman's Club had created, only to transform it into a "political hang-out for the friends" of the machine. Brake had become "but one of the lesser cogs in as foul a machine as ever was sta [sic] up by politicians to degrade womanhood and debauch government."[66] Wayne hoped to rally women Progressives to punish a former ally, now corrupting party-machine builder. Women's club leaders renewed their ambiguous commitment to nonpartisan political activism, and Protestant Progressives welcomed their shift away from a Democratic Party alliance.

In addition, women's club leaders found prohibition assuming new importance among their members. In the preceding elections, questions of structural reform or legislative protections for women workers had taken prominence over prohibition for many middle-class women. During the 1910 Denver city election, the Democratic party machine had stirred up support for the temperance issue that year in hopes of deflecting attention, especially among women, from the initiative and referendum. Party bosses in Colorado had long attempted to "befog" voters, claimed a sympathetic journalist, by directing "attention to a temperance issue when there are other big issues involved in an election."[67] In 1910 and again in 1912, prohibition measures lost by significant margins. By 1914, conditions had changed dramatically. The Anti-Saloon League, WCTU, and Republican Party all worked to cement a link between saloons and industrial warfare. In this election, prohibition had at last become the "big issue."

The arrival of Billy Sunday in Colorado that fall surely helped. Sunday staged a six-week crusade rallying prohibition activists across the state. The newly formed Denver Evangelical Association encouraged ministers to open their churches and provide funds to support Sunday's crusade. Juvenile court judge Ben Lindsey and other leading Citizens' Party members in Denver heralded both the evangelist and the promise of prohibition alike. Sunday, however, represented a narrowed religious vision. Where Bryan had sought to promote Christian morality in the service of social democracy, Sunday was concerned chiefly with saving individual souls. Prohibition appealed to evangelicals like Sunday because it seemed to promise social improvement through individual redemption. Challenges to monopolistic economic power or political manipulations by party machines did not find their way into Sunday's crusades. In fact, the evangelist received significant backing from the Rockefeller family, as Colorado unionists were quick to point out.[68] Sunday's brief popularity in the fall of 1914 highlighted the growing importance of prohibition among Protestant Progressives and women's club members, as economic justice receded.

The election results of November 3 confirmed the growing rift between the erstwhile allies, clubwomen and trade unionists. Republican law-and-order candidates swept the state behind the leadership of Carlson, and the prohibition initiative won by a narrow margin. In a dramatic reversal of fortunes, the 1914 election was a disaster for organized labor, as every candidate associated with unionism suffered defeat. As a Boulder editor wrote, "a great majority of the people went on record against the anarchy of the saloon as well as the anarchy of the union."[69] Carlson won easily with 129,096 votes to Patterson's 95,690. Progressive Party leader Costigan finished a distant third with only 33,320, polling less than half his 1912 total. Carlson and the prohibition amendment received almost the same number of votes in the election. Rural voters and the urban middle classes, formerly sympathetic to the Progressive Party, deserted Costigan for his Republican challenger in 1914. While most unionists opposed the prohibition initiative, workers split their votes among Democratic and Progressive Party candidates.

If unionists were isolated after the election, clubwomen too suffered from internal divisions. Female candidates, largely associated with the Progressive and Democratic parties, faired as poorly as male unionists. One clubwoman remarkably observed after the election: "The suffragists of Colorado have lost the illusions of youth. In the wisdom of maturity they admit that women are very human—quite as human as men. They vote and play the political game much the same as men."[70] After the triumph of Carlson's masculine law-and-order campaign, female Progressives struggled to unify the women's vote.

A few weeks after the election, the miners voted to end the strike in the coalfields. Governor Ammons then authorized the reopening of saloons in the former strike zone.[71] Without unions, it seemed, mine workers could safely return to the saloon, at least until the implementation of statewide prohibition in January 1916.

The election of 1914 proved a moral victory for prohibition advocates and a failure for labor Progressives. The religious vision of Billy Sunday assumed greater importance than that of William Jennings Bryan. The labor Progressive challenge to corporate dominance over the state legislature and the hinterlands of Colorado achieved little. Corporate and Republican leaders rallied Protestant Progressives in order to isolate protesting workers and sidestep investigations into electoral manipulations. Earlier Protestant reform hopes to remake masculine citizenship in broad terms focused in 1914 only on transforming individual workers. The third-party challenge led by Costigan met with a significant rebuke that year, from which it never recovered. The coalition of labor and women Progressives that had enjoyed important successes between 1910 and 1912 continued to unravel.

Protestant Progressives, however, savored their success. Colorado had adopted statewide prohibition with its promise of civic renewal. The saloon appeared less a cog in the dominant network of party machines and corporations, as it had under Mayor Speer, and more a site for sparking working-class radicalism. As war raged in Europe, union and women's club leaders struggled to regain their eroding influence and revive a challenge to corporate abuses of politics. Wartime conditions inspired both new hopes for reform and new labor conflicts, especially in Denver.

Three

The Denver Tramway Crisis and the
Struggle for Masculine Citizenship

Just six years after the horrific violence of the Ten Days' War after Ludlow, class warfare erupted in Denver. On August 5, 1920, an angry mob surrounded private guards employed by the Denver Tramway Company to break a five-day-old strike. Trapped inside the South Denver tramway facility on Broadway, more than one hundred strikebreakers feared the swelling crowd outside, which threw stones and lit a perimeter fence on fire. Guards then fired shots from inside the tramway facility, killing two nineteen-year-old men who were running away from the scene. Several others were wounded, but after midnight the police restored order and the crowd dispersed.[1]

The next evening, a crowd outside the East Side tramway barns again harassed and jeered strikebreakers. When a car loaded with reinforcements attempted to join the strikebreakers in the facility, bricks crashed against the radiator and smashed the windshield of their vehicle. In quick response, the strikebreakers opened fire on the crowd, killing five and wounding eleven, including several children. There were no striking workers killed or injured in these confrontations. When questioned later about the violence, the lead strikebreaker quipped, "All I can say is that we started on the defensive, but we answered as good as they gave."[2] With city police ultimately unable to cope, the mayor and governor appealed for federal help. On the seventh day of the streetcar strike, US Army soldiers arrived and declared martial law over the city of Denver.

The city's church leaders swiftly called for an investigation. They created the Denver Commission of Religious Forces, which included chiefly Protestant Progressive activists along with Denver priest William O'Ryan and Jewish community leader Mrs. Ray S. David. The commission hired three national figures to review the situation and propose recommendations. Prominent social work activist Edward Devine joined Father John Ryan and Dr. John A. Lapp, both directors of the Department of Social Action of the National Catholic Welfare Council. Several months later these investigators issued a report that suggestively asked whether "industry is normally war?" Condemning the "transfer [of] the police power of government to privately controlled agents who [were] irresponsive to the claims of justice," they urged the Denver public to assume its proper responsibilities. The handling of tramway fare and wage issues within the realm of partisan politics had been "especially pernicious." Had the public established "regulation of the street railway system" to ensure its solvency "and a living wage to its employees the whole unhappy conflict might have been prevented."[3]

The postwar violence in Denver reveals the limits of Progressive reform in the city. The defeat of Mayor Speer in 1912 had inspired great hopes among religiously inspired reformers. Enlightened Christian virtue was to replace selfish partisanship as a guide for city officials. The next year Progressives secured commission government for Denver, officially uncoupled from partisan alignments. Protestant activists hoped for the closure of saloons and prohibition of alcohol. These religious Progressives had significantly weakened the party system in the city in hopes of mobilizing the voting public for disinterested political action.

By 1920, Protestant Progressives had lost influence over city administration and the popular press. They offered little resistance as private tramway employees claimed police power. The city lacked a meaningful process for regulating public utilities or for resolving class conflicts. The dispute over tramway wages that began in 1918 became a battle over the character of Denver's public life in 1920. During the tramway strike Denver workers struggled against a conception of the public interest defined and represented largely by employers and consumers. Labor Progressive hopes for a broader view of the public interest gave way to defensive battles against the coercive arm of the state. Newspaper editors, Tramway Company managers, and Denver's mayor successfully advanced the short-term interests of the riding public over worker hopes for a living wage. Court injunctions only confirmed the lack of political influence for union workers in postwar Denver.

The strikebreaking tactics of the Tramway Company additionally sparked a contest over the gendered character of public life in the city. As more deliberative, peaceful strategies for settling the strike failed, the aggressive, warlike masculinity of the strikebreaking force prevailed. The imposition of martial law only confirmed the militarization of the tramway dispute. Unionists countered with a vision of the city's long-term responsibilities to protect consumers and male workers. Their more restrained ideal of working-class manhood faced a crucial challenge.

THE TRAMWAY UTILITY AND THE URBAN PUBLIC

From the start, the Denver tramway dispute revived the efforts of Progressives to define the needs and interests of the municipal public vis-à-vis private utility companies. The Tramway Company occupied a strategically important and visibly prominent presence in Denver. It tied the city together while also helping to segment urban space in its construction of new lines and streets. Even before the strikes began, Denver Tramway Company operations raised important questions about the boundaries of public authority and limits to streetcar regulation. As municipal utilities and quasi-private businesses, streetcar companies occupied a confusing middle ground, much as railroads during the late nineteenth century.[4] Although privately owned, streetcar lines required a franchise to operate on public streets and were subject to further regulation by city government. Protestant and labor Progressives had long sought to advance the city's authority over the Tramway Company.

Initially, regulations of utility corporations were quite modest. Denver's streetcar system was typical in this regard.[5] In 1899, the Denver City Tramway Company emerged from a merger of rival tramway lines to establish a monopoly over the city's streetcar service under the ownership of William Evans. The consolidated Tramway Company still operated under the terms of an 1885 franchise that required the company to provide "service," vaguely defined, on specified streets, to pave between and slightly outside the tracks it laid, and to charge only a five-cent fare. As one contemporary critic noted, "no provisions were inserted furthering and protecting the rights and interests of the public." Denver's Home Rule Charter of 1904 represented an effort to increase public oversight of this private company. The charter required city voters, not simply the city council or mayor, to approve of utility franchises. On May 15, 1906, Denver voters approved a new franchise for the Denver Tramway Company by only seventy-five votes amid widespread accusations of fraud. Speer loyalists cast ballots for the dead and stuffed ballot boxes, in collusion with the Tramway Company, to push the utility-friendly franchise through. The new franchise required the company to compensate the city $1.2 million for its access to public streets but essentially allowed the company to determine future expansions. Paving requirements and the five-cent fare were extended twenty more years. The city reserved to itself all "police functions" on the streets.[6]

Although city oversight of the tramway was technically rather narrow in its franchise agreements, Denver residents assumed this contract included a host of obligations to the public. Chief among these was a duty to provide reliable, efficient, and profitable service at a five-cent fare. Many residents additionally assumed that since the community at large helped create the value of such a public utility, the public should have a say in the distribution of profits arising from its operation. The long-term public interest in streetcar service also implied the payment of sufficient wages to allow workers to meet the rising cost of living and fares adequate to ensure financial solvency for the company.[7] Reconciling these competing obligations was never easy, especially since they remained more implied than defined in minimal franchise agreements.

Mayor Speer had observed the performance of streetcar service while mayor from 1904 to 1912. During those years Evans preferred local oversight by Speer, with whom he maintained a working relationship, to possible state regulation. Protestant reformers, however, demanded more centralized regulation of Denver's utilities along with an end to their close ties to the city's Democratic machine. After the failure of two utility regulation initiatives on the 1912 ballot, Democratic legislators in 1913 passed a bill to create a state Public Utilities Commission (PUC). Utility directors fought the bill but Governor Ammons signed it into law.[8] Progressive reformers hoped that the PUC would at last curb utility meddling in city politics.

THE COMMISSION GOVERNMENT
EXPERIMENT AND UTILITY REGULATION

In addition to the PUC, Progressives held high hopes for commission government in Denver. This structural reorganization of city government promised to limit the pervasive influence of utilities in Denver politics and promote public morality. After ousting Speer from office in May 1912, reformers grew impatient with Mayor Arnold. They had hoped for economy in government, reductions in taxes, and expansions of police and public health services. Arnold disappointed on all counts. Pressure for commission government resumed in late 1912, and voters at last approved this charter revision in February 1913. Voters abolished the mayor and bicameral city council. Soon after, Arnold fired Josephine Roche, bringing down a torrent of criticism from his erstwhile Protestant allies. In May 1913, Denver elected five nonpartisan commissioners from the city at large. Protestant Progressives hoped these new officials would advance economy, efficiency, and morality in city government.

The commission proposal included provisions long championed by religious Progressives. The ballot would include no reference to party. A preferential system in principle limited the electioneering tactics of parties. Voters could indicate their first, second, and third preferences of candidates for a specific office. A $1,000 cap on campaign financing was intended to limit corporate influence. The weakening of the traditional party system created new opportunities for a wide range of interest groups. The Ministerial Alliance, the Clean Denver Men's Committee, the Christian Citizenship Union, and city newspapers each endorsed a slate of candidates. Ten unionists in Denver Trades and Labor Assembly joined with a large group of Chamber of Commerce members to create the Denver Voters' Federation. This federation endorsed three candidates for each of the five commission posts. Unionists did not endorse a separate slate of candidates. Tellingly, a revived Municipal Ownership Committee, headed by longtime Protestant Progressives, endorsed candidates without consulting organized labor.[9] Ultimately, 115 candidates ran for six posts, creating much more confusion than Progressives had envisioned.

The election disappointed Progressives. Costigan, Lindsey, and Roche chose not to run for city office, given statewide commitments or health concerns. Voters only elected one commissioner with ties to the Christian Citizenship Union. Printer Otto Thum was a founding member of the state labor federation and longtime supporter of Costigan and the moral reform goals of Protestant churches. He became Commissioner of Property in the new government. Two other Protestant Progressive candidates trailed far behind the victors in the races for commissioner of finance and of safety. Mayor Speer's city engineer, whom Arnold had defeated for mayor just a year before, became commissioner of improvements. Women's club candidates who ran on behalf of "city mothers" for commissioner of social welfare lost to a relative outsider on the Denver scene.[10]

Once in office, commissioners pleased few. Reformers had created unrealistically high expectations for commission government. They promised dramatic tax reductions on the one hand along with expansions in services such as improved policing, poor relief, and the containment of gambling, saloons, and prostitution. Commissioners did not fulfill these demands. Four commissioners had ties to the Speer machine and thus raised suspicions among reformers about their political independence. Additionally, business elites harassed the commissioners, sought to dictate budget decisions, and undermined their efforts. This antagonism highlighted a key difference between Denver's commission experiment and that in other Progressive Era cities. Elsewhere commissioners typically enjoyed the support of businessmen, who hope to place city government in the hands of expert managers. To make matters worse, Denver commissioners wrangled over patronage and turf wars ensued, further eroding public support. The structure of this new government form left unclear just how executive decisions would be made. Few effective regulations of utilities emerged.[11]

When popular frustrations with the commissioners reached a peak in 1916, Speer reemerged with his own charter revision and broad support from business and labor leaders. Protestant Progressives mounted only a minor campaign to oppose the old boss. After four years out of politics, Speer returned to power in May 1916 under a strong-mayor charter with few utility regulations.[12] In his final term, Speer backed the municipal purchase of the water utility after years of court wrangling over the 1910 initiative, but at an inflated price that reformers considered too favorable to the private owners. With Speer back in power, the Tramway Company had less need for active participation in city politics. Commissioners had secured little lasting change to the city's administration and failed to create a viable alternative to party politics in Denver. That failure would hamper efforts to resolve the complicated tramway dispute.

Mayor's Speer's brief return to power also boded ill for the prospects of labor Progressivism. Elected along with a new charter that restored a strong mayor, Speer was able to appoint four city council members directly. The charter empowered the Civic and Commercial Association, formerly the Chamber of Commerce, to appoint four more aldermen. Granted only one appointment, organized labor chose a member of the barbers' union. Once in power, Speer quickly abolished the commission's civil service rules and began cutting the city payroll to reduce expenses. The *Denver Labor Bulletin* complained that Speer further squeezed workers by giving in to business pressure to reduce the daily wage on city contracts.[13]

The shifting political landscape in Denver also reflected a changing cast of characters. Many Protestant Progressives either moved from Denver or passed away in the 1910s. Long-time Progressive activist Thomas Patterson sold his newspaper, the *Rocky Mountain News*, to Chicago grain speculator John Shaffer. Costigan became a tariff official in Wilson's administration and continued to serve through most of the 1920s. Ed Keating left Denver in 1911 to operate his own newspaper and then represent Pueblo in Congress. Harry Fisher moved to Salt Lake City, leaving the Christian Citizenship Union without his leadership. Central Presbyterian Church minister Robert Coyle resigned in poor health and in the face of criticism for his pro-labor preaching.[14] Creel moved to New York before assuming the leadership of the Committee on Public Information in Washington during the war.

In these same years, corporate elites consolidated the business lobby in the city. The Civic and Commercial Association grew increasingly influential, absorbing a formerly independent Taxpayers' League and Real Estate Exchange. Corporate elites, including the CFI president and Tramway Company manager, could again exert new pressure within an expanded business association. By the time Speer died in office in May 1918, long-standing Progressive hopes for significant utility regulation had grown remote.

WHO CAN REGULATE THE TRAMWAY COMPANY?

Still, worker frustrations with the Tramway Company in the summer of 1918 revived interest in the public regulation of the utilities. Streetcar workers formed a union in July 1918 to press their claims for higher wages in light of wartime inflation. General manager Frederic Hild conceded that some level of wage increase was necessary but insisted that the company could not afford a pay raise unless it could collect a higher fare.[15] To raise fares, the utility needed government approval. The question was, which government body had the authority to approve a fare increase? In August 1918 the Tramway Company appealed to Denver's city council, the state PUC, and the National War Labor Board (NWLB) for permission to raise fares.[16] The NWLB began hearings in Denver in late September 1918. By that time both the city council and state utilities commission had authorized a temporary one-cent increase to six cents.

After gathering testimony from union members and Tramway Company officials, the NWLB in November awarded the streetcar union a wage increase retroactive to August that amounted to nearly three times the amount put forward by the Tramway Company. Board members Frank Walsh and former president William Taft personally urged the city council and PUC to maintain the six-cent fare to cover the increased cost of the wage increase.[17] According to the NWLB, increased wages and fares were both in the best interests of the municipal public. Although the NWLB could not enforce its fare decision, its wage award would become the standard in negotiations among unionists, the company, and local government officials over the next two years.

Initially, however, the NWLB ruling precipitated what tramway manager Hild called "a crisis." The company could not support the "tremendous" increase in wages on a six-cent fare. "All returns to stockholders were cut off nearly four years ago and not one penny has been paid to them since," Hild insisted.[18] Thus the company urged the city council and PUC to approve a fare hike to seven cents. The tramway union backed the company in its request. While the city council deliberated, attention focused on the PUC. On December 17, 1918, the PUC approved the new seven-cent fare, after a year-long investigation of Tramway Company finances.

Although PUC officials insisted the fare hike was justified, it triggered a range of protests. Accompanying its report on the PUC decision the next day, the *Denver Post* featured a front-page Steele cartoon (Figure 3.1). There the tramway petition for a fare increase appeared as begging for alms at the door of the state PUC, represented by a thrifty matron appalled at the beggar's

3.1. *Beggars Shouldn't Be Choosers* (DENVER POST, DECEMBER 18, 1918)

"nerve."[19] The state agency assumed a feminine image, here an older woman. While she might be strong within the space of her institutional "home," she was certainly not a figure ready to take to the streets to uphold the interests of the riding public against the Tramway Company. The PUC, in Steele's cartoon, expressed the frustration of the riding public with the "nerve" of the Tramway Company's petition for higher fares. Nonetheless, the Tramway Company began collecting a seven-cent fare on January 1, 1919.

Working-class opposition to the fare hike exploded the next day. As the workday drew to the close, about 500 employees of the Union Stockyards, the Denver Rock Drill Company, and the Union Pacific shops boarded streetcars but refused to pay more than five cents. When union drivers halted operation of the cars, they were ejected by the crowds who had formed "Five-cents or nothing" clubs. A few men from the crowd took control of several streetcars and drove them downtown before they were abandoned. Soon the business district was jammed with empty streetcars and some boys began smashing windows and tearing off fenders. Tramway workers attempted to rescue cars but were rebuffed and occasionally assaulted by a crowd growing to nearly 10,000. In a few instances, the crowd tore caps and coats from the tramway conductors and tossed them into bonfires made out of the wooden fenders. The police were unable to make arrests, given their small numbers on the scene. Eventually the Tramway Company cut off power to the cars until the crowd dispersed, resuming service only after midnight. Smaller and less violent protests continued for the next few days.[20] Many workers suspected collusion between tramway union Local 746 and the company, linking the wage demands of the union with the fare petitions of the tramway.

Reporting on the "Five-cents or nothing" protests in the following days, most press accounts focused attention on problems with the PUC. Because the commissioners were appointed by the governor and not subject to popular approval through election, they were "too autocratic," insisted one labor editor. Labor-sympathetic members of the Colorado legislature even introduced bills in the days following these protests to require direct election of utility commissioners. *Denver Post* editor Bruce Gustin noted that court challenges to PUC decisions had taken years to resolve. Many of Denver's workers did not see the PUC representing the interests of tramway consumers.[21] Hoping to deflect public scrutiny of the PUC, the Tramway Company printed a statement that cast the rioters as Bolsheviks, foreigners, or workers who had enjoyed their own wage increases during the war but now sought to deny others similar wage gains.[22] Ultimately the protests signaled the potential consequences of consumer frustrations with what many workers considered an illegitimate negotiation between the PUC and the Tramway Company. These members of the riding public lacked deliberative access to those negotiations. They eerily anticipated the popular response to the strikebreaking activities of 1920 when the Tramway Company again enjoyed backing from government officials who failed to secure the support of the consuming public at large.

Confusion as to the source of power for setting fares abounded: did the PUC or the city council possess the ultimate authority to regulate utility rates? Finally, the Colorado Supreme Court undercut the PUC in a January 1919 decision that insisted that under its Home Rule Charter, the City of Denver exclusively possessed such power. Following the court decision, the Tramway Company lowered its fare to six cents to bring it into compliance with the previous city council ordinance.[23] The court also nullified the PUC valuation of Tramway Company property, which the commission had determined after a year's investigation. The project to determine the value of tramway property in order to decide upon a reasonable fare also became the city's sole responsibility.

Despite earlier Progressive hopes, the utilities commission had failed to shift the authority for regulating utilities from local to state government. Colorado was unusual in this regard. Most states successfully transferred utility regulation from city to state governments in the 1910s. Business leaders often supported this effort in hopes of creating a more predictable and stable context for their operations. The movement to establish state PUCs tended to undercut the municipal ownership movement in other locales.[24] Yet in Denver, resolution of the tramway impasse would depend again on city politics rather than the presumed expertise of a state board.

The city then turned to a financial evaluation of the tramway system. This was a thorny and hotly contested political task. It could nonetheless serve the public interest, many argued, by establishing a basis for determining fares and wages. In spring 1919, Speer's successor created a Tramway Adjustment committee of fifty-five business and labor representatives (the Committee of Fifty-Five) to ascertain the company's financial status. Dominated by members of Denver's Civic and Commercial Association, this committee asserted a valuation of tramway assets slightly higher than that of the PUC. Labor members vociferously objected, since this justified overcapitalization and a higher fare. Union reports of the committee soon called it a "farce," complaining of endless "wrangling" over petty motions and fake posturing by some members as "champions of the people."[25]

The final report, issued in late May, was rejected by all the union members of the committee as too favorable to the Tramway Company. It urged the city to release the Tramway Company from franchise obligations such as street paving while guaranteeing a certain of rate of return for investors.[26] City attorneys quickly challenged the valuation in court. In a series of confrontations over the next several years, city and Tramway Company attorneys would offer widely divergent assessments of the costs of tracks and paving, electrical systems, rolling stock, and other items. One observer noted that Denver's Tramway valuation became the longest and most aggressively contested such process ever conducted over a municipal utility.[27] City efforts to determine the value of tramway assets failed to establish a legitimate basis for settling fare petitions and arbitrating the wages dispute. Confusion about the nature of city regulation of utilities came to shape the campaign to elect a new mayor.

MAYOR BAILEY AND THE STRIKE OF 1919

In May 1919, Denver's riding public had a chance to vote its views on the tramway controversy. The mayoral and aldermanic elections would determine the city's representation in its negotiations with the tramway. Some candidates raised broader questions about municipal ownership of the streetcar utility. But most prominently, the campaign turned on the simple issue of a five-cent fare. With little concern for the long-term service of the Tramway Company or the wage demands presented by the unionists, the winning candidate promised the return of a five-cent fare.

During the mayoral campaign, Denver's workers briefly debated the question of municipal ownership. One union candidate called for a three-cent fare on the tramway lines and called for public ownership of all utilities.[28] Yet as Election Day approached, workers focused attention on the front runners: former commissioner of public safety Dewey Bailey and corporate attorney Cass Herrington. Both had initially sought the endorsement of Denver's Republican Party, but Herrington opted to run as an independent when Bailey received his party's nomination. According to the major newspapers, Bailey was a scheming ward politician, machine candidate, and prohibition opponent. As commissioner of public safety under Mayor Speer, Bailey had lent police authority to Denver's anti-labor employers' association in several recent strikes. Herrington, by contrast, promised to bring nonpartisan administration of city affairs and high ideals to the office. In a speech to the members of Local 746, Herrington insisted that workers had a right to union recognition. After Herrington's speech, union orators urged members to support Herrington since he stood for the "principles of union labor" during the recent war. The Anti-Saloon League also endorsed Herrington's candidacy.[29]

Yet Bailey had pledged to restore a five-cent fare on tramway lines if elected. As public safety commissioner during the recent "Five-cents or nothing" riots, he had also refrained from providing police protection for tramway efforts to collect a seven-cent fare. His election on May 20 by a substantial plurality suggests the importance of these positions in voter's minds. Traditionally Democratic working-class districts, especially around the stockyards, supported Bailey by a margin of three to one, while Herrington outpolled Bailey in residential precincts dominated by Protestant Progressives.[30] Editorializing on the election returns, the *Labor Bulletin* editor wondered how Bailey had won without the support of any of the "great organizations" in

Denver. Employers associations, labor unions, "the church element," the "drys," and the big newspapers all backed other candidates. Bailey's win suggested that "the individual voters refused to be bound by the actions of organizations to dominate their political beliefs." The tramway fare issue loomed far larger than Protestant Progressive concerns.

No labor candidate won a seat on the city council. All those candidates echoing Bailey's pledge to restore a five-cent fare were elected. Although it was "hard to say where the labor vote went to," a union newspaper editor mused, "Mr. Bailey evidently must have received a portion."[31] Despite this support for Bailey, organized labor lacked much influence on the city council and with the new mayor. The erosion of Speer's Democratic machine left union workers without an effective means of advancing their interests at city hall.

Mayor Bailey promptly followed through on his campaign pledge to lower streetcar fares, rallying council members to pass a five-cent fare ordinance and repeal what council members called the "war-time emergency fare" of six cents on June 30. This reduction in fare precipitated a long-threatened rollback of tramway wages and the first strike by Local 746. With the announcement of the city council move, *Labor Bulletin* editor Ralph Moser voiced his fear that "labor is going to be the 'goat' in the Tramway controversy."[32] Tramway workers respond to the wage-cut proposal by voting overwhelmingly to strike. Union leader William O'Brien demanded solely a return to the federal wage award and promised that union members were "anxious to inconvenience the public as little as possible. . . . There will be no violence, but we will not permit the cars to run."[33]

The 1919 strike successfully tied up the streetcar system for four days with broad public support. Tramway Company managers attempting to run trains met large crowds of unionists who put crews off and returned the cars themselves to the barns. Company officials surrendered quietly to unionists and pickets proved effective in keeping the public from the trains. During the strike, major newspapers featured photos of young men biking their sweethearts around town. The *Denver Post*, for example, ran a photo with the caption: "Denver mermaids won't let a little streetcar strike interfere with their swimming." The "fair bather" arrived at Washington Park beach on the handlebars of a lifeguard's bike.[34] Strike conditions seemed to call forth common courtesy and even chivalry on behalf of a riding public depicted most often in feminine terms.

Having made no advance plans to recruit strikebreakers, tramway officials quickly scrambled to hire sufficient numbers of replacement workers while rejecting offers from Kansas City and St. Louis detective agencies to provide professional strikebreakers. One company official said: "[T]he strikers have the most efficient system of picketing I have ever seen. Outwitting them appears to be out of the question. We have tried every scheme we know and we have been frustrated." Labor editor Moser commented on the public mood during strike: "[E]verybody took the matter good-naturedly and the serious inconvenience experienced by the masses was made sport of."[35]

The union enjoyed public sympathy since responsibility for the strike focused on the other players in the struggle. The press almost unanimously held the Tramway Company and city authorities accountable for the strike. *Rocky Mountain News* editor John Shaffer contended that the riding public had largely accepted the six-cent fare "until the matter became a political issue at the recent municipal election." Now, *Denver Post* editor Gustin insisted that Mayor Bailey and tramway chief executive Charles Boettcher had "the power to settle the Tramway situation" inside an hour. Bailey had created the current problem with his five-cent fare pledge and Boettcher had proved too intractable. "Both men should be recalled," the editor continued. Boettcher should make way for "a competent, broad-minded man. Mr. Bailey should be recalled to make room for a man who has the ability to handle this city under the present form of government which puts the entire power in the hands of one man." Bailey was clearly no Robert Speer. For their parts, the new mayor and the tramway chief executive hurled accusations at each other. "Let the Tramway company pay its employes [*sic*] the former wage. Then let the company petition for an election" to determine the fare, insisted Mayor Bailey.[36]

In response to the mayor's charges that strikers were acting in collusion with the company to press for a higher fare, union leader O'Brien insisted that the members had "absolutely nothing to do with the amount of car fare collected. . . . That is none of our business and it is not our fight." The union's successful separation of the wage and fare issues, and consumer frustration with the Tramway Company and Mayor Bailey, helped the union control the action on the streets. In this context, tramway manager Hild remarkably declared that professional strikebreakers "induce ill-feeling, rioting and sometimes bloodshed. We don't want anything of that sort. It creates bitterness that cannot be dissipated for years."[37]

After an all-night negotiation on the third day of the strike, the mayor and sympathetic council members promised to push for a temporary return to a six-cent fare until a special election in October would decide the fare on a more permanent basis. In exchange, tramway officials agreed to restore wages to the NWLB levels that workers received before the imposition of a five-cent fare. The Tramway Company agreed to carry out a petition campaign to secure support for the fare increase, with conductors asking for signatures of riders. Although union leaders were not present at these negotiations, city and tramway officials issued the surprising public statement at their conclusion that "[t]he strike on the Tramway has been settled by unanimous consent of the mayor, his cabinet, the city council, and officials of the Tramway

Company."[38] In the view of mayor and Tramway Company, the union did not figure as a political player in the resolution of the fare issue.

Instead, tramway officials met separately with union leaders to discuss wages. The two sides agreed to return to NWLB wage levels with a future wage increase to be arbitrated. Shortly after the provisional settlement, however, union leader O'Brien insisted that members would not circulate the Tramway Company petition for a six-cent fare ordinance, despite the company's agreement with the city.[39] O'Brien again insisted on a separation between the fare and wage questions. While the union had stood its ground, successfully resisting a wage cut, streetcar workers had not received broad recognition of their wage demands. The municipal public still viewed the interest of Local 746 as secondary to its short-term consumer concerns with the Tramway Company. Efforts by the union to decouple its interests from those of the company continued.

In the months that followed the strike, unionists began to press harder for a more favorable political solution to the tramway situation — municipal ownership. Without the countervailing influence of Mayor Speer, Denver Trades and Labor Assembly delegates embraced city ownership of the streetcar system. Labor editor Moser insisted in August 1919 that municipal ownership was the only way to secure honest, economical service and eliminate bribery and corruption. During the strike the Denver Trades and Labor Assembly reasserted its commitment to a city-run streetcar system. The prospects for municipal ownership were not entirely remote. In June and September of 1919, the mayor's office had featured articles in its *Municipal Facts* magazine on Seattle's recent purchase of its streetcar lines. City ownership there promised to "lower the costs of operation," "reduce the costs of accidents," and increase wages. In September the city labor assembly began circulating petitions to put a Plumb Plan proposition for municipal ownership of the streetcar system on the October ballot.[40] Glenn E. Plumb, national counsel for the railway employees union, had that year called for the federal government to purchase railroad properties at fair values, subject to judicial review. Yet in Denver, the labor petition failed to secure enough signatures to make it onto the ballot.

Tramway workers continued to insist that the wage issue had to remain separate from fare measures. City labor federation members pledged to oppose any fare ordinance "where the question of wages for the Tramway men is included. Organized labor is opposed to laws that will set wage scales" for employees. Local 746 leader O'Brien expressed his opposition to the October ballot measures that would shift the wage question "from the Tramway company to the voters of the city." Seeking to clarify his position, O'Brien continued, "We are employed by the Tramway Company, and the wage paid us is strictly a question between the Company and the men." Yet Local 746 members did in fact quietly urge riders to support the "Service-at-Cost" plan in the coming election.[41]

As the October special election approached, the Committee of Fifty-Five began a campaign on behalf of its "Service-at-Cost" plan. The committee paid for frequent advertisements that insisted that this ballot measure, with its appointed board of control, would give the city control over the streetcar system without having to buy the property. Labor would have a member on the three-person board. And the plan would leave the Tramway Company no power to raise the fare, even creating financial incentives for lowering the fare. In light of the five-cent fare restoration and strike, the plan gained new supporters. *Post* editor Gustin enthused that the plan would ensure "peace and prosperity" and mean a vote against a future strike of the tramway men.[42]

On October 22, city voters faced two measures: the "Service-at-Cost" plan or an elastic six-cent fare measure. Drawn up in negotiations between the city and company during the 1919 strike, the latter plan would have established a six-cent fare that could be raised or lowered in direct relation to wages paid tramway employees. Those wages, in turn, would depend on the average wage paid streetcar workers in five comparable cities, St. Louis, Omaha, Kansas City, Minneapolis, and St. Paul.[43] Critics of the "Service-at-Cost" plan noted that it would nullify the existing franchise agreement and relieve the Tramway Company of its minimal obligations. It would also guarantee the company a specific return on investment, regardless of its performance.[44] Denver's labor leaders publicly rejected both the "Service-at-Cost" and "Elastic-Fare" plans, since both subjected the wages of union workers to public regulation.

The results of the citywide vote only perpetuated the uncertainty of the tramway situation. A light turnout of only 21,000 out of a possible 80,000 voters rejected both fare proposals. The Service-at-Cost measure lost by a narrow margin with support coming especially from wealthy Capitol Hill and those precincts with the heaviest concentration of tramway employees and their families. Opposition to the measure was strongest in working-class neighborhoods in west Denver where the stockyard workers resided.[45] Union workers broadly opposed city government regulations of wages. With this failure to secure popular approval of a fare and wage regulation system, the Tramway Company and Local 746 resumed negotiations over wages.

Yet public sentiment in Denver was shifting in 1919 under the influence of Red Scare campaigns and the open-shop movement.[46] The *Denver Post* waged its own anti-radical campaign, targeting union labor in the city. One Steele cartoon in the fall 1919 featured a feminine serpent representing "I.W.W. Bolshevism," which offered a sexually seductive appeal to the upright workingman (Figure 3.2).

3.2. *The Thing for Labor to Fight* (DENVER POST, OCTOBER 24, 1919)

This and other images, the paper had suggested, might lure workers into an orgy of violence and destruction and thus were just what "American Labor Unionism" had to fight. Denver businessmen expressed new hostility even to union labor. The Denver Commercial and Civic Association, the Kiwanis Club, and the Lions' Club all approved open-shop resolutions in spring 1920. This signaled a significant shift away from earlier cross-class cooperation within the Committee of Fifty-Five.[47]

As fear of radicalism escalated in Denver, the Tramway Company and union attempted to arbitrate their differences with few interventions by city authorities over the next seven months. Unionists continued to insist on a wage increase and the Tramway Company unsuccessfully pressured the city council to approve a fare hike.[48] Bailey's administration could not establish the value of tramway property and did not support city purchase of the streetcar system. Denver's workers were divided and unable to advance a clear vision for utility regulation or settlement of the dispute. Electoral politics, the city administration, and Tramway Company and union negotiation all failed to resolve the conflict. A second strike appeared unavoidable by the summer of 1920.

MALE CITIZENSHIP AND THE SECOND TRAMWAY STRIKE

Talk of a second strike by the tramway union that summer led city authorities to petition the Denver District Court for an injunction. City attorneys argued that the public interest demanded a government commitment to minimize disruptions to urban routines. District court judge Greeley W. Whitford quickly agreed to the city's request. He issued a convoluted order that both the Tramway Company and its workers "desist and refrain from ceasing to run and operate" streetcars. Whitford insisted that the company not cut wages or discharge "competent employees." The judge commanded workers not to strike.[49] With this court order, the prospect of a strike assumed an entirely new aspect. The injunction left the Tramway Company free to employ strikebreakers to ensure compliance with the order. Yet the union appeared to have few legal options except watchful waiting. The short-term convenience of consumers assumed paramount importance for Whitford.

Before submitting their petition to the District Court, city attorneys had consulted with several members of the executive board of Local 746 who understood mistakenly that the suit would apply only to the company, compelling it to operate cars and preventing a wage cut. When Judge Whitford heard the case, the union did not formally oppose the city's request for an injunction. While the company appealed Whitford's remarkably sweeping order, union leaders largely ignored it. Denver labor leader William Thornton advised Local 746 members that "no court can enjoin men from striking for a reasonable wage increase. . . . No man in this land can keep men from quitting their work. The temporary restraining order issued against the men is absolutely worthless and no power over them whatever."[50]

With wage negotiations between Local 746 and the company producing no resolution in July, union leaders consulted their attorney, Wayne Williams, about the relevance of Whitford's restraining order in the event of a strike declaration. He advised the executive committee against striking, fearing that it would alienate the public and appear to defy the court order. The union would be better off seeking the dissolution of the order through court appeals, Williams argued.[51] Yet the leaders of Local 746 had grown increasingly frustrated with the lack of resolution to the wage dispute and fearful that the company would ultimately secure an end to Whitford's injunction on terms unfavorable to the workers. Without the injunction in effect, they anticipated another wage reduction in the months ahead with postwar unemployment conditions still worse than they were at present. Moreover, the injunction case did not address the lack of a working agreement between the company and the union, even one calling for further arbitration.

Thus, at a meeting that began late on July 31, the union voted to strike for a second time. Two-thirds of union members were present for what became an all-night session. Union president Harry Silberg, ex-president William O'Brien, and city labor federation member and arbitrator William Thornton spoke. Silberg reviewed the most recent series of failed negotiations with the company. O'Brien insisted that the company was determined to break the union. Thornton noted negotiations with the company had failed repeatedly and the union could expect no resolution from court or municipal action. Although none of the speakers directly urged a strike, Thornton concluded his condemnation of all recent reconciliation attempts with the question, "What are you men going to do about it?" The answer came: "tie 'em up" and "pass the hat" for a strike vote. Eight-hundred eighty-seven chose "yes" to only eleven against.[52]

The union quickly shut down streetcar operations in Denver for the next two days. Along with DTLA leaders, Local 746 would struggle unsuccessfully to define the obligations of the municipal public in terms of a living wage for workers and city ownership of Denver's streetcar utility. The second streetcar strike proved ill-suited to these political tasks. But with its strike vote in 1920, Local 746 led Denver's union leadership into an intense contest over the responsibilities of the public and character of male citizenship.

Among the most influential participants in this struggle were newspaper editors. Most Denver editors affirmed the material interests of the municipal public in terms already defined by the mayor and district court. This was a remarkable shift from the 1919 tramway strike. Consider, for example, the first few days of the second strike. *Denver Post* editor Gustin swung dramatically from his position in 1919. A year later, the editor contended that the strike was the work of an outside agitator, menacing the riding public. Amalgamated representative Allan Burt, called from Salt Lake City to assist Local 746, had put "the whole city into turmoil" by "fomenting and pulling off a strike among the employe[e]s of the Tramway." The city of Denver cried out for "release from the domination of this little band of 1,100 willful and misguided men." The public, insisted the *Rocky Mountain News*, would suffer from a "squeeze play" orchestrated by company and union. Even the otherwise sympathetic editor of the *Denver Express* blamed union leadership for the interruption of service.[53]

Although the *Post* had maintained a consistent hostility toward the Tramway Company during the 1919 strike, now the paper reported quite fa-

3.3. *A Bad One to Arouse (DENVER POST, AUGUST 4, 1920)*

vorably on the strikebreaking preparations of the company. "Hotel accommodations" in the "comfortable quarters" of the tramway auditorium awaited some 600 expected strikebreakers, the *Post* stated. Professional strikebreaker John "Black Jack" Jerome had arrived in Denver from San Francisco several days before the strike was called and was "in entire charge" of plans to combat the strike. In fact, the *Post* approvingly reported on the possible escalation of tensions into a war between company strikebreakers and the union.[54]

The needs of the public, according to the *Post*, demanded nothing less. A cartoon appeared in the paper just before the armed strikebreakers shot at protesting crowds. It pictured a brawny, disheveled, cigar-chomping man, representing "public sentiment" (Figure 3.3). He expressed his angry frustration with inflation, profiteering, and most prominently strike agitation. The last seemed most damaging to the public interest. With this working-class image, the *Post* likely hoped to appeal to an imagined mass of male workers who resisted radical "agitation" but hoped for action to curb the high cost of living, whatever its causes. The contrast in public imagery with the 1919 strike was dramatic. During that strike young men were pictured shuttling mostly young women about town. That streetcar tie-up seemed to create less a public hardship than new dating opportunities. The 1920 strike, however, might arouse the potent power of a masculine "public sentiment," here in opposition to striking workers and radicalism.

Beginning with the first test of strength between the strikebreakers and the strikers, the press engaged in a struggle over the masculinity of the combatants. Gender became the field on which a contest to defend the urban public unfolded. On day three of the strike, Black Jack Jerome led the first streetcar out of the tramway building and through the business district in defiance of the pickets. In the eyes of *Post* reporter Ryley Cooper, that first car run appeared almost staged for the movies. The crowd was tense, but "Black Jack determined. He stood erect and defiant, while across his breast was slung a revolver in a new holster and a bandolier of cartridges. He was 'Black Jack' John Jerome, playing the part that his name gave him, heavy, forbidding in aspect, a three days' growth of black, stubby beard covering his face, his steady eyes set straight ahead, his lips drawn in a straight line."[55] Cooper saw Jerome living up to his sobriquet, which reflected his reputed skill as a card player. An armed gambler now appeared poised to save Denver from a radical cabal. Protestant Progressives did not comment on the irony.

The *Post* reported that as many as 25,000 walkers cheered " 'Black Jack' Jerome and his strike busters." Labor papers placed only a few hundred Jerome supporters on the streets, with most strikers held back by police. Nonetheless, a *Post* daily editorial, titled "The Public Speaks," insisted that such cheers "told more than anything else could tell the attitude of the common people of Denver toward the streetcar strike and toward the strikers." The editor brazenly promised that the "strike is doomed to fail."[56]

If the heavily armed Jerome assumed a reassuring image of male resolve for the *Post*, the mass of strikebreakers became mere "boyish adventurers." Instead of the "heavy, hurly men" focused on fighting that *Post* reporter Ryley Cooper had expected to find on his tour among the strikebreakers, he met "a bunch of boys at heart, adventurers by nature more interested in learning about local colleges than in knocking in the heads of strikers." Still, one said, "[W]e'll fight if the time comes to fight. . . . Our job is to pull a streetcar company thru its troubles with as little damage as possible."[57]

Jerome had in fact recruited a number of University of California students to assist in his fight.[58] Historians have recently begun to explore the use of college youth as strikebreakers. Stephen Norwood has insightfully noted the various points of opposition between many young, elite college men and organized workers in the early twentieth century. Strikebreaking by college youth, especially football players, became a test of masculine mettle on the urban frontier. Given popular press coverage of the street fighting associated with major urban strikes by longshoremen in San Francisco, flour millers in Minneapolis, and the police in Boston, Jerome could offer his associates their own chance to demonstrate their muscular physicality.[59]

For Denver's *Labor Bulletin*, however, armed strikebreakers suggested an entirely different style of masculinity. Reporting on Jerome's activities in a Fresno streetcar strike just months earlier, the *Labor Bulletin* noted that "Black Jack" had shot a bystander, a real estate broker, in the neck and been briefly jailed. The editor asked, "Are we going to have our wives and daughters insulted by thugs, criminals, and ex-convicts" like Jerome? Such dangerous figures invoked paternal obligations of union men to protect their dependents. In contrast to the "style of man the Tramway Company" recruited as strikebreakers, the strikers were "law-abiding citizens, who own their own homes, and pay taxes for the support of the city." In an open letter, Local 746 leaders further insisted that the company had "nagged, ragged, fired our men, [and] subjected them to all sorts of petty annoyance," provoking a defense of union manhood. The union had to take a stand against the "thugs and toughs" who had come to terrorize the Denver community.[60]

The *Denver Express*, which enjoyed a broad working-class readership, offered a similar defense of rank-and-file union manhood. The editor declared that striking workers "are honest, substantial citizens, good friends and neighbors. . . . Denver wishes them well — wants them to have good wages, wholesome homes." Strike supporters insisted that reasoned restraint, not passionate anger or a rush to violence, characterized the strikers. And indeed, the streetcar workers were among the most conservative of Denver's organized workers. Yet even a moderately sympathetic paper like the *Express* could not resist a critique of union leaders. The editor lectured the executive committee for its failure to await a political settlement of the tramway dispute: "The ability to defer immediate gains or pleasures in favor of larger returns later is the faculty which distinguishes the civilized man from the savage; the full grown man from the child."[61] Hoping to rescue the rank-and-file men of Local 746 from public scorn, the *Express* editor presented them as misled manly citizens in contrast to their impetuous, childlike leadership.

By the third day of the 1920 strike, the lines of the contest over masculinity on the streets of Denver were clearly drawn. For workers especially, this reflected a struggle over the nature of masculine citizenship. Leaders of Denver's working class took to the streets in hopes of demonstrating their commitment to a restrained, rational vision of male citizenship. After Jerome's initial run,

Denver's citywide union federation organized a parade of 600 union men and women, led by three servicemen in uniform bearing the U.S. flag. With this collective walk through Denver's main streets to city hall, workers insisted upon their citizenship rights. This public march ended in a meeting with the mayor to present a settlement proposal. Foremost among the workers' demands were the disarming of the strikebreakers and an end to police protection of tramway cars.[62] These workers contrasted their own orderly civic activity with that of armed strikebreakers who had illegitimately seized police authority to oppose union demands with threats of violence.

The mayor remained largely defiant. Surprisingly, he disputed both union allegations and even *Denver Post* reports that the strikebreakers were armed. He pledged continued police protection for tramway strikebreakers and maintained that the streetcar union was to blame for the strike. His job was to ensure continued service for consumers. Bailey asked, "What kind of city administration would this be, if it allowed 1,100 men to run this city?"[63] Reporting on the mayor's meeting, *Post* editor Gustin lamented the passing of the days "when labor paid due deference and respect to the rights of the people." Now the "labor agitator says, as the capitalists used to say, 'THE PUBLIC BE DAMNED' . . . 'TO HELL WITH THE PEOPLE.'" The peaceful march of workers with a petition for city hall had become for the *Post* "a storm . . . with insolence and with the purpose of intimidation." Bailey appeared "a real American mayor," who "stood pat" and "never faltered" in his "vigorous" defense of "the People" in opposition to the strikers.[64]

By day five of the strike, a skeletal streetcar service had resumed, with armed strikebreakers and police escorts. Still hoping to persuade city hall to disarm strikebreakers, strikers and sympathizers again petitioned Mayor Bailey for intervention. A worker delegation met briefly with the mayor while outside city hall a crowd of 1,500 strikers and other union supporters gathered peacefully. The collective voice of Denver's organized workers did not hold sway with the city's chief executive.[65] The strikers and leaders of Denver's working class had continued to seek a peaceful and deliberative resolution to the tramway impasse.

Other Denver residents were no longer willing to wait for negotiations. The character of public life came to resemble more that of the aggressive strikebreaker than the restrained unionist. As the second rally at city hall dispersed, the peaceful expression of solidarity with Local 746 gave way to a series of violent attacks on Denver's streets. A new and growing crowd of workers, including boys, ex-servicemen, and railroad employees, coalesced into a rioting mob. Estimates placed as many as several thousand rioters, hundreds of police, and dozens of strikebreakers on the streets during the late hours of Thursday, August 5. The mob's targets—tramway property, strikebreakers, and the *Denver Post*—reveal a certain order in what initially appeared to onlookers as a chaotic rampage. The rioters displayed some sympathy for the strikers by attacking the explicit enemies of Local 746. Armed strikebreakers in particular provoked violent reaction, while the police became inadvertent victims of the mob. Yet the violence irreparably damaged the prospects of the strikers for advancing their vision of public responsibility, decent wages, and municipal ownership of the streetcar system. The mainstream press worked to link unionists with radicals, rioters, and potential revolution.

The growing crowd just a few blocks from city hall halted two streetcars around six o'clock in the evening. A strikebreaker fired one shot before protesters "began to take their full revenge," noted an *Express* reporter. In five minutes the cars were reduced to ruins. Three strikebreakers and two boys were badly injured. The crowd then allowed the police to herd them down the streets. Nearly two hours later a crowd of "more than 2,500 excited men and boys" halted three other cars and attacked the strikebreakers. Although none of the rioters seemed to have a gun, "every conceivable weapon was brought into play" as they beat any strikebreaker they could grab "into a state of insensibility." The police were helpless to stop the assaults. Because they had orders not to shoot, the officers devoted their energy to shielding and rescuing strikebreakers. Meanwhile hundreds of men heaved several streetcars over onto their sides in front of the Cathedral of the Immaculate Conception on Colfax.[66]

From the church, the mob headed to Champa Street for an attack on the *Denver Post* building at about nine-thirty that night. After breaking every front window, the rioters wrecked the offices, unraveled rolls of paper into the streets, and attempted to set fire to the structure. The press machines remained unharmed behind a few locked doors. Few employees were present in the building, and those remaining quickly fled the mob. The *Post*, able to publish an edition the next day, insisted that men in army uniform and young boys had led the assault on its property.[67] But the crowd support for the destruction suggested a violent protest against the influence of this hostile paper. The paper had come to frame the public debate about the strike in terms so antagonist to the strikers that the crowd lashed out in heated, if only momentary, protest.[68] Reporting on the shootings at the South Denver Tramway facility that followed the attack on the *Post* building, the *Express* editor was distressed as "gay parties of men and women, apparently sight-seeing and joy-riding," replaced the dispersing crowd. "Lovemaking and rioting went hand in hand and scenes in autos were disgusting."[69] Sexual disorder compounded the chaos on the streets.

The August 5 riots particularly led to critiques of the police for unpreparedness and soft handling. The surrender of police power to private guards had left the city vulnerable and exposed, argued critics. The mayor called for 2,000 volunteers to guard the city, and members of the American Legion overran city hall to sign up.[70] The press celebration of the legionnaires in the subsequent days suggests the extent to which a wartime mentality gripped the city. The attempt to balance competing economic interests had disintegrated into violent attacks and counterattacks.

Waging its own battle to restore order, the mainstream press again invoked reassuring conceptions of masculinity. The *Express* found solace in the sight of the legionnaires, "husky, big, strapping fellows," deputized and armed by the city with sawed-off shotguns. *Rocky Mountain News* editor John Shaffer went further: the volunteer force of legionnaires stood "around the bulwark of our civilization, defending the ark of the covenant of liberty. . . . These are the Minute Men of today." This volunteer force reflected the "discipline of war" and displayed a "refreshing snap and vim as they directed traffic and kept the streets clear and safe."[71] Despite the presence of these additional deputized police, violent confrontations between strikebreakers and tramway opponents continued. By the end of the next day's clashes, the police had made more than 100 arrests for rioting, and few of these were striking workers. More than fifty people were injured and seven lay dead.[72]

In the aftermath of the rioting, editors competed in a struggle to defend or impugn the manhood of the strikers. The editor of the *Labor Bulletin* defended both the innocence and manly restraint of the striking unionists, insisting "they were the first on the scene [of the rioting] to stand courageously . . . in the face of gunshot, 'Black Jack,' and a frenzied mob, with death staring at them," pleading "with a mass of humanity gone mad to refrain from bloodshed."[73] The *Post* editor saw in the rioting a descent into revolution. Invoking widely circulating images from the Red Scare, the editor shrieked that "Bolshevism, Sovietism and Anarchy, with gun and torch, have leaped from bloody and ravished Russia to our beloved land." The sacking of the *Post* was but a prelude for further violence. "Revolution, and its red flag and blood-stained sword, is not a hideous nightmare, but is at the door of every man today." The tramway's own *Bulletin* outdid the hysterical *Post*. Alleging that even faster than law-abiding strikebreakers had come to town, "another element was coming to Denver, one that knew no law save ruin, one that recognized no spirit save that of the mob, one that understood nothing but bloodshed and rioting to the gaining of its end. It was the I.W.W.!" Like "the vulture swoops toward the carrion or the wolf to the call of his kind," the "gaunt men, narrow-eyed men, bearded men, treacherous men" of the IWW swarmed into Denver and overtook the otherwise conservative streetcar union to provoke the "spilling of blood."[74] In the eyes of tramway supporters, only the reassuring presence of federal troops had rescued Denver from anarchy and revolution.

News editor Shaffer saw the riots as the unfortunate consequence of the opposition between the striking unionists and the municipal public. Despite the rioting, Shaffer saw a victory for the "people," as he defined them, in coming to know "their own power and collective strength." Lawlessness may have prevailed for a moment, but "class consciousness has been given a severe rebuke." The strikers had unsuccessfully challenged not so much the tramway corporation as the "traveling public," which had emerged "master in its own house." For Shaffer, a certain contract had bound union workers to the municipal public. Doing "injury" to the community, strikers had "ignored their relationship to the public as employe[e]s of a public utility . . . bound by franchise contract to serve the public and keep its cars going."[75] Shaffer blurred the terms of the franchise agreement here, since the tramway company was the legal party to the contract, not its workers. Still his reading of an unofficial contract between union members and the public would reappear in a court battle over Whitford's injunction. The strike by Local 746 positioned the union in opposition, contended Shaffer, to the interests of Denver's municipal public.

After two nights of murderous violence, the governor called for federal military help to secure the streets. By Saturday, August 7, federal troops from Fort Logan, Colorado, had assumed control of the streets of Denver as Colonel Ballou declared martial law. Among Ballou's first orders was to disarm Jerome's strikebreakers. With this initial order, Ballou won important respect from the city's workers.[76] The rioting ceased as more and more federal troops arrived in Denver in subsequent days. Although the army ended the aggressive tactics of the Tramway Company, the company nonetheless assumed a clear advantage in negotiations with the union in this militarized context. Armed, violent conflict rather than expert arbitration had decided the outcome of a wage dispute within a municipal utility.

The workers' vision of restrained male citizenship, reminiscent of that advanced by Protestant moralists, lost out in the struggle against the aggressive strikebreaker. The public that various Progressives had hoped to mobilize in nonpartisan activism against corporate utility interests here appeared hopelessly fragmented. Many became spectators to the illegitimate assumption of police power and manipulations of the Tramway Company. Others exploded in riot against the symbols of injustice and distortion.

WORKERS IN A DIVIDED POLITICAL WORLD

With martial law imposed on Denver, it became increasingly clear that the Tramway Company would rid itself of its union workforce. Local 746 first declared an "armistice" in its confrontation with the Tramway Company. Yet several days of conflicting declarations followed. After some union meetings came the announcement that the strike was over; the men were willing to return to work on any terms. After other gatherings, union members pledged that the strike would continue until the company rehired all members of Local 746 and fired the strikebreakers.[77] Tramway manager Hild steadfastly maintained that workers would only be rehired as individuals. Replacement workers would remain on the job. The union and its executive committee struggled to define a clear course of action in large measure because of actions in Denver District Court.

Several days into the strike District Judge Whitford had summoned the executive committee to account for the strike order, which appeared to violate his injunction. City attorneys asked Whitford to compel the strikers to desist from picketing, recall the strike order, and allow the Tramway Company to run cars. Even before Whitford could make his decision, Mayor Bailey ordered the arrest of union picketers. The shift from his response to the 1919 strike was nearly complete. Just before rioting began on day five of the strike, city attorneys argued before Judge Whitford that the union members worked for an industry "affecting the public interest." Although Colorado law granted workers in private industry the right to strike, the city insisted that tramway workers did not enjoy such a right, given a contract binding them, along with the company, to uphold the terms of the franchise and maintain continuous service. Whitford threatened to jail the executive committee of the union for contempt unless the strike order was recalled and the men returned to work.[78] This put the executive committee in the unenviable position of urging Local 746 members to end the strike to satisfy Judge Whitford and still press the company for the realization of union demands.

For the next month, members of Local 746 and their sympathizers retained some hope that they might alter their position in relation to the municipal public. The *Express* broke a revealing story about strikebreaker responsibility for the murders during the rioting. General Leonard Wood, who had assumed command of the troops in Denver from Colonel Ballou on August 10, began an informal investigation into the shootings, the paper reported. He contended that the company's use of strikebreakers had been a "colossal blunder." As noncitizens of Colorado, these men were illegally armed and not properly deputized. While touring the scenes of violent confrontation with Governor Shoup, tramway officials, and Black Jack Jerome, Wood branded Jerome as "unscrupulous" and "cowardly," suggesting that strikebreakers would be "indicted for murder" for the shootings on the sixth day of the strike.[79] Wood's comments bolstered labor claims that strikebreakers lacked any legitimate authority and were little better than armed criminals. The *Labor Bulletin* ran the *Express* story in vivid detail several days later under the headline "Women and Children Were Shot Down by the Thugs and Strikebreakers Imported by the Tramway Company."[80]

The *Labor Bulletin* ran a series of articles in subsequent weeks highlighting the incompetence and unscrupulous character of the replacement streetcar workers. The numbers of streetcar wrecks soared in the weeks following the strike, the *Bulletin* noted, even taking the lives of several pedestrians. Unionists continued to protest inadequate and dangerous streetcar service well into October. The *Express* also gave favorable notice to police investigations that traced the cause of an August and September crime wave to the men imported as strikebreakers. After "filling the places of the strikers, they were cheated out of their money by Black Jack Jerome and have vowed vengeance" on the city.[81] Local 746 and its sympathizers worked for weeks to win back the support of public opinion and alter perceptions of the Tramway Company.

Still the company refused to consider any offers from Local 746. Even union appeals to the governor for arbitration were rebuffed. An official from the US Conciliation Service spent a month in negotiations between the company and Local 746 but was ultimately unsuccessful. In November, Local 746 met a final time to call off the strike. Tramway officials followed that announcement with the introduction of a new company union, patterned after Rockefeller's famous plan at Colorado Fuel and Iron.[82]

All the while, the executive committee of Local 746 battled in court over the right to strike. Although the union intended this second strike fundamentally as an assertion of members' political as well as economic rights, court action against strike leaders threatened worker citizenship in postwar Denver. Judge Whitford's contempt hearings in particular rested on a pre-liberal, almost feudal understanding of worker obligations to the Tramway Company and the city as a whole. The urban public, in this view, had bound the tramway workers in ways that denied them political and economic freedom.

Roughly a week after the US Army arrived in Denver, Judge Whitford sent the union leaders to prison for contempt. Defense attorney Williams petitioned the Colorado Supreme Court for the release of the men, on the grounds that Whitford's injunction had been illegal. At last, the union addressed Whitford's restraining order, presenting a broad defense of workers' rights to strike in Colorado. Williams's defense challenged Whitford's pre-liberal interpretation of workers obligations to the company and the city as a whole.

So important did the *Labor Bulletin* deem this case that it reprinted Williams's defense briefs in full in the fall of 1920. The crucial issue, insisted the editor, was a question of "freedom or slavery for workers." Williams's brief directly challenged Whitford's "no-strike" injunction as based on common-law precedents that no longer held the force of law. First, he noted that Colorado law dating to the 1880s had rejected the common-law rule that a labor union was a form of conspiracy. The attorney for the union leaders reviewed common-law doctrine that viewed workers solely in terms of their ascribed, dependent status. Bound to a master, the worker under common law lacked the power to negotiate terms of employment or to terminate employment at will.[83]

This review of common-law doctrine did not merely sketch past obligations that bound workers; it illustrated the constraints still imposed upon workers by judges such as Whitford who resorted to common-law traditions. Under the enduring common-law regime of master and servant, judges prescribed obligations upon employees, based on their dependent status. Employers, or in common-law parlance, "masters," could enforce a property interest over the worker's labor and seek court protection in the form of an injunction to prevent outsiders from luring a worker away from his employment in the form of a strike.[84] On the basis of just such reasoning Whitford had imprisoned the executive committee of Local 746.

City attorneys alleged and Whitford agreed that both the Tramway Company and its union workforce were bound by a franchise obligation to maintain service for the public at large. The municipal public thus became the employing party in that contract that bound the executive committee. Whitford's injunction clearly relied on common-law doctrine in the attempt to protect this contract from outside interference or termination, except by the employer—in this case the city residents. The power to alter the contract rested only with the employer, not the employees, according to Whitford.

The experience of the executive committee in district court highlights the divided political world of Colorado workers. As scholar Karen Orren has argued of the late nineteenth century, the worker as public citizen enjoyed the franchise and the power to shape legislative action while the worker as private employee often remained bound by an outdated judicial doctrine that demanded loyalty and obedience to employers.[85] The leadership of Local 746 confronted just such a divide in 1920, with Judge Whitford using his court authority to insist foremost upon workers' common-law obligations to their employer. The needs of the consuming public for uninterrupted service undermined the citizenship rights of streetcar workers.

Williams's defense brief thus sought to secure and protect workers' right to strike in either a private business or a "public" industry like the tramway.[86] Regardless of whom the court determined to be the employer in this case, Williams could argue, the workers retained a contract right to quit work of their own accord. If contract principles governed political relations, Williams argued, so they should apply to the relations of the workplace. Worker citizenship included fundamental economic rights as well as political ones.[87]

The Colorado Supreme Court, however, did not rule on Williams's view of contract principles nor on the vision of worker citizenship that it informed. This debate would feature more prominently in labor struggles against the Colorado Industrial Commission in subsequent years. In mid-September Colorado Supreme Court justices ordered the release of the executive committee members, without comment, after the men had spent thirty-three days in prison.[88] State interventions on behalf of consumers would continue to undermine worker citizenship rights in the years ahead.

While the judicial system limited worker rights, it absolved Tramway Company strikebreakers of any wrongdoing. A month-long grand jury investigation concluded in late September 1920 that not a single person should be indicted for the killing of seven and wounding of more than one hundred city residents during the riots. The grand jury did, however, indict three labor leaders, including William Thornton and former Local 746 leader William O'Brien, for "inciting riots." These men easily established that they were nowhere near the street fights that erupted during the strike. But they had given speeches to Local 746 members on the night that the men declared a strike. Labor editor Moser asked poignantly, "If the courts are only used to prosecute the workers and not the employers for any misdeeds they have done, is it any wonder that the workers are losing respect for the courts?" All three charges were quickly dismissed for lack of evidence at the men's initial hearings in court.[89] Nonetheless, judicial reactions to the tramway crisis only affirmed the divided political world of union workers in the postwar period.

The outcome of the 1920 strike highlighted the erosion of labor Progressivism in Denver. In that conflict, the mayor, the Tramway Company, and the major newspaper editors had worked to define the needs of the consuming public in terms of uninterrupted service at all costs. Armed private guards assumed public police powers to protect those needs and defy striking workers. The contest between strikebreakers and strikers became a battle over the nature of working-class male citizenship. Street-fighting urban outlaws advanced the tramway's economic and political goals with violence and intimidation while unionists unsuccessfully relied on a more restrained, deliberative vision of manhood. Court action to uphold the needs of consumers further threatened the political rights of workers. Military occupation ultimately highlighted the inability of Denver's governing institutions to negotiate a democratic solution to workplace problems of postwar adjustment.

The tramway conflict also demonstrated the limits of both Progressive reform and Denver's strong-mayor system. Protestant reform challenges to Mayor Speer and his centralized administration had resulted in little overall change to the structure of city government. Workers had often opposed these reforms, relying instead on Speer and his machine for a measure of influence at city hall. Although Speer had unofficially arbitrated labor conflicts, he left no machinery for adjusting disputes after his death. Progressive hopes for utility regulation at the state level came to naught. The Public Utilities Commission could not establish its authority for regulating utilities like the Tramway Company. Workers struggled to assert basic citizenship rights against the coercive power of city government. The city and courts insisted on a view of the public interest defined only in terms of consumers. The authors of the Denver Commission of Religious Forces report on the strike concluded that "labor should be paid a good living before money receives its hire." Despite the national campaign of Father John Ryan for a living wage, this endured as a largely vain hope into the 1920s.[90]

Four

The Consuming Public and the Industrial Commission

In his 1906 Annual Message to Congress, President Roosevelt urged support for a bill to mandate the government investigation of labor disputes before allowing workers to strike.[1] In an "age of great corporate and labor combinations," the president insisted that "the public has itself an interest which can not wisely be disregarded; an interest not merely of general convenience, for the question of a just and proper public policy must also be considered."[2] Congress at the time was unmoved. Yet Roosevelt's proposal signaled a growing Progressive movement to compel the investigation and arbitration of major labor conflicts. This movement peaked in the years soon after World War I. National advocates for government mediation insisted that an impartial commission of experts could peacefully negotiate workplace disputes and spare the consuming public the contests of will and force associated with major strikes. The federal arbitration of railroad and mining conflicts established important precedents.[3]

National mediation boards, however, rarely assumed the power to compel compliance. Such efforts were more prominent at the state level, especially in Colorado and Kansas. In 1915, Colorado legislators largely implemented

Roosevelt's Progressive proposal, creating the first state board with powers to ban strikes and lockouts pending an investigation in industries affected with a public interest. Soon after the war, Kansas expanded on the Colorado precedent with a compulsory arbitration board to regulate a host of industries deemed essential to the public.[4] Administrative Progressive programs for state mediation of labor conflicts in the postwar period were particularly bound up with questions of compulsion in the public interest.

In fact, crucial to the fate of the Colorado and Kansas experiments were competing efforts to define and represent the public and its interests.[5] These mediation boards drew government bureaucrats, organized labor, large and small-business owners, farmers, and middle-class reformers into negotiations over the interests and boundaries of the public. Before 1914, Protestant Progressives in Colorado had wielded great influence over the scope and goals of nonpartisan public action in challenges against party machines and corporate lobbying. After the massacre at Ludlow a new cadre of industrial relations experts defined the public interest in less moral terms. With an emphasis on cross-class harmony and scientific investigation of labor unrest, mediation Progressives in Colorado and Kansas followed the lead of national figures such as John Commons at the University of Wisconsin and Paul Kellogg, editor of the influential *Survey* magazine. Their vision of the public interest informed the creation of the Colorado Industrial Commission (CIC) and the Kansas Industrial Court.

The most consistent and fundamental struggle for the public interest occurred between these government boards and organized labor. In the immediate postwar years the CIC and Kansas Industrial Court sought foremost to represent the consumer. Responding to the surge in strike activity between 1919 and 1922, these boards sought to protect the consumer, check inflation, and end disruptions to life's routines.[6] Commissioners argued that only state compulsion could ensure negotiation between capital and labor to protect the consuming public.

Organized workers strongly disagreed. The consuming public, unionists insisted, had no rights superior to those of workers to earn a living and resist employer oppression. Labor leaders argued that these boards taught consumers how to oppress workers. Unionization and protective labor legislation were far better tools than expert investigation for equalizing the balance of power in the workplace.[7] The right to quit work collectively, they contended, was essential to democratic freedom. It was a citizenship right superior to the consuming public's right to convenience. The Colorado labor department, empowered to enforce protective labor laws, could enhance union strength and worker citizenship. In responding to the challenge of compulsory arbitration with its focus on the interests of the public, union leaders advanced a vision of labor Progressivism at odds with the mediation experts.

CREATING THE COLORADO INDUSTRIAL COMMISSION

Colorado legislators, similar to President Roosevelt, came to favor compulsory investigation in response to a dispute in coal mining. Throughout the Colorado coal strike of 1913 and 1914, the Colorado Fuel and Iron Company (CFI) consistently refused to recognize the growing influence of the United Mine Workers of America (UMW). Progressive legislators considered compulsory arbitration as the only way to bring employers like the CFI to the negotiating table.[8] The Ten Days' War and subsequent investigation of the strike by the US Commission on Industrial Relations (CIR) convinced many Colorado voters of the need for state intervention.[9]

The US Commission on Industrial Relations was itself divided over the causes of industrial unrest. Between August 1914 and the release of final reports a year later, labor Progressives like commissioner Frank Walsh increasingly stressed inequalities in American society and sought to mobilize public outrage over corporate domination of workers' economic and political lives. Recommending the public recovery of mineral rights in the Mountain West along with new legislative guarantees of worker freedoms without employer interference, Walsh inspired labor Progressives in Colorado with hopes of creating a new politics of industrial democracy. Fellow commissioner John Commons, however, placed great faith in the promise of impartial, expert, nonbinding commissions that might investigate disputes over working conditions or labor legislation.[10] Commons would have the greater influence in the West.

In Colorado, Progressive Party leader Ed Costigan increasingly shared the concerns of Walsh. In 1914, the Progressive attorney defended striking Colorado coal miners against charges of murder. Judge Ben Lindsey traveled to Washington to speak in defense of these union workers. In that fall campaign for governor, Costigan called for the creation of an industrial commission to investigate labor disputes but also proposed to declare coal mines public utilities, thus making them more easily subject to state regulation. The Progressive candidate also wanted to renegotiate public leases to coal companies to define working and safety conditions. Costigan noted how flagrantly coal operators had violated state labor laws for years. Former president Roosevelt lent his support.[11] Yet the prohibition initiative that year overshadowed Costigan's proposals. Governor-elect Carlson consulted with Commons in December as he began drawing up a bill to create an industrial commission for Colorado.

In late January 1915, Republicans in the state House and Senate introduced the new governor's industrial plan. Carlson envisioned a commission of "nonpartisan" experts empowered to investigate labor disputes, to administer state labor laws, and to oversee a new workmen's compensation program that relied on private insurance. Such a board would better serve the public, Carlson argued, than negotiation by "partisan representatives" from capital and labor. Carlson had further consulted with Rockefeller's adviser and former Canadian labor minister MacKenzie King about Canada's labor board, which investigated disputes in public utilities. Members of Denver's Civic and Commercial Association helped Republican legislators such as William Eaton draft the initial bill for the legislature, drawing upon King's and Commons's proposals. They broadened the scope of the Canadian law to allow investigation of all industries "affected with a public interest." The governor's bill also proposed to abolish the Bureau of Labor Statistics and transfer its duties to the new commission.[12]

Senate Democrats, with encouragement from labor leaders, opposed the plan to provide workmen's compensation via private insurance companies and the proposal to eliminate the state labor department. The labor bureau at the time was staffed with Democratic appointees who had begun to uphold labor legislation for male and female workers. These Senate Democrats, led by George Lewis of Victor, gained the support of Republican senator William Candlish of Leadville and ultimately persuaded the governor and Republican House to spare the state labor department and create a state insurance fund for workmen's compensation. To secure Republican support for these measures, Candlish strengthened the coercive powers of the new Industrial Commission.[13] Because the state workmen's compensation program was linked in the end to the industrial commission plan, labor leaders had little choice but to accept the latter in order to secure the former. Besides, the labor department had survived the legislative wrangling and might serve as an ally for workers in the state bureaucracy.

As passed in 1915, the Industrial Relations Law created the nation's first system of compulsory investigation of labor disputes. Three commissioners, appointed by the governor, were empowered to subpoena witnesses, business records, and union meeting minutes. Carlson appointed a legislative ally of the CFI and long-time Speer loyalist Hiram Hilts and Republicans Joseph Bell and George Densmore to serve. The law required employers and workers to give commissioners thirty days' notice of changes in working conditions or the intention to strike. Most concerning for workers, the CIC could ban strikes or lockouts for the duration of its investigations.

The industrial commission law promised to usher in "a new era of peace and prosperity," according to Shaffer at the *Rocky Mountain News*. No longer would Colorado "be the doormat for foreign agitators and selfish corporations or require the interference of Washington bureaucracy."[14] While John D. Rockefeller Jr. and the executives of the CFI launched their widely publicized and highly influential employee representation plan, government officials in Colorado offered their own, often overlooked solution to the problem of industrial warfare.

EARLY CHALLENGES TO THE INDUSTRIAL COMMISSION

In the first years of its operation, workers remained cautiously optimistic that the industrial commission law would prove helpful and that commissioners would act impartially. Two commissioners appeared at the August 1915 Colorado State Federation of Labor convention, pledging their desire to improve relations between workers and employers.[15] The compulsory features of the law were not initially invoked in labor disputes, and most workers expected that they could be repealed. But soon union dealings with the Industrial Commission undermined hopes that it would protect the working public.

In July 1916, 200 members of Denver's Bakery and Confectionery Workers Union, two-thirds of them women, struck a biscuit and a cracker factory following a decision by the Industrial Commission that rejected their demands for increased wages. The commission insisted that the Denver companies had to compete with eastern firms paying lower wages, and thus Denver workers could not reasonably expect a wage increase. *Labor Bulletin* editor Clint Houston complained that the CIC decision recognized employer costs as superior to worker needs. The "beggarly wage" of $3.50 to $5.00 per week for women workers needed redress from the Industrial Commission. Many of these women were breadwinners for their families, Houston insisted. The editor faulted the commission for failing to establish and enforce women's minimum-wage standards.[16] These female members of the working public deserved greater consideration from the commission. Without CIC support for union wage demands, the strike soon failed.

The cracker case significantly shifted worker perceptions of the Industrial Commission and its interventions on behalf of the working public. Soon afterward, American Federation of Labor legislative representative Grant Hamilton returned to Denver to lead opposition to the CIC law. In speeches to the Denver Trades and Labor Assembly and the state federation of labor, Hamilton contested CIC claims that it represented "the public." That "mysterious, invisible public" of the Industrial Commission was in fact "composed of those who stand behind the cashiers' desks in our banks or behind the counters in our counting rooms." Instead of this narrow constituency, Hamilton insisted that the public protected by the Industrial Commission ought to include workers. At its 1916 convention in August, the state labor federation, clearly swayed by Hamilton's lobbying, voted to support a campaign to repeal the industrial commission law entirely.[17]

Growing worker opposition to the Industrial Commission shaped the fall 1916 election campaign. The Denver and state labor federations urged Democratic candidates to support a repeal of the law and secured a repeal provision in the party platform. Democratic gubernatorial candidate Julius Gunter did not openly advocate repeal but promised to evaluate the CIC law if elected. The Democrat had served as district judge in Trinidad, where he established important connections with the Democratic machine in southern Colorado before winning election to the state Supreme Court. A modest and lukewarm campaigner, Gunter most importantly promised to look to Wilson as a model for his own Democratic administration of state government. Colorado unionists strongly opposed Carlson and gave Gunter and the Democrats a broad endorsement in the fall.[18] Nationally, former Industrial Relations commissioner Frank Walsh successfully rallied workers to President Wilson's Democratic campaign. Many Colorado workers, even former Socialists, supported the Democratic Party ticket that year.

Once in office, however, Governor Gunter referred to Colorado's industrial commission law as "sound in fundamentals but susceptible to improvement." In meetings with the state labor legislative committee, Gunter insisted that he would take no official stand either for or against the law.[19] Still, when labor allies Senator Samuel DeBusk from Trinidad and Representative Arthur Meyer, a printer from Denver, introduced the repeal bill during the 1917 legislative session, unionists breathed a sigh of relief.

Joint Senate and House hearings on the repeal bill that winter marked the high point of labor's hopes to shape public opinion. On the evening of February 19, hundreds of workers packed into the legislative hall, even spilling out into the gallery in order to hear the speeches offered in support of the repeal bill. Grant Hamilton spoke first. Hamilton argued that the CIC law revived "Roman absolutism," enabled a state bureaucracy to invade private union meetings, and was based on flawed Canadian precedent that actually provoked strikes rather than prevented them. In his testimony and subsequent pleas on behalf of the repeal bill, Hamilton sought to protect union activism and contract negotiations from state intervention. He frequently invoked the principle of contract as a metaphor for individual freedom and voluntary cooperation.

In contrast, Hamilton posed the condition of status, under which workers owed some obligation to their putative superiors. Even philanthropists and social welfare advocates in recent years had worked to limit contract freedom and voluntarism with "benevolent coercion." Welfare legislation of the Industrial Commission sort would in the end "result in a new bondage — bondage to officialdom. . . . [Freedom] has always come thru repealing legislative restrictions, not thru enacting legislation."[20] Despite his appeals to liberal ideology, Hamilton did not favorably impress the legislators in attendance. His concluding comments in fact suggested that workers should defy the law if they could not repeal it. The chair of the hearing, Senator Lewis, was after all co-sponsor of the industrial commission law. The law's other sponsor, Senator Candlish, sat directly next to Lewis. The senators could hardly contain their hostility toward Hamilton by the end of his testimony.

Edward Costigan followed Hamilton but aroused far less ire. Insisting that he represented not labor or capital but "the general public," Costigan admitted that his views of the CIC had changed since his campaign for governor in 1914. He noted that John Commons, who had helped draft Colorado's workmen's compensation program, disliked the compulsory provisions of the CIC law. Ralph Easley of the National Civic Federation and even MacKenzie King had come to oppose them. A twelve-year experiment with compulsory arbitration in Australia had failed to prevent strikes or ease labor unrest. Australian critics had found that compulsory arbitration became a "one-sided instrument of oppression" and taught "the public how to oppress" in ways reminiscent of the Reign of Terror in revolutionary France.[21] The CIC law posed dangers to not only worker liberties but the very public it was intended to protect. Costigan's testimony continued to demonstrate his shift from an advocate of moral to labor Progressivism.

In the days after the first hearing on the repeal bill, a state labor committee urgently requested that its affiliate unions lobby their legislators. Yet the Senate had stalled over Gunter's nominees to the Industrial Commission. When the Senate at last voted on the repeal proposal in late February, the vote was twenty-eight to four against. Soon afterward, the House also rejected repeal. Republicans had overwhelmingly voted to retain the Industrial Commission. Senators Lewis and Candlish even attempted to add a provision to the industrial commission law that would have revived the common-law charge of conspiracy against striking workers. Their provision passed the Senate but was defeated in the House.[22]

Legislative failure generated protests against Democratic lawmakers and their betrayal of labor support in the 1916 election. The state labor federation published a roll-call vote of the repeal bill vote to guide workers in the next election. Some workers urged recall campaigns against prominent Democratic senators. Governor Gunter was indicted in the labor press for his disregard of worker demands and loyalty. *Labor Bulletin* editor Houston insisted that at the next election Colorado workers would "officiate in the last sad rites over the remains of the Democratic political organization whose death was superinduced by the gangrene of broken faith and duplicity."[23] The failure of repeal likely led some unionists to oppose Gunter's primary run in 1918 and to vote Republican in that fall's general election.

Yet with American entry into war in April 1917, prospects for defying the industrial commission law assumed an entirely new aspect. Professions of patriotism and support for the wartime mobilization efforts by Governor Gunter led many unionists to adopt a more conciliatory approach toward the commission. The war also witnessed the creation of federal mediation boards and national trade agreements under federal oversight. In this context, many non-union workers turned to the CIC for assistance. During the war, the Industrial

Commission actually worked to the advantage of many non-union, especially female workers. The 1917 legislature passed a women's minimum-wage law, which helped to guide CIC investigations. A number of women struck for higher wages and settled with employers along lines recommended by the Industrial Commission. Given wartime inflation, the commissioners tended to approve worker demands for wage increases. Supporters of the CIC went so far as to argue that commissioners had accepted a kind of wardship on behalf of such workers. Underpaid, non-union employees received compensation more in accordance with their needs.[24] Union workers, however, remained suspicious of the commission and looked elsewhere for state support.

LABOR PROGRESSIVES AND THE BUREAU OF LABOR STATISTICS

The modest backing some non-union workers received from the CIC was overshadowed during the Great War by the more active interventions of the Colorado Bureau of Labor Statistics. Although Governor Carlson had initially hoped in 1915 to move the bureau under the authority of the CIC, it remained an independent administrative outpost for labor-friendly appointees in state government. The Wilson landslide in 1916 helped elect Democratic candidate James Noland as Colorado's secretary of state. Given the curiously diffuse administration of Colorado government, Noland had the power to appoint the director of the labor bureau without consulting the governor. In a move that encouraged labor Progressives, Noland appointed William Morrissey, railroad unionist and labor reporter for the *Denver Post*, to serve as acting commissioner of labor. Under Morrissey's leadership, the Bureau of Labor Statistics became a key site for enforcing the protective legislation that labor Progressives had long advocated. Morrissey's interventions on behalf of the working public offer a striking contrast to the state Industrial Commission.

The Colorado labor commissioner was clearly inspired by federal wartime agencies. The National War Labor Board legitimated the central demand of working people for a measure of influence over working conditions. Although the federal board was technically a voluntary agency empowered only to hold hearings and present evidence, its aggressive field staff and executive support from Wilson gave the board some coercive power vis-à-vis employers. Soon after creating the National War Labor Board, the Wilson administration launched the War Labor Policies Board with Felix Frankfurter in charge. By the summer of 1918, the War Labor Policies Board formulated standard clauses for workers on federal government contracts that mandated an eight-hour day and the observance of state labor laws. Frankfurter's board took fewer defiant stands against anti-union employers than Walsh's board, however. While historians have sketched a fairly clear picture of the operation of these federal labor boards during the war, their negotiations with state labor boards remain unclear.[25] In Colorado, the operation of the wartime state labor bureau highlights the effort to reconcile state-level police powers for protecting workers with the fleeting promises of federal government support for industrial democracy.

The Colorado Bureau of Labor Statistics assumed increasing responsibilities with the passage of each new protective labor law. In 1912, voters approved initiatives to limit male miners and women working in mill, factory, and retail positions to an eight-hour day in the interest of public health. The state labor commissioner at the time sought to expand the types of women's work covered under the law to include clerical positions. While a district court judge approved this extension of the law in 1914, employers of such female workers rarely observed the hours limitation. Efforts to enforce laws to require factory inspections for workers' safety, to prohibit employers from discriminating against union employees and from hiring strikebreakers under false pretenses, to secure a minimum wage for women workers, and to collect wages unfairly withheld by employers all kept the small staff in the bureau quite busy. Labor bureau officials perpetually complained about inadequate appropriations and enforcement mechanisms.

In day-to-day operations, the legislature left the state labor chief wide latitude in terms of which laws to enforce and how aggressively to do so. Thus Morrissey's Republican predecessor largely relaxed many labor laws, especially the women's hours law. He found that this law exerted what he considered a "hardship upon both the employer and upon those that the law was intended to protect," especially in seasonable work like canning, hotels, resorts, and department stores during the holidays.[26] Soon after Morrissey assumed control over the Bureau of Labor Statistics in March 1917, employers begged for exemptions from the women's and miner's hours laws, citing the emergency of wartime. Morrissey, however, saw the potential influence that the bureau could have, especially during the war, to expand upon the precedents set by federal agencies to improve working conditions.

In contrast to his Republican predecessor, Morrissey insisted that the women's eight-hour law should not be suspended during the war. He instead recommended that canneries, laundries, and sugar-beet processors should hire more female workers rather than lengthening hours for their existing employees.[27] Although employers inveighed against Morrissey, the labor bureau chief insisted that gradually "the trend of public sentiment seemed to sustain our stand."[28] By summer 1918, Morrissey could point to federal support for his position—that from Frankfurter at the Labor Policies Board.

Union leaders praised Morrissey for his work. Although he found the Bureau of Labor Statistics in a "chaotic state" initially, noted one labor reporter, the new chief began a "vigorous law enforcement policy" in 1917. *Denver Labor Bulletin* editor Clint Houston enthused that for the first time since the bureau was created, "Morrissey is making of this department something more than the political sinecure it has been under previous administrations."[29] The principles of fairness and toughness were set against complaints about earlier partisanship and laxity in celebrations of Morrissey's work.

The labor bureau director also rejected employer requests to suspend the male miner's hours law during the war. In these years, Colorado unionists continued to press for an expansion of hours legislation to cover additional male workers. For example, the Denver labor federation president argued in March 1917 that the Allies' demand for steel created ideal conditions for passing an hours law for steelworkers. As a former factory inspector for the Bureau of Labor Statistics, Mitchell had participated in the 1912 campaign for the miner's eight-hour law. He noted that although labor advocates dropped steelworkers from inclusion under that initiative, they had agreed that a later campaign would be necessary on their behalf. Spring 1917 offered a good time for securing such a law, the labor president argued. Plus, protective legislation would enhance prospects for unionizing the industry.[30] As with miner campaigns for the hours law in the 1890s, labor Progressives did not see unionization and protective labor legislation as mutually exclusive goals for working men.

State labor leaders continued during the war to lobby for the extension of the eight-hour law for other male laborers so long as the Bureau of Labor Statistics would remain the agency charged with their enforcement. As the chief union lobbyist noted, "the laws necessary for the protection and safe guarding of the lives, health, and comfort of those who labor" must be "improved, amended, and enlarged to keep pace" with changing conditions for all workers.[31] Although these proposals came to naught during the war, union enthusiasm for hours protection highlights a faith in the potential of the labor bureau.

The interventions the labor bureau made on behalf of male and female workers in these years are most clearly visible in the case of Western Union employees. In May 1917, Morrissey insisted that Western Union offices in the state comply with the women's eight-hour law, even though the state law did not explicitly include telegraph operators under its provisions. By requiring the company to uphold the eight-hour day for 200 women operators and clerks, Morrissey expected roughly 400 male employees to benefit in like manner. Thus he hoped to use the gender protection as a surrogate for explicitly class-based strategies. In this, his action was hardly unique among Progressive Era reformers.[32]

But the war created opportunities for Morrissey. Colorado employees of Western Union joined the Commercial Telegraphers Union of America in a national organizing campaign in the spring of 1918. When the company's antiunion president, Newcomb Carlton, ordered managers to fire union employees, Denver officials complied. Amid union threats of a nationwide strike, the

National War Labor Board intervened and pressured Carlton to reinstate employees. Carlton defiantly refused.[33] Into this fray jumped Colorado Bureau of Labor Statistics head Morrissey. He first appealed to President Wilson directly, rather than Governor Gunter, on behalf of the discharged operators. On July 16, 1918, Wilson nationalized the telegraph lines, backing the federal labor board and legitimating its authority to settle labor disputes during the war.

Several days later, Morrissey felt confident enough to indict Colorado managers of Western Union with violations of the state's Anti-Coercion Act. The 1911 measure prohibited employers from firing workers solely on the basis of union membership. Morrissey highlighted the fact that one of the "discharged employe[e]s was 21 years of age and sole support of a widowed mother and two sisters." The state's protective law could thus aid a female breadwinner as well as her dependents, Morrissey implied. Western Union managers admitted that they violated the anti-coercion law and were released on bond.[34] Although Morrissey, following his predecessors, had largely relied on moral suasion and voluntary compliance in his enforcement of labor laws up to this point, the coercive power of the national labor board offered a promising precedent for the state Bureau of Labor Statistics. Under wartime conditions, he sought to harness the police power of the state in the interests of the unionizing public, which included both male and female workers.

Unfortunately for labor Progressives, political conditions changed dramatically with the end of the war. Because the district courts were closed during the final months of the war, the Western Union case did not come to trial until 1919. As the National War Labor Board retreated from its aggressive stance on behalf of union workers in the postwar era, labor commissioner Morrissey lost a key ally. When the company managers had their day in court, the district court judge agreed with their contention that the anti-coercion law violated their Fourteenth Amendment right to due process.[35] On appeal to the Colorado Supreme Court, justices in 1920 sustained the lower court ruling. Worse still for reformers, the court also overturned a 1912 initiative designed to allow the popular recall of judicial decisions. Conservative court authority remained supreme, despite earlier reforms to enable the voting public to circumvent a hostile judiciary. The wartime emergency only momentarily enhanced the enforcement power of the Bureau of Labor Statistics. Yet worker hopes for the agency endured, bolstered in the postwar period by Morrissey's tireless advocacy.

POSTWAR INVESTIGATIONS OF LABOR DISPUTES

In contrast to the state labor bureau, the Colorado Industrial Commission directly challenged union workers in the postwar period. From 1919 to 1922, the Colorado Industrial Commission struggled to arbitrate major labor disputes that were not easily contained within the state's boundaries.[36] These disputes revived the contest over the needs of the public. Colorado voters hoped for an end to the protracted strikes, bloodshed, violence, and destruction of property of Colorado's early years of industrialization. Commissioners saw themselves working for peaceful reconciliation between potential economic combatants. Yet labor Progressives sought to recast the needs of the public in terms of economic justice and basic citizenship rights: a minimum wage for women workers, union freedom to negotiate contracts and wage strikes, and political freedom from corporate intimidation in the remote hinterland regions of the state.

The postwar period in fact witnessed a national debate about what role the public should play in labor disputes. In 1920, US senator Miles Poindexter reintroduced a measure to prohibit railroad strikes pending an investigation of the national Railroad Labor Board to protect the traveling public. In response, American Federation of Labor secretary Frank Morrison complained that such concern for "the public" did not include attention "to the wages paid to the workers or the conditions under which they work, but rather with the continuous operation of industry so that [the public's] wants may be supplied without interruption." The key issue, as another labor official noted during the Senate's hearings on Poindexter's bill, was "Who is going to define the public? We are a part of the public. And who is going to say that the representative chosen for the public really represents the public?"[37] This question struck to the heart of the Progressive vision of "expert" investigation and arbitration. Colorado's industrial commissioners confidently insisted that they defined and best represented the public in labor disputes. During these years of postwar adjustment, the CIC would increasingly use its coercive powers to enforce its vision of the public interest.

Until 1919, Colorado commissioners had largely relied on persuasion rather than coercion to secure participation in their investigations. They had at times tolerated both labor and employer defiance of the CIC law without pressing for indictments. Most commonly, workers or employers refused to testify during CIC investigations of disputes.[38] Additionally, unions such as those representing the printers and cigarmakers had failed to give thirty days' notice of their intent to strike. More commonly, employers flouted the law by lowering wages without first notifying the CIC. Commissioners, however, continued to insist that workers and employers give thirty-day notice of any intended change in wages, hours, or working conditions. This requirement became the sticking point in a series of coal mining disputes between 1919 and 1922.

Workers in the southern coalfields in 1919 still endured the dominance of operators like the Colorado Fuel and Iron Company as they had before the Ludlow massacre. The United Mine Workers had consistently if unsuccessfully sought to abolish the CFI company union and establish a legitimate system of collective bargaining. Nationwide coal strikes in 1919 and again in 1921 offered Colorado organizers for the miners' union a chance to rally workers in the southern coalfields to assert their economic and political rights in this hinterland region.[39] Although the UMW had only gained a foothold in the southern mines, Colorado miners still benefited in 1919 and 1920 from federal government mediation and UMW strength in other parts of the country. Yet the Colorado Industrial Commission demonstrated far more attention to the needs of the state's consumers and coal operators than to the economic and political demands of workers.

Commissioners in these years consistently challenged miner decisions to strike and ignored demands for union recognition while working foremost to ensure an uninterrupted supply of coal. While strike conditions nationally had severely cut production, Colorado output remained fairly constant in 1919 and 1920.[40] CIC intervention, commissioners insisted, had made continuous output possible. Their work thus directly benefited the consuming public, as they saw it. The consumer of more than half the coal produced in this case, however, was the Colorado Fuel and Iron steel mill in Pueblo. Employers too had much to celebrate as a result of commission efforts to limit strikes.

The interventions of the Industrial Commission also pushed judges to narrow legal interpretations of the public interest to favor consumers foremost. After commissioners had begun prosecutions against UMW miners for striking without CIC approval in 1919, the miners appealed the case to the state Supreme Court. In April 1921, the Colorado Supreme Court overturned a lower court ruling that the CIC could not legally prohibit miners from striking. The high court instead affirmed the constitutionality of the thirty-day provision of the state Industrial Relations Act as a valid protection for consumers. Justice Denison's opinion stated that "Food, shelter, and heat, before all others, are the great necessities of life, and in modern life heat means coal." The interruption of business operations to provide these necessities cannot but affect the public, Denison alleged. The CIC had acted legally in restraining the coal miners from striking in 1919 as that industry was affected with a public interest.

Additionally, the Colorado Supreme Court found no evidence of UMW claims of involuntary servitude under the act. According to the court, an "individual workman may quit at will for any reason or no reason. There is not even prohibition of strikes. The only thing forbidden is a strike before or during the Commission's action."[41] That the timing of a strike might be a factor of overwhelming importance for workers did not figure in Denison's opinion. The Supreme Court affirmed the CIC's coercive power to curb worker rights on behalf of consumers. The Denver Tramway strike had worked in similar ways to narrow worker rights.

In 1921, the Industrial Commission again intervened in a southern coal strike to the advantage of mine operators and consumers. On August 30, CFI officials posted a notice that 30 percent wage cuts were to take effect the next day. Company unions had already agreed to the cuts, operators insisted. CFI officials gave no notice to the CIC, defying the Industrial Relations Act. A strike by the mainly non-union workers immediately followed until the CIC ordered a restoration of the old wage schedule pending an investigation. The United Mine Workers quickly seized the opportunity to enlist more than a thousand new members from Rockefeller's company unions. Mine union leaders urged the Industrial Commission to retain prevailing wage levels and to indict CFI operators for their violation of the thirty-day rule.[42] The commissioners began their investigation in Walsenburg on September 9. But with no interruption in coal supplies for consumers, the CFI violation of the industrial law did not require coercive action by the commissioners.

Still, commissioners collected widespread evidence from miners about the efforts within company unions to secure consent for the wage cut. Workers testified of coercion, intimidation, threats of closing mines, and the loss of jobs unless men signed petitions approving the decrease. Workers and operators offered wildly divergent daily wage figures. The CIC did not officially recognize the UMW in the investigation but heard from union members individually. UMW leaders nonetheless insisted that the CFI hold to the national bituminous coal commission award of 1920, which would maintain wages until April 1922.[43]

After nearly two months of hearings, the CIC announced its award in early November. Because the company had secured worker consent to the wage cut through its employee representation plan, CFI officials could lower wages up to 30 percent with CIC approval. Widespread complaints of CFI intimidation did not alter the commissioners' decision to back the company. Considering miner skill and training as well competitive pressures on CFI operators, the CIC accepted company claims that miners were overpaid. The company received no fine or indictment for violating the thirty-day rule, and the commission ignored the fact that CFI had broken the national coal commission agreement. The nationwide demand for coal had begun to fall, as it would throughout the decade from its 1920 high, and coal operators insisted that wage costs had to come down as well. Two weeks after the commission ruling, the CFI implemented its wage cut. Again the majority of its workers walked out. Most assumed that since the CIC took no punitive action against the CFI for violating the Industrial Relations Law, commissioners would similarly ignore the strike action without a thirty-day notice.[44]

Sadly, the striking workers were mistaken. An uninterrupted supply of coal was suddenly in jeopardy. Not only did the CIC indict strikers, but Republican governor Shoup sent the national guard to Huerfano County as a strikebreaking force. The governor responded chiefly to CFI rather than commissioner concerns. Even before the strike call and without any signs of public disorder, Shoup insisted that "tumult, riot, and insurrection" would prevail without the troops. Memories of the Ten Days' War clearly played a role. The governor mobilized the Colorado Rangers, as the guard was called, and declared martial law over the county just after the CIC ruling. Troops were kept in the county for more than a year. UMW organizers were prohibited by the Rangers from entering CFI property or holding open meetings. Mine owners praised both the "upstanding, virile body of men" recruited to protect their properties and Governor Shoup for his "fearless stand for law and order."[45]

The imposition of martial law in the southern coal districts severely curtailed political freedom for the striking workers. For Walsenburg editor John Coss, "the iron heel of military despotism" reigned. The state Rangers declared most public meetings illegal, censored the press, and converted the county court house into an armory, compelling the district judge to hold court in a small adjacent office. The Rangers' presence enhanced rather than eased a warlike mentality in the region. Many county residents insisted that the Ranger occupation threatened the very working public it was intended to protect.[46]

Throughout this period of military occupation in the coalfields, industrial commissioners happily reported that the ineffective strike activity of the UMW had not cut into coal output significantly. The CIC claimed credit for enabling southern mines to operate at "practically full capacity during the entire time of the disastrous coal strike throughout all the other states of the Union."[47] Again, continuous production, not a democratic challenge to the overwhelming dominance of corporate elites, was in the public's best interest, according to the CIC. Together with the state national guard, the CIC created more instability and resentment than lasting industrial peace. Although inspired by Commons's vision for impartial, expert investigation, the CIC worked to the short-term benefit of consumers and employers.

JAILING STRIKING PACKINGHOUSE WORKERS

Industrial Commission interventions in meatpacking disputes worked in similar ways. The conflict between packers and workers, like that in coal, reflected a need to contract supply following the wartime boom. During and immediately after World War I, Pueblo and Denver packinghouse workers, like those in Chicago and Kansas City, had joined the Amalgamated Meat Cutters and Butcher Workmen's Union in record numbers. The president's Mediation Commission provided an incentive. Colorado packers, both affiliates of the Big Five as well as smaller independent producers, generally observed national arbitration agreements in wartime.[48] After the war, however, the packers launched an aggressive open-shop campaign, and the Colorado Industrial Commission played a key facilitating role.

With the national packing arbitration agreement set to expire in September 1921, the packinghouse union launched a new organizing drive in Denver. By October, the organizers had secured many new union members from the ranks of Denver's 800 packinghouse employees. Denver's packers, including Swift, Armour, Cudahy, Coffin, and Mountain States, followed the national line in refusing to consider union demands as the arbitration agreement ended. Workers feared news of a wage cut. In light of Colorado's industrial commission law, Swift and other Denver packers gave the board thirty-day notice in November of proposed wage reductions. Although Big Five wage cuts went into effect in Chicago on November 28, in Colorado packers agreed to wait until the CIC conducted its investigation before reducing local wages. Before the commission held its initial hearing, however, the Amalgamated in Chicago declared a national strike on December 5. Denver's union workers walked out too, without giving the CIC thirty days' notice.[49]

Colorado's commissioners then began their own campaign against Denver's packinghouse workers. Commissioners based their interventions on a view of the public interest that clearly favored the packers. Although Colorado workers had responded to a national strike call, the CIC began local prosecutions for a violation of the thirty-day clause of the industrial law. Commissioners petitioned Denver district judge Clarence Morley for an injunction, which he promptly granted, to order the local leaders of the Amalgamated to call off the strike at once. The Amalgamated district president and Denver Local 641 leaders defied the order only to face charges of contempt in district court. While Chicago witnessed rioting and police firing upon picketers and strike sympathizers, Denver was calm during the strike. The city labor federation pledged to support the packinghouse workers in their fight against the packers, the CIC, and district court.[50]

Meanwhile, the CIC held hearings to investigate both the packers' proposed wage cut and the strike action by Local 641. At the CIC hearings conducted toward the end of December, attorneys for Swift and other Denver packers appeared along with subpoenaed union representatives. The packers presented carefully prepared records and charts, alleging falling prices and losses incurred as a result of the current wage scale. The CIC granted the packers of Denver their requested wage reduction as "reasonable" under prevailing economic conditions.[51]

On January 4, 1922, district court judge Morley found the union leaders guilty of contempt, sentencing them to up to sixty days in jail. Meatpacking was another industry affected with a public interest, Morley insisted, and the strike had threatened consumer supplies. Local union leaders had "acted unlawfully" when they heeded the strike call of national officers in Chicago in violation of the CIC law. "The men might as well have listened to a similar order promulgated in Russia . . . which has no respect for the laws of this state."[52] Morley's ruling revealed the punitive potential of the industrial commission law at it fullest. With its leaders in jail and employers promoting company union plans, Local 641 struggled to keep the strike alive through the end of January. Denver packers ignored the federal mediators sent from Washington. On February 1, the Amalgamated executive board in Chicago conceded defeat. While Chicago packinghouse workers had especially been divided along racial lines during the strike, Denver's workers had to contend more fundamentally with hostile interventions by the district court and Industrial Commission.

Denver unionists were divided about how best to respond to the landmark prosecutions of workers under the CIC law. This was the first time that the industrial commission law had been used to send workers to jail. Some labor federation members urged direct defiance of the industrial law and organized public protest meetings for late January. The more conservative members of the federation prevailed, however, in killing a direct-action resolution. These "law-and-order" members, as they called themselves, insisted that lobbying efforts to repeal the industrial commission law would falter if the central union publicly called for the violation of state laws.[53] The more conservative city labor federation members successfully urged city officials to deny a parade permit to the direct-action advocates, squashing the possibility for a broader public protest of the commission. Although frustrated by the coercive intervention of the CIC, Denver's labor leaders could not agree on a demonstration to assert workers' civic rights.

With striking meatcutters jailed, indictments against striking coal miners, and division among labor leaders, it was evident to many unionists in the winter of 1922 that the CIC had successfully reinforced the open-shop drive of Colorado employers. The commissioners had defined the public interest chiefly in terms of consumer convenience, mobilizing the coercive power of the state government to enforce that view. This view of the public interest, and a coercive mediation board to represent it, gained national popularity in the postwar years, particularly as a result of the Kansas experiment.

THE KANSAS INDUSTRIAL COURT
AND COMPULSORY ARBITRATION

What Colorado pioneered, in terms of a commission to represent consumer interests in labor disputes, Kansas refined with its Industrial Court. Where Colorado lawmakers had empowered their state board with compulsory investigation powers, the Kansas Industrial Court marked the first nationwide test of the idea of binding arbitration. The Kansas experiment drew national attention, as a number of states, and even the federal government, considered similar programs to contain the industrial unrest of the postwar era. Moreover, the Kansas court, along with the CIC in Colorado, marked the apex of the Progressive impulse to promote cross-class harmony by means of the investigation and arbitration of labor disputes. Yet again, state intervention to ease labor unrest and balance competing interests favored consumers at the expense of workers' civic rights.

The Kansas Industrial Court also grew out of disputes in coal mining. UMW Local 14 president Alexander Howat and 12,000 union miners in the southeast region of the state completely shut down the coalfields in late 1919 in response to a national strike call. Centered in Crawford and Cherokee counties, Kansas coal-mining communities, unlike their counterparts in southern Colorado, constituted nearly a closed shop by 1919 after decades of intermittent, bloody conflicts and strikebreaking by the operators. In the preceding four years alone, Kansas mines had witnessed more than 700 strikes, most reflecting the struggle of the UMW for recognition. The hard-drinking, tempestuous Howat had forged a tight organization among the overwhelmingly foreign-born miners in this region. The county seat of Crawford County, Girard, was home to several national socialist newspapers including *Appeal to Reason*.[54] In this region, considered by most Kansans to be a "Little Balkans," new immigrant, union miners and their families had developed a strong class critique of not only the economic inequalities in the mining camps and company towns but also the state government, given its regular support for the operators.

The small bituminous coal industry in Kansas was owned by a few individuals and corporations and dominated by Central Coal and Coke. Kansas operators had banned together under the Southwest Coal Operators' Association. With the end of the federal wartime arbitration agreement, operators in Kansas, like those in Colorado, had hoped to resist pressure for wage increases and oppose union expansion. After repeated operator refusals to consider arbitration during the 1919 strike, Kansas governor Henry Allen declared a state of emergency and seized control of the mines in December. Allen then secured ex-servicemen and college youth to mine coal under military protection. These "keen, kindly, clean-faced young chaps, dressed in their uniforms" did more than break a strike, according to the governor. They "were proving . . . that government does have the right to protect the public" from the putative aggressions of a "labor czar" like Howat. Allen's celebration of the masculine student-strikebreaker provides another example of a national trend in these years.[55] Yet Allen envisioned a state agency to perform this gendered work on a more permanent basis.

In January 1920, Governor Allen convened a special session of the state legislature, dominated by representatives from farm districts, which quickly rallied to his proposal for an industrial court with compulsory arbitration powers. At Senate hearings on Allen's measure, both union and corporate representatives expressed serious concerns about the bill. Former Industrial Relations Committee co-chair Frank Walsh testified that the proposed anti-strike provisions would so limit the right of workers to strike as to constitute a kind of involuntary servitude. Legislators were unmoved and overwhelmingly approved the plan. The new court was to ensure continuous production in specific industries that broadly affected the consuming public: food production, clothing manufacture, fuel, transportation, and utilities. Like the Colorado Industrial Commission, the Kansas court was composed of three members, appointed by the governor. As in Colorado, these appointments reflected partisan alignments in state government more than legal or professional qualifications. District judge and early court advocate William Huggins became presiding judge. The governor appointed his former campaign manager and newspaper owner Clyde Reed to serve. Progressive editor William Allen White was nominated but declined appointment.[56]

Although building on Colorado precedents, the Kansas experiment in compulsory arbitration was in many ways unique. The Kansas board not only had the powers to prohibit strikes and lockouts pending an investigation but also had the authority to impose a settlement regulating working conditions and wages that bound both workers and employers. The court was further charged with enforcement of the state's protective labor legislation. Defiance of court orders could result in as many as two years in jail and a fine of $5,000. Unlike in Colorado, the Kansas legislature explicitly defined those industries that were affected with a public interest and thus subject to court authority. The Kansas act also revived common-law obligations of master and servant, defining unlawful worker "conspiracy . . . and inducement and intimidation of others with intent to cause suspension of operation" of specific industries. Union workers in Kansas viewed the law as a direct challenge to the basic principles of unionism.[57]

Not merely content with the court's creation, Governor Allen launched a broad public relations campaign on behalf of the Kansas experiment. In a series of articles and speeches throughout 1920, Allen expanded on his notion that the court offered the best defense of public health, welfare, and security during industrial disputes. Allen in fact likened the threat of industrial strife to that of organized crime. The rights of the general public, "of women and children . . . to an adequate supply of the bare necessities of life are superior to the right of labor or capital to stop production in the interests of selfish quarrel."[58] Strikebreakers too needed the benevolent protection of the Kansas court, Allen argued, in order to fulfill their manhood and resist the assaults of union strikers. Allen liked to cite the case of one strikebreaker, Ernest Guffy, who had chosen to work alongside soldiers during the 1919 coal strike but was "terrorized by . . . union comrades." The union pressured his grocer and landlord not to deal with him. American Federation of Labor unionists talked of worker freedom, Allen contended, but not of the freedom of the strike-breaker to work.[59]

Governor Allen agreed with a number of Progressive thinkers who viewed consumers as the only group that represented the whole of society. *New Republic* coeditor Walter Weyl had insisted in 1912 that "[i]n America to-day the unifying economic force, about which a majority . . . is forming, is the common interest of the citizen as a consumer of wealth. . . . Despite his over-whelming superiority in numbers, the consumer, finding it difficult to orga-nize, has often been worsted in industrial battles." Similarly, the future New Dealer Rexford Tugwell contended that consumers have a public interest in certain industries that amounts to a right to "appeal to the courts, without a legislative act directing regulation, for redress." Courts could fairly compel businesses affected with a public interest to provide "adequate service at rea-sonable rates." Allen saw the Industrial Court in such terms: that is, empow-ering the consuming public, which was the only true "public," through state regulation over business and labor.[60]

Allen spoke before numerous chambers of commerce, the New Jersey and New York legislatures, and employers' associations along the East Coast. Clamor for legislation along Kansas lines followed in the Nebraska, Missouri, New York, and New Jersey state legislatures. One reporter observed, "Never before in the history of the United States has there been so widespread a movement [for anti-strike and compulsory arbitration proposals]."[61] In his 1921 Annual Message to Congress, President Warren Harding even called for a federal industrial court to handle labor disputes "which menace the public welfare. . . . [T]he strike, lockout, and the boycott are as . . . disastrous in their results as war or armed revolution in the domain of politics." In 1922, US sen-ator Kenyon introduced a bill to create a National Coal Mining Board, which would have effectively introduced compulsory arbitration in the industry.[62]

The court's presiding judge William Huggins generally echoed Allen's emphasis on the threats to vulnerable feminine consumers and non-union men. He equated the economic pressure of strikes and lockouts with block-ades. Such "acts of war . . . punish the poor, the weak, the aged, the help-less, the women and children." Huggins acknowledged that the interests of the worker and employer were linked, although secondary, to those of the general public. Again continuous production was paramount. To that end, "skilled and faithful workers and ample capital should always be available." While recognizing union representation under very narrow circumstances, the court would, Huggins clearly hoped, come to replace the union as a tool for workers to achieve justice. Even the American Federation of Labor (AFL) came in for attack. Invited in 1923 to address the Denver Civic and Commercial

Association, Huggins contended that Gompers and other "conservative labor leaders" posed a greater menace than Bolsheviks with their ambitious program to "make an employe[e]'s job more sacred than the right of the owner to the use of his plant."[63]

Organized labor offered its own response to Allen's and Huggins's public of dependents in need of Industrial Court protection. In May 1920, Samuel Gompers debated Governor Allen before a packed house in New York's Carnegie Hall. The AFL leader took two views of Allen's argument that the Kansas court was needed to advocate for the public interest. On the one hand, Gompers declared that the consuming public had no rights superior to a worker's own right to live and defend his or her rights against employer oppression. Yet Gompers also argued that there was no public wholly separate from workers and employers, save paupers or wards of the state. The public, as Gompers saw it, was in fact one-quarter union, while "Governor Allen's public seems to be for most part an employing and non-union public."[64] Unionists struggled repeatedly and unsuccessfully to challenge the champions of administrative labor boards in their definitions of the public interest.

More locally, Howat and his Kansas supporters repeatedly defied the Industrial Court on the ground with wildcat strikes. Just three days after the court began its operations in 1920, 400 coal miners in Crawford County announced their intention to strike. The immediate grievance of the miners was a violation of their working agreement by the Southwest Coal Operators' Association. More significantly, the miners intended to defy the Industrial Court. Judges began investigations at once, although Governor Allen also instructed his attorney general to seek an injunction in district court prohibiting the leaders of UMW District 14 from calling a strike in an industry of such public importance. The district court in Crawford County granted a permanent injunction against the miners and also prosecuted Howat and the other leaders of District 14 for refusing to testify before the Industrial Court.[65] Finding Howat guilty, the district court jailed him for contempt, and thousands of Kansas miners promptly struck in sympathy. Howat appealed his case to the Kansas Supreme Court and was released on bond.[66]

The tempestuous leader of District 14 consistently viewed the Industrial Court as the official, repressive arm of the state Coal Operators Association. Throughout the summer of 1920, Howat's court fight symbolized the union struggle against a consuming public defined in hostile terms. At its June national convention, the AFL voted overwhelmingly to support Howat in his defiance of the Kansas law, even though Howat's independence within the UMW had generated significant concerns among the union's leadership. The convention pledged to support workers in Kansas and Colorado against antistrike legislation. By 1922 the AFL executive committee decided to create a legal bureau to collect and publish court opinions on legislative programs such as the Kansas Industrial Court and the "equally obnoxious and dangerous" Colorado Industrial Commission.[67] Yet Gompers and other AFL leaders would struggle continuously to define the public interest in labor disputes in terms of worker citizenship rights.

WHO DEFINES THE PUBLIC INTEREST?

Although Colorado commissioners and Kansas judges insisted that they represented the whole public, not merely "partisan" interest groups, they too easily conflated the interests of the consuming public with those of large, open-shop employers.[68] Critics of compulsory arbitration noted that corporate employers who defied board orders to reduce hours or increase wages did not affect the welfare and comfort of consumers. Yet when workers struck to force compliance of a board order or simply quit work in defiance of the CIC or Industrial Court to seize a moment of strength vis-à-vis their employer, the consuming public was easily aroused in opposition.[69] The CIC and Kansas Industrial Court could then claim to champion the injured public by indicting the strikers. Industrial Court judge Huggins in particular pledged to fight the AFL policy of rewarding friends and punishing enemies that would "subject the power of government to the selfish ends of a class."[70] The Industrial Court and CIC also resorted to court injunctions to enforce their orders against small-business owners and unions more often than large corporate firms like the CFI. And neither the CIC nor the Industrial Court consistently elevated worker rights to a living wage or working conditions above the demands of the consuming public for uninterrupted production or service.

Despite their lofty rhetoric, the Colorado Industrial Commission and Industrial Court failed to balance group interests as mediation Progressives had hoped. In a *Survey* article on the Kansas Court in April, journalist John Fitch lamented that the competition of group interests gave way under the Kansas court to the imposition of a narrowly defined public interest. The court sought to determine that interest by relying chiefly on legal rules and precedents. Compulsory arbitration of the Kansas sort meant an effort to stop economic controversies between organized groups by simple declaration. Yet the growing awareness and acceptance of the principles of collective representation associated with interest-group politics offered a counter example, Fitch argued. "Divergent interests exist and will continue to exist. . . . To forbid a group the right to exercise its group strength" in the economic as well as political realm would create conditions of "servitude."[71] Collective bargaining in industry resembled interest-group lobbying at state capitols, Fitch implied. The main question in both cases was one of organized representation of interest.

Fitch subsequently argued that the Kansas court undermined any collective response of union workers but treated workers only as individuals. The public as envisioned by the court was merely a loose aggregation of workers, employers, and consumers. The court did not recognize group negotiations within a broader public. Rather than simply stopping strikes, Fitch argued, state agents might work to remove the cause of strikes and encourage voluntary collective bargaining. "[I]f that can be done strikes will take care of themselves, just as typhoid fever will if you look after the water supply."[72] Without addressing the root cause of strikes or attempting to recognize and balance group interests, mediation Progressives would fail to secure industrial peace.

The CIC and Industrial Court also envisioned the consuming public in ethnic and spatial terms and worked to shield it from outside pressures and influences. The largely native-born, Anglo populations of these states appeared to need protections from the foreign-born immigrants working in industrial and mining districts. Only 12 percent of Colorado residents were foreign-born immigrants in 1920. In the southern coal districts, the percentage was often twice as high. English and Italian immigrants predominated with smaller numbers of East European and Mexican workers. In Kansas, mining communities included Italian, German, French, and Belgian immigrants along with many from the Austro-Hungarian Empire.[73] When unionized, Colorado and Kansas workers were linked to national organizations in national industries like coal, meatpacking, and the railroads. Both state boards struggled unsuccessfully to contain local confrontations that arose from nationwide strikes in these industries. Union organizers who followed national strike calls, like meatcutters in Denver, were subject to legal action for violating state board orders. Given the difficulties of treating each state as a distinct economic zone, supporters of the CIC and Industrial Court welcomed proposals to expand their arbitration models on a national scale in the early 1920s.

Yet there remained one conception of the public interest upon which arbitration commissioners and organized labor could in principle agree. The Colorado Industrial Relations Act and Kansas Industrial Court Law drew in part upon a republican "public interest" tradition in US law to which many workers were sympathetic. As one Industrial Court judge argued, his authority rested on the same police-power principle that guided legislatures in regulating businesses that affect the public or in creating workmen's compensation, health rules in factories and mines, minimum wages for women and children, and prohibitions of child labor.[74] Although the Colorado Supreme Court had increasingly defined the "public interest" in terms of consumer needs, the Kansas Industrial Court drew upon this tradition in one significant case to advance the needs of the working public.

The case began in 1921 when 300 union workers at the Wolff Packing Company in Topeka filed a complaint with the Industrial Court over pending wage cuts and hour increases. With the termination of the federal wartime agreement in meatpacking, Wolff managers insisted that labor costs had to decrease for the firm to survive. The Industrial Court investigated working conditions and industry competition, ultimately affirming worker rights to a "fair wage" prior to any return on capital investment for the packer. Here was a principle that union and non-union workers alike could endorse. The Industrial Court exceeded the requirements of the state's minimum wage, which applied only to women workers at the time, and extended the principle to male workers as well. Wolff Packing appealed the decision with the aid of the Federation of Kansas Industries, contending that wages within the firm were not a public concern. In June 1922 the Kansas Supreme Court remarkably held that "an industry . . . that cannot be operated except at the sacrifice of its employees ought to quit business."[75] Despite its unremitting hostility toward Howat and the UMW, the Kansas Industrial Court had won a significant victory for workers hoping for state recognition of a "fair wage" principle. The Wolff Packing case promised to expand state regulation of wages and hours based on the principle of the public interest.

But the Kansas ruling did not stand for long. Upon appeal by Wolff Packing, the US Supreme Court found in 1923 that the Industrial Court lacked the authority to impose its "fair wage" principle and had abridged the employer's freedom of contract rights without due process. Challenging the public-interest argument directly, Chief Justice Taft insisted that "one does not devote one's . . . business to the public use or clothe it with a public interest merely because one makes commodities for . . . the public." Two years later, the Supreme Court denied the Industrial Court the authority to regulate hours as well.[76] The public-interest tradition could not sustain such an extension of state government power on behalf of the working public as the Kansas Industrial Court envisioned. Although labor leaders had frequently complained that the Kansas court law created a kind of industrial slavery for workers, it was to the possible enslavement of capital, noted one critic, that the Supreme Court took exception.[77]

More broadly, the Supreme Court decision undermined the principle upon which the state arbitration movement rested. The Colorado Industrial Commission would also proceed more cautiously as a consequence. At the same time, organized labor in Colorado mobilized to discredit the experiment in the political arena. Given the prominence of the interventions of the Industrial Commission in the early 1920s, Colorado unionists increasingly developed their political tactics in light of arguments about the public interest.

COLORADO WORKERS AND POSTWAR ELECTORAL POLITICS

The immediate postwar years saw workers nationwide experimenting with new electoral tactics. Colorado was no exception. Given union frustrations with the Industrial Commission in Colorado and the wartime Democratic

Party, labor Progressives attempted to rally workers for a class-based challenge at the polls in 1920.[78]

The 1920 campaign initially revealed divisions over political tactics among labor leaders. Some AFL loyalists within the Colorado labor federation insisted that nonpartisan action was preferable to direct cooperation with the Democratic Party. Labor was partisan, insisted AFL president Samuel Gompers, to principles and not to any political party. Workers should campaign on behalf of the people against privilege. "The trend of the times is distinctly non-partisan," claimed *Denver Labor Bulletin* editor Ralph Moser. The splits within the state Democratic Party only reinforced the editor's conviction that nonpartisan action was essential.[79]

Yet early support for nonpartisanship in Colorado gradually faded. The promise of a farmer-labor alliance was more appealing. The Non-Partisan League (NPL) of North Dakota appeared to show the way. Initially a group of North Dakota farmers, the NPL highlighted agrarian discontent with the Republican-dominated government in 1915. Tapping former Socialists to lead the revolt, the Non-Partisan League worked to capture the Republican Party in the 1916 and 1918 primaries. Although not technically creating its own party structure, the NPL gained control over North Dakota government and launched an ambitious experiment in state ownership of banking and distribution networks. Working with the Industrial Workers of the World, which had effectively organized harvest workers in the state, the NPL also initiated a labor program with broad appeal to workers.[80]

Attempting to expand its success after 1916, the NPL relocated its headquarters to St. Paul, Minnesota, in January 1917. There the NPL generated a great deal of support, especially among farmers. Yet the more heterogeneous economy in Minnesota made an NPL sweep of the state more difficult than in North Dakota with its one-crop, export-dependent economy. The Minnesota GOP launched an offensive to crush the NPL, drawing upon state government agencies during wartime to intimidate supporters and limit their access to public space. Still, NPL candidates made a strong showing in Minnesota's GOP primary of 1918. Organized labor in Minnesota allied with the NPL in August 1919, creating the Working People's Political League.[81]

NPL organizers from St. Paul appeared in Colorado in 1918, and the next year a number of union activists promoted a farmer-labor alliance for the 1920 election. Several leaders of the state labor federation worked to link NPL tactics with the nonpartisan program promoted by the AFL's national leadership. In 1920 the AFL had launched a "radically new and important departure from its previous tactics," according to one sympathetic observer. AFL unions could now focus energies on the primary elections in an effort to capture a major party, following the lead of the North Dakota NPL. This would mean a new application of the "rewarding friend, punishing enemies" policy, one that would wrest control of primaries from the party machines.[82] While Colorado labor Progressives committed the state's federation to an NPL alliance, they increasingly advocated a campaign strategy at odds with the theoretical goals of AFL nonpartisanship. The practical effort to capture the Democratic Party was not easily reconciled with a principled attack on partisanship.

Increasingly, Colorado labor leaders planned for a party takeover. The internal weakness within the Democratic Party offered a promising context for this approach. The party primary in September proved a success for the NPL-state federation of labor alliance. The NPL coalition secured the nomination of nearly its entire ticket. The farmer-labor takeover had given the insurgents the appearance of legitimacy, the apparent endorsement of a major political party. But the victory quickly generated opposition in the press. *Rocky Mountain News* editor John Shaffer alleged that the results of the primary confirmed only that the NPL "boll weevil" had attached itself "to the Democratic tree." The mainstream press insisted that narrow class-consciousness, inspired by "un-American agitators," now guided the remnants of the Colorado Democratic Party. The *Express* editorialized that Colorado Democrats would "function as a class party directed from outside the state by a salaried organization centering at St. Paul."[83] The Republican Party not only promised stability, law, and order but also claimed to represent the broader public against a special interest.

On Election Day 1920, even the "perfect weather" appeared to conspire against organized labor's capture tactics. The unseasonable temperatures and the presidential election drew an unusually high number of voters, who handed the Democratic ticket a bitter defeat. The popular juvenile court judge Ben Lindsey was one of the few Democrats elected as Republicans swept to victory. Tramway injunction judge Greeley Whitford easily won election to the Colorado Supreme Court. The Republicans secured overwhelming majorities in the state legislature. Incumbent Governor Shoup won reelection on a pledge to maintain the Industrial Commission and its coercive interventions against miners on behalf of consumers. The vote was a repudiation of the capture tactics of the NPL-labor alliance, as the Democratic candidate for governor failed to carry a single county.[84] Labor Progressives appeared too narrowly partisan to appeal to the broader public.

Two years later, however, public sentiment toward the Industrial Commission had begun to shift. Governor Shoup's handling of the coal strikes and the CIC prosecution of meatcutters dominated the campaign planning of union activists. At the May 1922 labor federation convention, delegates focused their political agenda on renewed demands for repeal of the CIC law. They elected to the presidency of the federation an outspoken critic of the CIC who advocated defiance of the industrial law. Delegates also demanded an end to the state's Ranger law, citing Governor Shoup's use of the state guard as a strikebreaking force in the recent coal strike. Sympathetic observers accused the CIC of financial mismanagement and argued that taxpayers suffered additional burdens as a result of the commission and the Rangers. Yet the convention also returned to the AFL's "friends and enemies" approach, endorsing candidates in both the Democratic and Republican primaries.[85] Labor leaders sought to appeal more broadly to growing public concerns about the warlike conditions that followed CIC and state police interventions.

As the September primaries approached, attention focused especially on William Sweet's bid for the Democratic nomination for governor. William Sweet was in some ways an unlikely choice on which to pin labor Progressive hopes. Born to wealth and devoting his working life to finance, Sweet was also a Social Gospel follower, advocate of prohibition, and supporter of Protestant Progressivism. He directed the Denver YMCA for many years before his gubernatorial campaign. He backed the Christian Citizenship Union crusades against the Democratic machine but did not play a leadership role in that religious organization.

After the tramway crisis in August 1920, Sweet had organized a rally on behalf of striking workers that thousands attended. With that rally, Sweet hoped to spark a challenge to "anti-labor movement which is being furthered by the *Denver Post*, the *Rocky Mountain News* and the *Denver Times.*" In what seemed to many observers at the time as a preelection campaign rally, Sweet defended tramway unionists as "intelligent and fine-looking" men deserving continued support from Denver citizens.[86] In the 1922 primary campaign, the Democratic Sweet pledged to amend the Industrial Relations Law to repeal its compulsory features and abolish the state Rangers. These promises were key for securing union support.

When Sweet won easy nomination in the September 12 primary, workers were delighted and mainstream Denver newspaper editors appalled. *News* editor Shaffer alleged that Sweet, the "parlor Socialist," had gathered "malcontents and dangerous elements . . . bent on trouble." Yet Sweet had also argued against the CIC and Rangers on the grounds of fiscal conservatism, committing himself foremost to cost-cutting bureaucratic consolidations and tax reduction. He advocated key reforms of labor Progressives while appealing to Protestant reformers as well. The Republican candidate emerging from the primaries, former mine worker and later attorney general Ben Griffith, insisted that the state police was necessary to preserve law and order during strikes.[87] Griffith had actively supported the Colorado Progressive Party under Costigan. Yet as the Progressive Party disbanded in 1916, Griffith drifted back to the Republican fold.

The Sweet-Griffith contest highlighted enduring differences over the legacy of administrative Progressivism. Organized labor formulated an effective appeal to voters that insisted that the coercive commission posed a significant danger to public peace. They noted that the commission had been unable to settle peacefully or fairly national disputes in coal, meatpacking, and the railroads. CIC interventions in fact worsened rather than improved relations between workers and employers. Griffith urged voter support for the continuation of the CIC, backed by the coercive power of the state militia. If labor disputes could not be averted, the Republican suggested, then the state must retain the authority to force a settlement.

The campaign for governor largely turned on perceived links between labor conflict and public danger. Rather than simply deciding on Republican or Democratic candidates, voters would choose "peace or war," according to *News* editor Shaffer. For his part, Sweet insisted that the state Rangers posed the danger. They were provocative, expensive, and dangerously un-American, inspired by a "war psychology" that no longer held. He also pledged to change the Industrial Relations Law to repeal its compulsory features and to ensure that organized labor and business could each nominate a representative to the commission. Former Governor Carlson countered that warlike conditions would return to Colorado if Sweet were elected. His proposals, Carlson alleged, would "emasculate the Industrial Commission by permitting its domination by capital and labor, the special warring interests," thereby eroding the power of the public over the commission. For Republicans, Griffith stood for "mediation and peace" rather than class legislation and industrial war.[88]

On November 7, 1922, a narrow majority of voters chose Sweet. Although some workers expressed concern in the final days of the campaign that Sweet was little more than a rich dreamer, most working-class districts in Denver, Pueblo, Huerfano, and Las Animas counties supported the Democrat.[89] In the midst of a nationwide agricultural recession, many rural counties also gave Sweet a plurality. The Democrat drew additional support from a number of clubwomen encouraged by his calls for stiffer enforcement of women's protective labor legislation. Yet Colorado voters ensured that Sweet would face Republican majorities in both the state House and Senate.[90] The promised abolition of the CIC would require an unlikely defection of Republican legislators.

Still, the governor's race proved in significant part to be a repudiation of the Rangers and the aggressive tactics of the CIC. Sweet had successfully tainted these institutions in the voters' minds with unnecessary expense and potential danger to public peace. And the governor-elect had outdone his Republican rival in calls for sweeping tax-code revisions. His focus on easing the tax burden while reducing government expenses highlights the importance of fiscal policy for Progressive politics in the 1920s.[91] During the Sweet campaign, union and farmer leaders alike had complained of the expansion of state payroll under the Republican Shoup, with employees occupying "palatial suites in the new and entirely unnecessary adjunct to the Capitol

Building," wrote a farmer-labor critic. Rather than cutting government and reducing expenses, friends of the "millionaire governor" Shoup had increased taxes for farmers and homeowners "to an alarming degree."[92]

As governor, the Progressive Sweet chiefly cut government costs and consolidated bureaucracy. The labor press offered its support of Sweet's effort, arguing even that a mushrooming state bureaucracy in preceding decades had been the result of Republican patronage politics and "wanton extravagance." Sweet proposed a sweeping reorganization of seventy-two state bureaus and the creation of new ones, modeled after federal cabinet departments, which would have placed the CIC and the state labor bureau under the same director. Most Colorado unionists endorsed Sweet's plan since it also included a repeal of the anti-strike features of the Industrial Relations Act and a provision that the payment of a living wage be the first consideration in CIC awards.[93] Even though Sweet's plan did little to secure union influence over the state's labor bureaucracy, labor Progressives remained cautiously optimistic.

Sweet's reorganization plan met with resistance, however, in the Republican-controlled legislature in the spring of 1923. Most opposed the plan on patronage grounds, and others were unwilling to consider so significant and potentially destabilizing a reshuffle of state administration. Senate Republicans countered with their own more modest reorganization bill, which also stalled. In the end, state lawmakers refused to abolish and consolidate so many bureaus at once, killing Sweet's plan. Administration reform bills would reappear throughout the decade, but party patronage concerns would continually undermine them. Progressive reforms left the two-party system intact and its devotion to patronage unchallenged. Even the CIC survived the 1923 session, despite Sweet's efforts to repeal its coercive powers. Legislators also opposed Sweet's bill to abolish the state Rangers. With his Ranger repeal bill stalled in committee, Sweet issued executive orders to disband the hated force in late January.[94]

Thus Sweet was able to fulfill one of his two main promises to organized labor. The Rangers would not menace striking workers in Colorado. The CIC endured, although chastened by the *Wolff Packing* decision of the Supreme Court. The Democratic governor did appoint to the commission Protestant Progressive Thomas Annear, who helped shift the tenor of its interventions. After 1923, the interventions of the CIC eased as a detente emerged between commissioners and workers. Unorganized workers along with certain unions such as typographical, bakery, and building-trade workers made some successful uses of the CIC. Union workers continued to resent and resist the commission. Nationwide labor disputes subsided as well, leaving the commission to less thorny conflicts within the state. Labor Progressives in 1922 had at least cast the Industrial Commission and state militia in terms hostile to public peace.

Informed by the scientific faith of administrative Progressives, the state mediation of labor disputes had faced its most significant tests in the years immediately following World War I. To its supporters, compulsory investigation and arbitration promised to equalize the bargaining positions of capital and labor. The arbitration movement gained strength from wartime expansions of federal government authority over national industries deemed "essential" to the public — particularly mining and railroads.[95] The federal government's retreat from its wartime mediations created new spaces for state-level experimentation. In Colorado and Kansas, administrative Progressives promoted coercive experiments.

Yet these agencies focused predominantly on the needs of consumers rather than the economic or political vision of workers. These administrative Progressive reforms failed to balance group interests or enhance civic participation. Thus workers contested the compulsory features of these state mediation projects, offering their own vision of the laboring public and its interests. Labor Progressives argued for at least equal if not paramount consideration of the right to earn a living without harassment and freedom from state limits on personal liberty to strike. Union workers defied their industrial boards, appealed court decisions, and ultimately turned to electoral campaigns.

Five

Ben Lindsey and Women Progressives

On his national lecture tours, Judge Ben Lindsey often celebrated the political work of Colorado clubwomen. His collaboration with activist women was more interesting to eastern audiences because of early twentieth-century debates about women's suffrage.[1] Since 1893, Colorado women had voted on an equal footing with men. Women in Illinois and eastern states, by contrast, waited another twenty years for the vote in most elections. National women's suffrage campaigners in these years reported regularly on the Colorado experiment. Progressives were keen to highlight the achievements Colorado women secured with the vote.

During the 1912 congressional debate over whether to extend equal suffrage to the territory of Alaska, for example, Colorado congressman Edward Taylor credited the "influence and energy" of the state women's club federation for much Progressive legislation. The vote had empowered women to secure passage of a host of educational, juvenile court, protective labor, public health, temperance, and social welfare reforms. "It is the feminine interest in motherhood, in the child, and in the home," the congressman insisted, "that has compelled the passage of these laws." Enfranchising mothers meant "the protection of the home and the family relations, of childhood and woman-hood," and the "safeguarding of public health and morals."[2] As Taylor suggested, women's support for Progressive social reform was often linked with motherhood in Colorado.

In her 1914 address to the Colorado Federation of Women's Clubs (CFWC), president Lerah McHugh affirmed that clubwomen represented "the concentrated motherhood of America."[3] The Federated Women's Club Legislative Committee had from its earliest days devoted its primary attention to a maternalist agenda: education reforms, protecting child crime victims and reforming wayward youth in juvenile courts; women's and child-labor laws; mothers' pensions; and maternal and child health care initiatives.[4] Municipal housekeeping goals played a significant role in the agenda of Colorado women, as they reflected an expansion of motherhood beyond the domestic sphere outward to the city and state as a whole. Women's Progressivism in Colorado drew heavily on such broad goals, which acquired a radical edge in alliances with labor reformers.

Nonpartisanship remained a central demand of women's Progressivism. Club leaders like Sarah Platt Decker guided voting women along nonpartisan paths by endorsing civil service, creating independent associations, and attacking party machines. Denver's Civic Federation of 1895, the Women's Nonpartisan Association of 1908, and the Public Service League of 1910 all arose under women's leadership to offer voters alternatives to party mobilization. Decker and other leaders allied themselves frequently with male Protestant moralists who attacked Mayor Speer's Democratic machine for its ties to corporate utilities and saloon owners. Denver woman's club member and journalist Ellis Meredith also insisted that clubwomen should engage politically to ensure "that the city is made decent for childish feet."[5] Early club leaders invoked maternalist rhetoric not just to create distance from party leaders but ultimately to call for a restructuring of the political system.

In hopes of securing nonpartisan mobilizations of female voters, women Progressives cooperated closely with one of the state's most flamboyant male reformers, juvenile court judge Ben Lindsey. The alliance that Colorado clubwomen formed with Lindsey confirms the importance of cross-gender coalitions in the state. Activist women needed access to positions of political authority that men like Lindsey held, and he in turn relied heavily on the grassroots network that clubwomen mobilized.[6] Their alliance on behalf of child protection and maternal legislation revealed the potential of women's Progressivism.

BEN LINDSEY, MOTHERS' ALLY

With his muckraking manifesto of 1909, Lindsey cast himself as a defender of domestic life against "the Beast." The judge offered the most compelling example of the possibilities for circumventing party machinery in seeking both office and influence. He credited Denver's mothers, female workers, and the Christian Citizenship Union with his success in a 1908 campaign for reelection as an independent when both parties snubbed him. Lindsey successfully appealed, as he put it, to "women—not so much their suffrage leaders or their [party] politicians—as the mothers in the homes and the working women in the factories and shops." The judge rallied the majority of the city's female and union voters who "saved the juvenile court" on several occasions and circumvented party machines. With his tale of defiance in the face of elite and machine opposition, Lindsey attempted to set himself up as a model for independent political action by others concerned about protecting the home and family. In other speeches and writings, and occasionally with the endorsement of papers like the *Denver Post*, Lindsey joined the outrage of moral reformers to the specific concerns of women's crusades against political corruption. By 1912, his national reputation for juvenile court reform made him a figure few women's club leaders could afford to ignore.[7]

Lindsey did share with many Colorado clubwomen a belief in the developmental model of childhood and a commitment to protecting and nurturing children at various stages. This model particularly reflected the work of psychologist G. Stanley Hall and the Child Study Movement advanced by the Mothers' Congress around the turn of the century. Hall argued that children passed through developmental stages that retraced human evolution. At each stage children required specific environmental support and certain kinds of maternal guidance in order to fulfill developmental goals.[8] In terms of broad social and economic reforms, this project meant curbing child wage labor, compelling school attendance, transforming the school experience, structuring play, and redefining delinquency. Lindsey embraced many of Hall's views and applied them in his effort to distinguish juvenile delinquency from adult criminal behavior.

Lindsey came at times to embody the court and its mission for redeeming wayward children caught by social and economic forces that led them astray. The "kids' judge," as he liked to be called, proposed an alternative view of delinquency that stressed environmental conditioning rather than inherent moral failings, and he sharply differentiated the operation of his court from that of criminal courts in the state. Lindsey also saw his court as the leading force in a crusade to curb the corrupt influences in society that fostered delinquency. As George Creel tellingly argued, Lindsey made his fight appear "real and vivid by linking Special Privilege with Vice and Crime and connecting political corruption with the sufferings of little children." Lindsey thus advocated temperance, bans on child labor, compulsory school laws, mother's pensions, and extensions of juvenile court authority into many aspects of family relations.[9] Lindsey, along with most activist women, forcefully linked challenges to party machines with calls for state protection of children.

In his early years as judge, Lindsey's juvenile court became a platform remaking masculinity. Lindsey stressed the promise of his court for building male character in boys endangered by the seductions of urban life on the one hand and the problems of industrialization on the other. He emphasized a rugged physicality and authenticity, intra-male loyalties, and the potential for benevolent state intervention to shape delinquent working-class and middle-class boys into men. The home was "infinitely more responsible for juvenile crime than the school," Lindsey observed in 1908.[10] The judge laid special blame upon fathers who neglected their children, allowing boys to frequent gambling halls or daughters the back rooms in saloons. His court worked to rehabilitate male juvenile offenders by building their masculine character.

Lindsey also cast his project in less traditionally paternalistic terms. He nurtured "confidence and affection," converting the "Court of Probation" into a "Court of Approbation." He no longer put juvenile offenders in prison to be "punished, but on probation to be saved." Criminal courts based on the "doctrine of fear" contrasted with a juvenile court based on "principle of love." Many observers even characterized Lindsey's court as maternal. Lindsey himself later compared his court to "the ministrations of a good mother," arguing that it functioned "with kindness and yet firmness; to help and not to hurt; to uplift and not degrade." As one parent wrote to Lindsey, "Your words have been those of a father. Your conduct has been as tender as that of a mother."[11] Combining paternal and maternal roles, Lindsey hoped his court could assume a new mission as surrogate parent.

Work with female "delinquents" also provided Lindsey with an opportunity to fashion a masculinity grounded in reform. His extension of court authority to handle cases of adolescent female sexual activity marked a dramatic intervention by a male government official within an intimate realm of the domestic sphere. In his early years as a muckraker, Lindsey explored and exposed dangers to girls posed by saloons. Despite a law prohibiting the serving of alcohol to women, saloons kept back rooms where "young girls could be drugged and ruined and the 'white slave' traffic promoted."[12] Police protection for these saloons could be secured with political contributions to the Democratic party machine.

Lindsey and his assistants worked to address both the problems of individual women and the conditions that threatened their livelihood. Women's club leaders praised the judge for appointing matrons to look after cases that involved sexually active adolescents. In 1903, Lindsey first appointed a female assistant judge (who also served as clerk of the court), Mrs. Ida Gregory. She was "a mother and a good woman," insisted the judge. Lindsey and Gregory together heard all these cases. By 1910, Josephine Roche became a regular fixture of the juvenile court. She too assisted with cases involving female adolescents and began investigating the dangers that urban Denver posed to them. Roche and Lindsey campaigned against open prostitution but also for improved wages and working conditions for women.[13] Her 1912 appointment as inspector of amusements under Mayor Arnold allowed Roche new public authority to uphold regulations of saloons and dance halls on behalf of women and children.

Lindsey also worked to support working-class motherhood. In terms of court interventions, Lindsey focused attention on the economic challenges faced by some young mothers. When a department store detective caught a young pregnant woman shoplifting in order to provide items for her baby, Lindsey insisted that she should not be tried in criminal court. The right of the unborn child was at stake, he argued. "Was it not more important to save these young mothers for their children under the probationary orders of the [juvenile] court and redeem them to good citizenship, than it was by imprisonment to visit the mere vengeance of the state upon them whereby the state would be committing the injustice of legally stealing them from their children?"[14] Lindsey insisted that the juvenile court could implement a nurturing vision of state authority.

The judge also lobbied for political changes to assist mothers. He coauthored the successful 1912 initiative to create a system of mothers' pensions. Lindsey went on to argue that working women especially deserved state support immediately prior to and following childbirth. In a 1916 campaign speech, Lindsey reported that hundreds of young women worked "until a few days before the baby came. . . . And afterwards, when they were weak and suffering . . . they have to return to work. So sometimes the baby is adopted out or is deserted" when the young mother actually "yearns for it and wants to give a mother's love and care." Prospective mothers deserved "the rest which a horse is given and the state, playing the role of kind master, would enable her to secure it."[15] Newspapers quipped that Lindsey wanted horses' rights for women.

In these efforts, Lindsey enjoyed the broad support of clubwomen and Mothers' Congress members in Denver. When critics opposed Lindsey's court for teaching "children to defy any authority but its own," Denver's clubwomen responded with an affirmation of the judge and his gendered project in state building. In 1916, they formed the Women's Non-Partisan Juvenile Court Association to rally voters to back Lindsey for reelection. Urging readers to set aside "personal or political prejudice," the association highlighted the judge's "wonderful record of service" not just on the bench but in support of a host of clubwomen's reforms. On the eve of World War I, Lindsey emerged as the most visible advocate of the women's club agenda, and club leaders forged another nonpartisan committee in association with the Denver

Christian Citizenship Union to work for his election.[16] Linking his reelection campaign to that of President Wilson further enhanced his prospects in the Democratic landslide of 1916.

The following spring, women's club leaders again mobilized on behalf of Lindsey and his juvenile court. A recent state Supreme Court decision had ended juvenile court jurisdiction over adult cases involving minors. The "women of Denver," argued the *Denver Post*, lobbied the legislature in support of a bill, introduced by Republican and clubwoman Agnes Riddle, to restore "Lindsey's right" to handle cases of rape when minors were the alleged victims. When the Senate judiciary committee held hearings on the bill, chair Barney Napier turned over the meeting to Mothers' Congress leader Dr. Maude Saunders. Women's club leaders joined Ben Lindsey in endorsing the bill. Denver city attorney Foster Cline also voiced his support, arguing that young women were intimidated in criminal court and rarely testified about the "delicate details" involved in rape cases.[17]

Yet Lindsey's advocacy had become a liability among some conservative legislators who resented the judge's muckraking exposés and strident, antiparty moralizing. A *Denver Post* reporter commented in 1917 that legislators had confessed that "they do not like Judge Lindsey and are against anything he is for." Thus Lindsey's bills to extend juvenile court jurisdiction and to fund maternity benefits for working women, which clubwomen endorsed, were in for "hard sledding." Ignoring the merits of the bills, legislators in the Senate rejected them.[18] Still, women's club leaders in 1917 remained committed to Lindsey's work and his advocacy of their measures. Club leaders blamed partisan legislators and Governor Gunter for the defeat of their agenda. Women's club leaders were also unable to revive the pre-Ludlow alliances with Colorado unionists that had secured much political success in 1912.

CLUBWOMEN MOBILIZE FOR WAR

World War I generated new possibilities for women reformers. Although clubwomen had stalled in their reform projects between 1913 and 1917, the Great War enabled them to achieve new successes as they sought to operate outside the partisan fray. The Governor's Women's Council of Defense (WCOD) lent new legitimacy to private women's club networks in their claims to represent organized women in the state. Their wartime baby-saving campaigns, in particular, laid new groundwork for state interventions under the Sheppard-Towner program in the 1920s.

From his initial efforts to mobilize the state for war, Governor Gunter helped guide women's activism along sex rather than party lines. When he created a separate Women's Council of Defense in May 1917, the governor largely followed the precedent set forth by the national Women's Council of

Defense, led by Anna Howard Shaw. Yet a separate women's council made less political sense in Colorado where women had long operated as voters within the political parties. Nonetheless, their division along gender lines during the war served to revive hopes that clubwomen might mobilize politically as women rather than alongside men. And the women's clubs, with their bipartisan membership, were uniquely poised to lead this effort.

When Governor Gunter named his Women's Council of Defense, he appointed a significant number of women's club leaders, given their experience in organizing women for political action. More than half of his WCOD were clubwomen, along with a significant number of wives of Denver's corporate elites. Clubwoman and Democratic state senator Helen Robinson directed the women's Liberty Loan Committee while other clubwomen led local war-bond drives. Along with Robinson, a few party activists served on war committees, but they relied more on their club than party affiliations to rally the state's women. By war's end, more than 30,000 women in Denver alone had joined the WCOD, which one paper celebrated as a "nonpartisan patriotic organization" of women.[19]

Demonstrations and professions of patriotism were utmost on the minds of the executive members of Colorado's WCOD, and they defined loyalty in terms of their own agenda for war mobilization. The women's war council organized rallies in women's club buildings in support of food conservation and called members out to march in Liberty Loan parades. With their service on the WCOD, some affluent clubwomen improved public perceptions of the corporate elite. For instance, the press singled out the wife of CFI president Jesse Welborn with high praise for her "tireless" efforts on behalf of food conservation. Although her husband's reputation rested especially on his stubborn refusal to negotiate with striking coal miners and manipulation of the state's military and political institutions, his wife's war service created a new image of sacrifice for the common good during the war emergency. Dissent from the WCOD program brought swift rebuke from clubwomen. One club president was expelled from Denver's East Side Woman's Club for her refusal to support its Liberty Loan drive. Her "pro-German and revolutionary" offenses, according to a *Post* reporter, consisted chiefly of her pacifism and contention that the war burden, if there had to be one, "should be paid for by direct tax on excess war profits" as in England. She regretted that her "beloved" club "should have any part in piling billions . . . in debts on our children." Her statements led club members to report her to the Denver district attorney for disloyalty.[20] Clubwomen largely backed the program of the WCOD in its strident displays of patriotism. Setting the standards for feminine patriotic service, the directors of the WCOD claimed to represent the state's women in wartime. As with so many other wartime institutions, the WCOD narrowed the meaning of patriotism and stifled dissent.

Directives from the national WCOD broadly informed the work of the Colorado council. Anna Shaw charged state councils with rallying women to service. They were to promote food conservation, child welfare, and decent working conditions for women. Shaw felt certain women would safeguard "the moral and spiritual forces of the Nation."[21] In Colorado, the WCOD created committees to attend to these directives. When it came to program specifics, the WCOD allowed clubwomen to focus state resources on a number of their stalled Progressive Era campaigns on behalf of working women.

One such committee was devoted to protecting women in industry. Chaired by Denver Woman's Club member Jessie Munroe, the committee proclaimed an ambitious wartime platform: working women should receive equal pay with men for equal work; this should amount to a living wage; they should enjoy the eight-hour day and "sanitary conditions," but also agree to "no loafing" on the job. The committee renewed long-standing club demands that the legislature strengthen the women's eight-hour and minimum-wage laws.[22] Bureau of Labor Statistics chief William Morrissey also pledged to support the WCOD platform.

Yet wartime Colorado witnessed far fewer women joining the industrial workforce than other states, even though WCOD members, along with Morrissey, initially expressed fears that a wave of women might "unnecessarily" replace male breadwinners in the industrial workforce. The head of the women's division of the US Employment Service in Colorado estimated that 5,000 women did take up farm work to replace men, but less than 1,000 took up "men's" industrial work. These women were concentrated in machine tool, railroad, and chemical work. The US Employment Service predicted that women workers would "gladly return" to their homes when soldiers completed their war service. Given the relatively small number of women who moved into industrial positions, it is perhaps not surprising that Colorado experienced few of the gender confrontations among workers visible in cities such as Cleveland, Detroit, and Kansas City.[23] Nonetheless, the WCOD Committee on Women in Industry continued to focus state attention on the needs of unorganized women workers.

Those council members devoted to child health found the war created more promising opportunities to harness state resources. National campaigns to promote infant health conducted by the US Children's Bureau reached a peak during the war. Children's Bureau director Julia Lathrop was chair of the national WCOD committee on child welfare. The bureau designated 1918 as Children's Year and promoted a grassroots campaign to improve infant and child health. Approximately 11 million women participated in these campaigns at the local level.[24]

Members of the Colorado council effectively framed these programs in the language of patriotism and conservation. The chair of the state child welfare committee reported that it "took Uncle Sam twelve months to wake up to the fact that, while he had been trying to intensify and conserve his other crops, he had not been doing anything toward conserving his most important crop of all—his crop of babies." The federal government now asked "every grown up member of the community to stand in a parental relationship not only to his own children but to all children." The child welfare committee chair also echoed the maternalist call of Mothers' Congress president Hannah Schoff, who insisted in 1906 that "parents can never do their full duty for their own children . . . until they make it their business to see that all children have proper treatment and proper protection."[25] The state WCOD included both Mothers' Congress members and social workers who staffed state welfare agencies, like Gertrude Vaile. The WCOD defined women's patriotic service to the state in terms of support for child welfare reforms.

Under the auspices of the WCOD, several private philanthropic projects of clubwomen and the Mothers' Congress became state government programs. Most notable among these was the "baby-saving" campaign. Colorado clubwomen and PTA members had for several years held baby weeks in Denver and Pueblo to promote infant health. Between 1914 and 1917, the General Federation of Women's Clubs had urged members to utilize the resources published by the US Children's Bureau in order to sponsor clinics and demonstrations. These campaigns combined weighing and measuring tests with free medical exams for infants.[26] During the war, city governments approved public funding for the expansion of this private club work to rural counties across the state. Organizers discouraged private club fundraisers and instead sought increased state appropriations to carry on their work.

Soon after the war, the WCOD successfully lobbied the legislature to create a Child Welfare Bureau. The new Republican governor, Oliver Shoup, backed the proposal in his inaugural address, insisting that child welfare was "perhaps the most sacred subject with which our legislators have to deal."[27] The legislature approved the measure, along with another bill to provide state-funded medical exams for school-aged children. In July 1919, the Colorado Child Welfare Bureau officially began its work, continuing the baby-saving campaigns that clubwomen had initiated. This bureau coordinated the baby and maternity clinics already offered by a range of organizations across the state—the PTA, Red Cross, WCTU, and city governments. During the war, the Women's Council of Defense eclipsed Lindsey in importance as the key institutional site for clubwomen seeking maternal reforms. Here clubwomen briefly came closest to organizing their members along gender lines.

Successful in launching a new state bureaucracy devoted to child and maternal health, WCOD members hoped to rally public support for a broad postwar reconstruction program. As the war neared its end in the fall of 1918, clubwomen participants on the war council joined with unionists, social workers, juvenile court judges, and sympathetic academics and physicians to create the nonpartisan Committee on Social Legislation to promote Progressive measures. Labor unionists and state labor official Morrissey met with WCOD member Jessie Munroe to coordinate lobbying for labor bills before the next legislative session began. Led by social workers, the committee also advocated expansions of mothers' pensions and an overhaul of all state laws concerning children to enhance the powers of the juvenile courts. Members also endorsed the American Association for Labor Legislation proposal for state-funded health insurance.[28] The social welfare committee briefly revived the pre-Ludlow coalition of clubwomen and trade unionists, advocating state interventions in the private worlds of work and family. By October, the committee turned its attention to the fall election campaign, since its outcome would shape the political climate for their reconstruction program.

POSTWAR RECONSTRUCTION AND PROGRESSIVE REFORM

In the postwar era, club leaders again joined with Lindsey to advocate their shared political goals. Before the 1919 legislature, club leaders urged passage of "Lindsey bills," as they were popularly known, to extend juvenile court authority, ban child labor, and extend maternity benefits to working-class and rural women.[29] Yet even wartime concerns about poor health among army recruits did not outweigh the hostility that several key legislators bore Judge Lindsey. Again, senators killed the bills. Conservative legislators increasingly conflated the women's Progressive agenda with the person of Judge Lindsey.

In May 1919, the Women's Council of Defense at last disbanded. Governor Oliver Shoup had promised to appoint a committee to take over a key project of the women's war council: the review and rationalization of laws affecting children. A year later, Shoup selected seven juvenile and county court judges and invited them to draft bills dealing with delinquency, neglect, custody, and the age of consent. Although a number of women on the war council made clear their enthusiasm for the project, along with significant expertise, Shoup chose only male judges for this committee. Ben Lindsey would chair the committee. Yet before conferring with the other judges, Lindsey first met with women's club leaders in order to coordinate efforts. In September 1920, the CFWC leader Jessie Munroe joined Mothers' Congress organizers, state representative May Bigelow, and US Children's Bureau officials to discuss their mutual legislative agenda. Clubwomen advocated a renewed campaign for the maternity bill, the child labor ban, the extension of juvenile court authority, and a bill to mandate county-level funding for mothers' pensions.[30]

Yet Lindsey's campaign for reelection that year led to a revealing dispute about what constituted "political" action on behalf of women Progressives. In October, a new executive committee of the Colorado Mothers' Congress informed Lindsey of its recent decision that candidates for public office would no longer be welcome to speak at their meetings. Lindsey ignored the rule and arranged for several speaking engagements with Denver school principals, bypassing the leadership of the Mothers' Congress. When the Mothers' Congress president publicly condemned Lindsey for violating organizational rules, Lindsey attacked the executive committee: "I thank God it is not the rank and file of the Mothers' Congress or Parent-Teacher association" but rather leaders motivated by "small, sordid, jealous, political and . . . unwomanly" reasons who opposed the appearances. Running that year on a party ticket, Lindsey had threatened the nonpartisan commitment of the Mothers' Congress leadership. Lindsey insisted his speeches were "not for political purposes," nor was "the position of the Juvenile court judge" a political one. Partisan politics, Lindsey perpetually insisted, were not of significant concern to him. His interest was merely "in the childhood of this city that is being so fearfully neglected."[31] Nonpartisan campaigning, especially for a candidate who consistently outpolled the rest of the Democratic slate, was clearly becoming more difficult in the postwar period. Yet women's club leaders remained committed to the promise of a nonpartisan Progressive mobilization.

When the 1921 legislature convened in January, Lindsey and other members of the governor's child welfare committee presented their recommendations: twelve bills that called for familiar reforms such as extensions of juvenile court authority, maternity benefits, and revisions to statutes defining delinquency and neglect. The state women's club federation prepared a bill to ban child labor, which Lindsey's committee supported. Four women served in the state legislature that session, most of them women's club members. In March, CFWC legislative committee head Jessie Munroe and school superintendent and clubwoman Mary Bradford testified on behalf of the Lindsey bills.[32] Yet again, legislators rejected the entire program. Although nominally a Democrat, Lindsey operated more and more on the margins of the party and could count on little support from rural legislators and those with ties to mining corporations.

Club leaders were devastated. For the last several sessions, the legislature had shown "very little attention" to the women's club agenda, complained Mary Bradford, writing in the newly created CFWC magazine. "In the earlier years of full citizenship for women it was comparatively easy for Colorado women to obtain the legislative improvements that they desired." Colorado had presented "a model for the world in the legal safeguards that it extended to women and children. . . . Now, alas, some of our most humanely wise legislation has become inoperative, other of our laws of this character are threatened with repeal, and the new legislation demanded by the advance made in other states since 1901 seems at this writing doomed to defeat." Bradford's pessimistic assessment of clubwomen's influence did not directly mention the alliance with Ben Lindsey. But club leaders would increasingly seek independence from the controversial judge. How then, Bradford asked, might the state's women's clubs again "animat[e], inspir[e], and stimulat[e] to action the agencies of state government" responsible for protecting mothers and children?[33]

The answer lay in reviving nonpartisan, educational campaigns without such close ties to Lindsey. The 1919 and 1921 legislatures had been "too much of one party," complained a CFWC lobbyist.[34] Not explicitly naming the Republican majority for its postwar opposition to the women's agenda, club leaders nonetheless renewed a commitment to nonpartisanship. Although an alliance with the reform wing of the Democratic Party had proven especially fruitful between 1909 and 1913, women's club leaders in 1921 confronted a fragmented and bitterly divided Democratic Party still reeling from wartime conflicts over loyalty. CFWC pioneers like Mary Bradford hoped to revive the former dynamism of women's Progressivism with a return to the nonpartisan vision of early leaders like Decker.

TRAINING FOR FEMININE CITIZENSHIP

In April 1921, the Colorado Federation of Women's Clubs launched a new magazine, the *Colorado Club Woman*. Edited by the state federation president, the new publication offered a link between the Legislative Council and individual club members at a moment of declining political influence. "We are not taking our rightful places as citizens," Bradford wrote in the third issue. She urged readers to make "every club a training camp for citizenship." The Legislative Council would lead educational civics campaigns in the early 1920s to review the machinery of government, process of electing officials, and operation of the legislature. In this way, women's club leaders hoped to enhance the lobbying influence of what one termed "the maternal in politics."[35] At the same time, the women's Legislative Council forged new alliances without Ben Lindsey. During the 1923 legislative session, clubwomen at last achieved long-sought political success by expanding their coalition across class, religious, and ethnic lines.

After the bitter defeats of 1921, women's club leaders launched a new educational campaign to bring clubs into closer contact with the CFWC legislative lobby and to reinvigorate women's Progressive citizenship. The founding of the state League of Women Voters coincided with this new club campaign, and indeed, many club leaders belonged to the league as well. CFWC Legislative Council member Nettie Jacobsen sent out a questionnaire to clubs statewide and found that many were suspicious of political questions. Jacobsen emphasized that "legislation is not politics." Lobbying before the general assembly stood apart from partisan campaigning. The women's club lobbying could counter the "forces of evil" that were "always organized" at the State Capitol. Given a growing perception that clubwomen lacked adequate information about "the machinations of legislation" and the election process, leaders organized a series of civics workshops beginning in 1922.[36]

Among the first topics was the function of the Legislative Council itself. Director Jessie Munroe revived earlier descriptions of women's federation lobby as the "Third House" of the legislature. An earlier clubwoman had coined the phrase, in part to expand women's authority beyond the private "home" to the public statehouse. Munroe insisted that the women's lobby was "absolutely non-partisan" and limited in its activity to social welfare measures exclusively. The council, Munroe continued, "can only be the stroke oar . . . and if you would win, you must time your stroke to be in unison with the stroke oar," appealing to legislators in coordination with the state club federation. When addressing legislators, women "must be forceful, patient, tactful, persistent, and diplomatic," Munroe argued.[37] She hoped her review of the functions of the lobbying arm of the women's federation would renew club interest in its activities and focus member influence.

In appeals that would have pleased early activists such as Decker, the Legislative Council members also stressed the importance of the primary election for mobilizing women against the party machine. The direct primary had been a fundamental demand of early women's club leaders. The primary was the "*only place* where a careful selection" of candidates was possible, wrote Munroe. The "*true citizen*" rallies family and friends to vote then; the "*politician* looks only after the general election." Party machinery began with the primary caucus, and thus clubwomen had to mobilize earlier to secure the maternal reforms they desired.[38] The council organized additional meetings to review the initiative, referendum, patronage, and state charitable institutions. The women's federation lobby relied on a revived civics campaign to mobilize clubwomen for nonpartisan activism.

Largely absent from the agenda in these workshops were extended discussions of the National Women's Party and the feminist demand for equal rights in the 1920s. A small group of clubwomen did press for broader equality in these years. In 1923, for example, Colorado Springs clubwomen and feminist activist Lillian Kerr organized the western states' conference of the National Women's Party. Featuring Mrs. O.H.P. Belmont and Alice Paul, the conference drew a number of leading clubwomen to Colorado Springs, including the Denver mayor's wife, Adelia Bailey; Democratic legislator Alma Lafferty; and even labor leader May Peake, to hear the goals of what one female reporter termed "militant suffragism." The conference concluded with a suffrage pageant at the Garden of the Gods.[39] Yet despite the stirring rhetoric, the state's women's club leaders and working-class women campaigned against the Equal Rights Amendment (ERA) in 1924. They remained focused on juvenile court reform, maternal and infant health initiatives, child labor, and education reforms more than campaigns for sex equality.[40]

Women Progressives did extend their campaign across class lines in these years. A number of female labor leaders also belonged to the women's clubs and sought to extend the educational project to working women. The *Colorado Labor Advocate* in 1924 began publishing excerpts from the club-women's workshop meetings in a series of articles on women in "practical politics." The Women's Page of the *Labor Advocate* joined clubwomen in opposing the ERA in early 1924, since the measure would abolish "all the laws that we now have for the protection of women and children." In February 1924, laboring women organized the Women's Union Labor Political League, which drew its membership chiefly from the garment workers' union and wives prominent in male union auxiliaries. "Well informed, intelligent mothers mean intelligent children," argued the league secretary. "Our children, properly trained at home . . . may become the great labor leaders of the future," she continued.[41] The working-class women's league devoted much more attention to class-conscious consumerism than did middle-class women's clubs. The effectiveness of union boycotts, for example, lay significantly with working-class mothers.[42] Little evidence exists on the scope and specific activities of this league in these years, but its emphasis on training for feminine citizenship bears a striking similarity to that of the middle-class-dominated clubs.

In addition to appealing to working-class women, club leaders enlisted the support of more religiously and ethnically diverse sisters in the press for Progressive reforms. After the 1921 legislature rejected recommendations of the governor's committee on child welfare, clubwomen lobbied Governor Shoup to appoint a new group. In June 1922, Shoup selected representatives from several women's organizations, including the CFWC, the Parent-Teacher Association (PTA), Council of Jewish Women, and Catholic Daughters of America to join a few juvenile judges. Lindsey was not among those chosen. Yet the religious diversity was striking, given the early stirrings of the Ku Klan Klan in these years. The 1922 Child Welfare Committee was chaired by Colorado Springs superintendent of education Inez Johnson Lewis. After reviewing the bills proposed by Lindsey's committee, the new group endorsed eight of the previous fourteen and prepared for the 1923 legislative session. These measures were focused on extending jurisdiction of the juvenile courts and establishing the maternity fund for working-class mothers.

The civics campaign and broad alliances enabled club leaders to secure long-sought legislative victories that year. The election of Governor William Sweet in 1922 gave women activists, along with unionists, a sympathetic executive. He had secured a primary victory despite the open opposition of the

Democratic party machine, and he campaigned as a Christian Progressive.[43] Clubwomen contributed to his win in defiance of long-time party leaders. If clubwomen could ensure passage of their agenda through the legislature, Sweet promised his support. Clubwoman and teacher Louise Patterson joined the legislature that session but sat as a minority Democrat from Pueblo. Women from Denver and Teller County served as Republicans.

The Legislative Council of the women's club federation fully backed the recommendations of the 1922 Child Welfare Committee and also drafted its own child labor and education measures. The new council director, Annah Pettee, implored club members to join the campaign on behalf of the women's agenda. "If we, as club women, as mothers and grandmothers, do not take a decided stand for the best in protective and corrective legislation concerning the children of our beloved state, may I ask, who will?" Although not mentioning Lindsey by name, Pettee celebrated the "splendid resume of the juvenile court" with its "private hearings for children's cases"; probation programs; treatment of child offenders as "state wards to be protected" rather than criminals. Educator Mary Bradford and PTA president Maude Saunders stumped for the child-labor and school-reform bills along with union leader and clubwoman May Peake.[44]

When the legislature adjourned, club leaders rejoiced that four child-welfare bills had passed. With Lindsey maintaining a lower profile than usual and the governor's Child Welfare Committee mobilizing a coalition of club and working-class women, those bills extending the scope of juvenile court operations and providing maternity benefits became law. Yet the child-labor and education-reform measures failed. Although protesting that the rights of children should have been "protected against the greed of industry," Pettee expressed thanks to some forty clubs statewide that had "complied with all requests for letters to senators and representatives."[45] One editor commented that the maternity bill, initially proposed by Lindsey in 1916, was the first law to provide for state support of unborn children. The state benefit would give each child "a decent chance to be born, lest it be imperiled by . . . the death of its mother through poverty, sinfulness, or ignorance."[46]

In 1923, women Progressives had successfully mobilized a coalition to secure legislation. This would be the last time that Lindsey's juvenile court would anchor their political project. Their reforms, however, did not generate significant economic or civic benefits for working-class and rural mothers. County compliance with the state mothers' pension program remained voluntary with benefits woefully underfunded. The newly created maternity benefit program suffered from the same problems. Fiscally conservative legislators had conceded relatively little, and appropriations for maternal programs remained woefully inadequate throughout the decade. Despite the passage of new juvenile court and maternity benefit laws, CFWC legislative chair Annah

Pettee rued that in 1923 "partisan politics" had again undermined "constructive legislation, particularly in the interest of industrial justice."[47] Efforts to enhance protective labor laws for women and ban child labor had again failed in the legislature. These failures contributed to lively debate in Denver about the needs of the working mother throughout the remainder of 1923.

THE CHALLENGES OF WORKING-CLASS MOTHERHOOD

Following legislative approval of the new maternity benefits, the Denver City Council struggled to implement them. During these same months, several women working at the Zott laundry in Denver launched a campaign to require enforcement of the women's eight-hour law. Additionally, Ben Lindsey defied a Denver grand jury probe into abortion by refusing to disclose his contacts with working women who sought his council about unwanted pregnancy. These events suggest the outlines of a broader debate about just how state and city government should protect and empower working mothers. Although clubwomen joined in this contest, they increasingly stood apart from Lindsey and working-class women in their vision of reform. Hopes for a Progressive-style mobilization of women unified by a common feminine vision began to fade.

The Zott laundry case began when May Corse refused to work fourteen-hour days while receiving pay for only eight and one-half hours. Reporting her case to the state district attorney, the Bureau of Labor Statistics, and the Industrial Commission, Corse initially received little help. But then the city labor federation took up her case and others like it in order to press state officials into enforcing the women's eight-hour law. *Labor Advocate* editor Frank Palmer quickly cast the issue in terms familiar to labor and women Progressives. One Zott employee, he reported, was a widow supporting four children who was forced to work overtime without pay, yet feared for her job if she reported the hours' violation. Many cases were "too pitiful to mention," Palmer wrote, "with invalid husbands and children being supported . . . by wages of from $10 to $15 a week. Without the support of a strong union, these women are helpless." Male unionists, Palmer insisted, had to force the state to punish "a man who will take advantage of girls and women who have to work in a laundry." L. K. Zott, the laundry owner, threatened to fine or fire any woman who complained of working conditions. He argued that his female employees could themselves be indicted by state officials for exceeding eight hours of work in one day, if they reported the violation.[48]

In late October, the laundry women got their day in district court under Judge Orahood. A number of former and current Zott employees testified about pressure to work overtime without compensation under threats that they keep silent. Zott's attorney alleged that his client never gave "official authorization" for his employees to work more than eight hours. The attorney did not explain how the work would get done if women did not stay late. Then city attorney Rice Means intervened on Zott's behalf. He suggested, astonishingly, that the women "might go down to the laundry and *break in* so that they could work nights." Editor Palmer mused that he could not tell whether Means "was intentionally dishonest or simply assinine [*sic*]. Or both." Judge Orahood dismissed the case against Zott, claiming that the manager was not liable for the conduct of his foremen.[49] At the next city labor federation meeting, delegates appointed a committee to demand that Denver mayor Ben Stapleton remove Means and Orahood from office.

After the Zott trial, laundry women and the city union assembly appealed to women's club leaders for assistance. As during the campaign to secure an eight-hour law for laundry women nearly twenty years earlier, union leaders in 1923 hoped to enlist middle-class consumers in the effort to boycott employers like Zott. "The fact is," Palmer insisted, "hundreds of Denver girls are being worked overtime, some of them in unspeakably filthy and unhealthy surroundings and for pitiably low wages." By December, the labor paper reported that the Zott laundry had suffered financially as former customers on the South side of town patronized laundries not known for breaking the women's eight-hour law. In January 1924, labor unionist and women's club member May Hill addressed the CFWC Legislative Council on the Zott laundry situation. Club members pledged their aid, in every way possible, to secure the enforcement of the eight-hour day for women.[50] The vulnerable position of working mothers especially elicited club responses.

Yet their support in 1924 sounded more muted than it had in 1908. Denver's labor unionists continued to press for tougher labor laws to protect working women in these years. The leadership of the CFWC, however, waged no larger campaign to revive enforcement of the eight-hour law. Just the year before, the US Supreme Court had declared women's minimum-wage laws unconstitutional in *Adkins v. Children's Hospital*. Women's unique capacity for motherhood no longer justified labor protection, argued the justices. Denver working-class women hoped that debate about women's labor protections would assume new urgency in light of the court ruling. Yet unionist May Hill expressed disappointment with her middle-class sisters after attending sessions of the General Federation of Women's Clubs convention in June. Although the conference highlighted successful legislation for the protection of childhood, natural resources, and public health, Hill conceded, delegates paid little attention to the problems of women in industry that year. Controversy over the ERA likely led many delegates to remain silent on the issue. The professed desire of club delegates to protect motherhood did not extend to labor legislation. This lack of attention at the national women's club meeting posed a challenge to "the home women of Labor," May Hill argued, "to organize themselves into a protecting, cooperating power on the field of industry."[51]

The national women's club president at the time, Mary Sherman of Estes Park, confirmed Hill's assessment of the national federation. Sherman's pet project from 1925 through 1928 was a new "Department of the Home." Grounding club identity in domesticity was nothing new, but federation president Sherman sought to focus attention on homemaking as a topic for club energies. "[W]omen's club work and home interests are not antagonistic," Sherman proclaimed. The "better homemaker a woman is, the better club woman she will be." The Colorado federation heeded Sherman's call and created a Department of the American Home in 1926. While essential to middle-class ideals for motherhood, homemaking focused club energies inward rather that out to the needs of wage-earning mothers. Sherman urged federated clubs to undertake a survey of homemaking facilities, such as kitchen and laundry equipment, in urban and rural contexts. She also launched a campaign to petition the US Census Bureau to identify "home-making" as a productive occupation on the census. Secretary of commerce Herbert Hoover received a flood of letters in support, and in 1930 the bureau changed its classification of millions of married women from "non-productive" to "housewife." While granting public recognition to homemakers, the campaign did little to address the problems of wage-working women and government protections for working-class mothers.[52]

If May Corse and other Zott employees sparked a debate about the need for workplace protections for laundry women, Ben Lindsey, characteristically, cast a spotlight on even more controversial issues related to motherhood: abortion and birth control. In October 1923, Lindsey appeared before the Denver City Council to request a $25,000 appropriation to implement the Maternity Benefit Law, passed the previous spring. The funds were necessary to protect motherhood, Lindsey insisted, and to reduce the rate of abortion among working women in the city. When pressed, the judge refused to disclose his knowledge of abortion practices in the city but insisted that birth control offered the best way to empower women who did not desire pregnancy. Should the city fail to implement the new law, Lindsey threatened to open a birth-control clinic under the auspices of his juvenile court. Lindsey additionally pledged to protect any woman seeking birth-control information from publicity. In support of his request, Lindsey disclosed an anonymous letter from a Denver woman who sought an abortion when her husband, upon learning of her pregnancy, threatened to desert her. The woman wrote: "Motherhood must be guaranteed safe for women, or women, whether married or single, will resort to illegal operations, as I was forced to do. It is a question whether the state of Colorado is a woman's friend, or the doctor who performs the operation."[53] In Lindsey's view, state protections for motherhood meant both financial support and legalized birth control.

The judge linked maternity benefits and birth control in ways that resonated with working-class women. "Birth control is a class issue," argued union women's editor May Hill. Within a few weeks of Lindsey's appeal to the Denver City Council for maternity benefits, Hill heralded the arrival of Margaret Sanger in Denver. While wealthy women have access to birth control, Hill argued, "it is a crime to give the same information to the women of the poor. . . . Labor has always backed Margaret Sanger in her work and her fight for the same freedom for the poor which the rich have." Sanger spoke in early November at the Grace Community Church Open Forum to a crowd that included many working-class listeners. Yet Sanger's and Lindsey's proposals increasingly alienated middle-class clubwomen. At their 1923 fall convention, CFWC delegates debated a birth-control resolution and a proposed bill to legalize its dispensation. By a vote of forty-eight to eleven, club delegates voted down the resolution.[54] Clubwomen rejected Lindsey's plan and grew increasingly concerned about his frank discussions of premarital sexuality.

By 1924 new differences about how best to protect and empower motherhood divided Ben Lindsey, working-class women, and middle-class clubwomen from one another. The prospects of advancing women's Progressivism appeared increasingly remote in light of these divisions. Lindsey soldiered on, publishing increasingly controversial books like *The Revolt of Modern Youth* (1925) and *The Companionate Marriage* (1927), which openly discussed adolescent sexuality, birth control, and a proposal to treat childless marriages differently from those that led to parenthood. In the case of the former, the marriage might be easily dissolved if the couple found themselves incompatible, while in the latter case, the state might insist on formal divorce proceedings.[55] Working-class women struggled to legalize birth control, secure labor law enforcement, and promote class-conscious consumerism. After 1923, middle-class clubwomen increasingly sought to define the women's reform in terms of public health initiatives for mothers and children. The Child Welfare Bureau, rather than the juvenile court, became their anchoring site with the state bureaucracy.

THE CHILD WELFARE BUREAU AND MATERNALIST REFORM

The Child Welfare Bureau (CWB) politicized motherhood in more prominent terms than any other agency during the 1920s. With federal matching grants, Colorado increasingly assumed some responsibility for mothers' private health concerns. In the state, as across much of the nation, clubwomen participated more actively in these public health projects than they did on behalf of any other maternal reform. Yet the Child Welfare Bureau did not advocate a

Progressive mobilization of women. Rather than asserting a critique against party or corporate dominance in politics around which to rally women's non-partisan activism, bureau officials relied on a scientific model of expertise and largely ignored political inequalities. This shift toward professionalism and away from political engagement gave maternalism a less radical tone as the decade wore on. Infant and maternal health projects were separated from the earlier and more encompassing vision of Progressive women's club leaders.

The maternal and infant health projects that animated Child Welfare Bureau workers and clubwomen in the 1920s initially reflected the efforts of the Women's Council of Defense to advance Progressive goals during World War I. The war enabled Women's council members to politicize motherhood in new ways. US Children's Bureau director Julia Lathrop wrote in 1919 that care of children was a "patriotic duty second only to that of caring for our soldiers on the front." Even the conservative editor of the *Rocky Mountain News*, John Shaffer, argued that same year that the "war has taught people a great deal about child welfare and the value of the child and the necessity . . . of encouraging high birth rates, which can only be done thru generous state action."[56] The Colorado Child Welfare Bureau was designed very much with the war experience in mind. Although the bureau would receive a significant boost from the federal Shepperd-Towner program after 1922, its initial operations relied more directly on support from women's clubs and a modest state appropriation.

By mid-decade the CWB became a hub for women Progressives. From the start, the bureau operated under the auspices of the state Department of Education. This department had long been the province of ambitious clubwomen like state school superintendents Democrat Mary Bradford and Republican Katherine Craig. Governor Shoup solicited potential appointees for the CWB Board of Control from the PTA. The bureau was staffed with PTA leaders and club members such as Maude Saunders, Florence Dick, and Estelle Mathews. Saunders also chaired the CFWC child welfare department, created to support CWB activities. The Child Bureau even paid the salary of the PTA organizer for the state.[57] During the 1920s, the bureau also cooperated closely with the Women's Christian Temperance Union and local women's clubs.

These close ties were forged through a number of events. Clubs supported the traveling infant and preschool child clinics offered by the CWB, recruiting members to volunteer and perform advance publicity work. The Progressive Mothers Club of Colorado Springs, for example, devoted all its energy to "child welfare work." This included staging "Better Baby Weeks," weighing and measuring infants in their community and raising funds to provide milk for children in poor families. Clubs in Pueblo purchased a Child Welfare cottage during the war and then hosted CWB clinics into the 1920s.

BEN LINDSEY AND WOMEN PROGRESSIVES

Throughout the decade, the CFWC regularly endorsed and lobbied the state legislature on behalf of the health initiatives of the Child Welfare Bureau.[58]

With the passage of the Shepperd-Towner Act in November 1921, the federal government reinforced the focus on maternal and infant health. Beginning that December, Colorado governor Shoup assigned the CWB the task of implementing the Shepperd-Towner program for the state. With federal funding, the CWB annual budget swelled from $4,000 to $15,000 between 1923 and 1928.[59] Given the decentralized administration of Shepperd-Towner, state variations in implementation deserve more careful consideration. With its close ties to the PTA and unusual cooperation between male and female health care providers, the Colorado CWB offers a valuable site for examining the impact of this women's Progressive reform.[60]

The outlook and agenda of the PTA particularly informed the early work of the Colorado bureau. Among the Child Welfare Bureau's objectives were the promotion of parent education and fostering closer relations between the home and school. This included programs to "direct . . . the leisure time activities" of children; expand domestic science classes; "target . . . gambling devices"; and promote "better motion pictures." The PTA's concern with Americanization also shaped the bureau's activities. CWB staff launched "Mothers' Clubs" within immigrant communities to teach "household arts . . . English, history, economics, and home hygiene."[61] Both the PTA and CWB stressed middle-class domesticity, Protestant morality, scientific childrearing, and preventative medicine. The PTA's gain, however, was in important ways a loss for the state women's club federation. The former organization gained influence within the Child Welfare Bureau even as the women's club lost a measure of authority over the scope and direction of bureau policy. Women's club leaders assumed mainly supportive roles.

Given its close associations with the PTA, the Child Welfare Bureau reflected the shifting focus of the PTA over the decade. In prewar years, the PTA had viewed parent education as a lever for changing society by organizing mothers across the nation. Hoping to remake childhood, especially adolescence, as a developmental period for individualization and experimentation, prewar PTA leaders sought to create different adults. Lindsey especially represented this vision with his emphasis on protecting adolescents and treating juvenile "criminals" as merely delinquent. In the postwar years, however, the PTA focused largely on recreational and entertainment activities. Broader hopes for social reform dropped out of the agenda. Its parent-education program in the 1920s targeted mainly the parents of young children. Child psychology similarly shifted from a focus on adolescence to stress the importance of preschool years for children's social and emotional growth. Historian Steven Schlossman has found that leading psychologists in the 1920s believed that "personality traits were fixed and irreversible by age five or even earlier."[62] Not surprisingly, the CWB increasingly devoted its attention to the needs of infants and preschool-aged children. The broader, prewar agenda of women's clubs and the earlier PTA did not play a significant role in shaping the bureau's policy over the course of the 1920s.

For Child Welfare Bureau workers, the needs of young children were primarily medical and nutritional. By 1923 the focus of the CWB was on traveling health "conferences" or clinics it ran for young children. Because of their important role in conducting these clinics, male doctors and female nurses gradually assumed greater roles within the bureau. County medical associations were quite supportive, recruiting doctors who volunteered their services for the traveling clinics. CWB representatives began attending the state conventions of the American Medical Association as well. By 1925, the CWB had two full-time doctors on its staff, a pediatrician and an obstetrician, along with seven nurses. In contrast to the national medical association, which became hostile to the federal Children's Bureau and its implementation of Shepperd-Towner, state doctors remained largely supportive, even writing letters and giving speeches to counter attacks from colleagues in other states.[63]

During its peak year of 1925 to 1926, the CWB examined more than 10,000 Colorado children and offered prenatal services to more than 230 expectant mothers statewide. In biennial reports to the governor and legislature, CWB officials catalogued an extensive list of childhood abnormalities and diseases that they encountered. Frequently, officials found that as many as 95 percent of the children examined had health problems that necessitated further interventions. They organized follow-up conferences to attend not only to acute cases but also to problems with "teeth, tonsils, health habits, diet," and hygiene.[64] Rural and mining communities received particular attention.

In documenting child health concerns, the CWB worked to legitimate its own continued operation as well as map out the scope and nature of possible interventions by this maternal bureaucracy. CWB officials insisted that mothering, especially in remote rural and immigrant communities, required careful guidance, often from male physicians. Scientific and especially medical intervention, rather than political or economic reforms, defined the outlook of the CWB. When Dr. Roy Forbes of Denver traveled in 1923 to the mining community of Mt. Harris, for example, he expected to find better than average child health conditions, given the service of two company physicians. But "of the 123 children examined few were found to be well nourished and the incidence of maternal nursing was entirely too small," Forbes observed. "The children showed evidence of candy habit and both the American and foreign mothers exhibited a pitiful ignorance of dietetic and hygienic essentials."[65] Forbes assumed mothers in this remote community bore the chief responsibility for child health but did not consider their limited control over the social and economic conditions with which their families contended in these

corporate-controlled company towns. Neither the wages paid by mine owners nor minimal services provided by company doctors entered into consideration. As male doctors like Forbes assumed control over CWB programs,
state's women's club leaders lost influence. Their broader prewar critiques of
party and corporate manipulations of politics did not figure in CWB projects.

Consider the campaign against child labor, which had long energized
women Progressives. By the early 1920s, employer opposition and US Supreme Court hostility gutted earlier laws that regulated or banned child wage
work. Among these laws was the national Keating-Owen Act, co-sponsored by
Colorado Progressive Ed Keating, who in 1916 was serving a term in Congress.
In 1923, the General Federation of Women's Clubs endorsed a federal child labor amendment and urged state federations and local clubs to lobby state legislatures on its behalf. That December, Colorado lobbyist Annah Pettee wrote
that the "abolishment of child labor, the blackest blot on the fairest state of this
Union, should be the first Shepherd [sic] Towner act. This is the stepping stone
towards the realization of the original intent and purpose of this measure."
Children's wage work in the sugar-beet fields in northeast Colorado particularly worried state clubwomen.[66]

The state's union leaders similarly sought to rally workers to this campaign. When the federal Child Labor Amendment came before the state legislature in the spring of 1925, union editor Frank Palmer argued that it represented "labor's most important fight . . . in a decade" at the statehouse. Palmer
insisted that this was a "fight for the children of America — that everyone shall
have the God-given right to grow and play and live: that none shall be condemned to the grind of the factory before a happy childhood has built the
strength into his body to withstand the tasks of life."[67] The state labor federation, along with the Women's Union Labor Political League, joined with wom-
en's club leaders to pressure lawmakers to ratify the amendment.

The Child Welfare Bureau also focused public attention on child labor
but with different consequences. In the early 1920s, the US Children's Bureau
and its Colorado counterpart combined efforts to investigate child labor and
mother's wage work in the beet fields of Weld and Larimer counties. The
study found that compulsory school laws were widely violated as truant officers often turned a blind eye to offenses. Employers and beet-working families colluded to defy regulations. This practice allowed child beet workers to
fall far behind grade level in school. Worse still in the eyes of investigators,
sugar-beet labor had created health problems for children, including orthope-
dic abnormalities, flat feet, and eye and hearing disorders. Beet work by mothers, most of them Russian-German or Mexican immigrants, jeopardized preg-
nancies, led to the neglect of young children and infants, and thus also threatened child health. The report called for stricter enforcement of compulsory
school laws and new regulations to govern child labor.[68] Yet the state Child

Welfare Bureau devoted little energy to these campaigns, continuing to stress medical interventions as the best route for improving child welfare. This difference divided the influence of women reformers.

During the 1925 legislative session, the state women's club federation threw its full weight behind the child labor initiative while the Child Welfare Bureau remained silent on the proposed amendment. The Colorado "Ratification Committee" included lobbyists from the state women's club federation, the Denver Woman's Club, the YWCA, as well as leading female unionists like May Peake. Several women legislators and clubwomen, including Louise Patterson and May Bigelow, held hearings on the amendment in March but Child Welfare Bureau officials did not testify. Republican and Democratic clubwomen alike pleaded for approval of the amendment. But anti-statist hostility to the bill had grown strong in Colorado, as in the nation, given allegations that it would "centralize control of parental discipline in Washington." Anti-feminist activists joined Catholic leaders who mounted a public campaign against the amendment nationwide, invoking the specter of Bolshevism and centralized control over education. Several women's club members of the legislature voted for ratification, but the majority in both houses rejected the amendment.[69] The lack of Child Welfare Bureau support was a significant loss for the ratification movement. Women's club and union leaders were unable to make the child labor amendment a priority for the Child Welfare Bureau.

Instead, the CWB quietly continued its focus on infant and maternal health by means of medical and scientific interventions. In addition to the traveling health clinics, the bureau devoted a great deal of attention to licensing and regulating midwives. The experience of Colorado's Child Welfare Bureau workers suggests that the Rocky Mountain West may have implemented the midwife-training campaign in terms different from other regions.[70] Colorado witnessed a cross-gender coalition of male physicians and female health officials in support of midwife reform.

Spanish-speaking nurses working for the Colorado bureau consistently urged reliance on midwives in rural and immigrant communities, such as those in the San Luis Valley. Bureau nurse Lena Pecover, for example, insisted that the "midwife is a necessity," since few Mexican American families could afford to pay full fees to a physician for deliveries. Local doctors in this section of the state felt it was unprofessional to undertake charity deliveries and frequently sued patients to recover the full cost of their services. Yet Pecover urged local midwives to receive additional CWB training, as did Shepperd-Towner nurses nationwide. Pecover reported that several young Mexican American nurses eagerly participated in the CWB program. One Mexican American midwife, Florenda Giron, was anxious to train with the local doctors, Pecover reported. Although only thirty-four, Mrs. Giron had lost nine infants and realized "that her babies need not have died if she and they had had proper care." Some Hispanic women embraced the possibilities of the scientific medicine that CWB enthusiastically promoted. The CWB midwife training was also designed to ease logistical hardships. CWB doctors at the Alamosa Hospital offered to train Mexican American women in obstetrics and pediatrics and then administer the state midwife's exam, eliminating the need to travel to Denver to fulfill such requirements.[71]

Pecover and her colleagues both displayed sensitivity to the delicate nature of their work with Mexican American midwives. Although clearly advocating the scientific views of birth and childrearing rooted in the Anglo-American middle class, these CWB nurses also recognized the difficulties of forcing registration and training on older midwives. If the CWB brought judicial proceedings against such midwives to compel their participation, "they will probably continue to work on the sly when they are released, and to find them out will be most difficult due to the their great influence over the Mexican women," Pecover wrote to her supervisors. "It would also be much harder to teach the Mexican women the value of the physician and good medical care if we have enemies in these women." Pecover proposed to place a trained, Spanish-speaking midwife, with ties to the local physicians and hospitals, in each district and then "allow the unregistered woman to have a small income by assisting the registered one." The CWB nurse thought this plan meant "doing our part to meet them [unregistered midwives] half way" and put in place a "go-between for the Mexicans and the doctors so that the people will lose their fear of doctors."[72] Historian Sandra Schackel similarly found that New Mexico Shepperd-Towner officials, some trained in Colorado, worked to bridge the cultural suspicions that separated immigrant and Indian communities from the Anglo health-care establishment. Former head of the Colorado Visiting Nurses Association Elizabeth Forster, for example, worked alongside traditional Navaho medicine men when she moved to New Mexico in the 1920s.[73] Yet immigrant and Native American mothers and midwives always remained the less powerful partners in these negotiations over childbirth and motherhood.

During the decade, the Child Welfare Bureau both expanded women's participation in maternal reform and narrowed its focus. Relying especially on local women's clubs and associations, the bureau drew many women of varied classes and ethnicities into its maternal and childhood health projects. Cross-gender coalitions emerged as well. The CWB emphasis on mother and child health also generated new interest among men's voluntary associations. CWB doctors gave speeches before men's clubs about maternity and "the place the father should fill in the home" when the baby arrived. Aroused by CWB statistics of inadequate conditions, the Kiwanis clubs in 1925 sponsored a $2,000 investigation of maternal and child welfare provisions across the state.[74] CWB health initiatives increasingly dominated the women's reform agenda in the state.

Under the leadership of the Child Welfare Bureau, medical interventions to address childhood abnormalities replaced broader critiques of the economic conditions for wage-earning mothers and their families. Training programs for midwives and clinics to reach new mothers dominated an agenda that earlier included debate about birth control and state-funding for maternity leave. Julia Lathrop had argued that the "power to maintain a decent family living standard is a primary essential of child welfare."[75] Such concerns did not animate the CWB nor those middle-class women and men in the state who looked to the bureau, rather than women's club leaders, to define the scope of possible government action on behalf of children. Progressive-style mobilizations of clubwomen against party and corporate corruption became more difficult.

With ties to local clubs and the state medical community, the Colorado Child Welfare Bureau withstood the end of Shepperd-Towner funding at the federal level. Doctors continued to cooperate with CWB officials to offer health clinics, although at a reduced level, into the 1930s. The Child Welfare Bureau shaped the debate about the needs of mothers and children until the passage of the Social Security Act in 1935 when state legislators created a new Public Welfare Department to administer the New Deal program. Women's clubs supported the Child Welfare Bureau and gradually adjusted their political sights as the women's reform agenda narrowed over the decade. Continued lobbying on behalf of the Child Labor Amendment at last bore some fruit in 1931, when Colorado legislators ratified it. But Colorado joined only five other states as the momentum for a federal law had earlier ground to a halt.[76] The focus within the state women's club federation was shifting elsewhere.

In 1932, during one of the worst years of the Great Depression, the CFWC organized a Division of Mothercraft. Mothercraft, claimed the new chair, was "a course of instruction for girls in personal hygiene, home sanitation, and the care of babies; the underlying motive of which is to fill the souls of the school and college girl with the conviction of the beauty and sanctity of the home."[77] This project fit with efforts across the country to introduce home economics into the curriculum at the secondary and even university level. Motherhood had become less a political rallying cry than a craft for domestic fulfillment.

Reflecting on twenty-five years of suffrage for Colorado women in January 1919, *Denver Post* reporter Frances Wayne argued angrily that "women are not much better off than when the ballot was bestowed on them by the gallant men of Colorado." They started with a few designated female elected of-

BEN LINDSEY AND WOMEN PROGRESSIVES

fices, such as the superintendent of schools and token representation in the legislature, and remained confined there. Where "salaries are high and there is much patronage to dispense, the men are in command." Women's employment within the state bureaucracy was also circumscribed, and favored legislative measures like mothers' pensions and protective labor laws lacked adequate enforcement. Colorado women "have been too willing to work without reward, and . . . the time has come to *wake up* and demand something more than the right to vote."[78]

Wayne's pessimistic assessment of the value of the suffrage revealed an underlying frustration among Colorado women. Although the Women's Council of Defense members had used the emergency of war to focus state resources on an important piece of the women's club political agenda, much remained undone and largely ignored by male governors and legislators. Wayne's call to action, although not unusual in these years, remained vague. How might organized clubwomen enhance their influence and gain access to the power of government?

Women's club leaders in the 1920s worked to mobilize members for Progressive reform. They advocated nonpartisan, educational campaigns, tactical lobbying, and a reliance on institutional ties to the juvenile court and Child Welfare Bureau. Ben Lindsey's juvenile court promised to reconstruct and protect childhood as a distinctive and delicate developmental stage. Working-class mothers largely embraced these efforts but also demanded attention to protective labor laws and birth control.

The Progressive project of Colorado women, however, fell far short of its goals. Social welfare programs for mothers and children remained underfunded and subject to the autocratic control of county commissioners. Women's club leaders struggled to define a unifying vision, given different views of the needs of working mothers. The Child Welfare Bureau dramatically expanded health-care initiatives for new mothers and children but did not advocate broader state interventions to protect them. CFWC leader Annah Pettee mused after the 1923 legislative session that "[w]e find our economic and political reform a myth."[79] The modest social welfare bureaucracy that women Progressives had created by 1924 would soon face a crucial test.

Six

The Colorado Klan and the Decline of Progressivism

The year 1924 proved pivotal for Colorado Progressives. While most women's club leaders sought to mobilize members along feminine rather than party lines, Colorado labor leaders hoped to sustain a national movement devoted to the economic problems of farmers and workers. The promise of Robert M. La Follette's Progressive presidential campaign captivated unionists across the state. It inspired hope for a revival of the Progressive Party coalition of 1912.

Yet the rise of the Ku Klux Klan in Colorado shifted the political campaign season decisively. Beginning with an election to recall Denver mayor Ben Stapleton in August 1924, the Klan increasingly divided workers and came to briefly dominate state politics. The Klan too drew upon the legacy of Progressives, utilizing the direct primary to nominate its favored candidates and preaching moral reform. By the fall Klan crusades overwhelmed La Follette's statewide campaign. Religious appeals trumped those based on class interest. Klan promoters and opponents battled over the meaning of male and female citizenship, recalling earlier struggles between moral reformers and Speer Democrats. Progressives defended their reforms against a new, aggressively masculine threat—the Klan party machine.

COLORADO LABOR AND LA FOLLETTE PROGRESSIVISM

In the years after World War I, labor Progressives in Colorado achieved few victories. Governor Sweet had disbanded the hated Rangers but was unable to persuade legislators to eliminate the Industrial Commission. Labor legislation still lacked adequate enforcement within the state bureaucracy. Thus, a number of Colorado labor leaders responded to national calls to explore political alternatives. In 1922, members of the railroad brotherhoods, the stationary engineers, and the machinist unions organized a national Conference for Progressive Political Action (CPPA), which debated prospects for an independent third party. Sympathetic unionists in Colorado organized a state branch of the CPPA, which met in January 1924 and included farmer leaders along with former Progressive Party activists.[1] Colorado CPPA activists held out hope that farmers and workers might revive the state Progressive Party as an alternative to the two reigning parties. At very least they hoped to influence the platform and nominations of candidates by the state Democratic Party.

Denver labor leaders meanwhile organized their own political committee in February to challenge machine politicians among the Democrats. The committee initially focused attention on caucuses, how to hold and conduct them, and how to ensure registration of the results. These civics efforts closely resembled those of women's club activists. The federal government was not ruled by the president or Congress, argued *Labor Advocate* editor Frank Palmer, but by the precinct caucus. Union members should attend their local caucus and demand a voice in electing convention delegates, Palmer insisted. They must not allow the "old party workers" to enforce caucus rules "against our people." Because the Denver Democratic Party remained a fractured organization, union members easily dominated the May 8 caucuses, selecting the majority of the delegates to attend the county convention.[2]

At the Democratic Denver County Convention on May 19, labor delegates assumed majority control, inspiring hope that they might in turn shape the state party convention at Colorado Springs. But divisions among workers surfaced at that state meeting. Campaigning for reelection, Governor William Sweet generated significant opposition among CPPA activists. The governor's opponents also claimed that he exerted determining influence over the state labor federation, "bending it to his political plans without even permitting it to possess an influence in his administration." Sweet supporters among the state labor federation countered that industrial peace had prevailed under the Democratic incumbent. This in turn meant "greater economy since there has not been a nickel of state money spent in either breaking strikes or guarding property." Several CPPA leaders remained unmoved and rejected Sweet's bid to lead the state Democrats.[3] The incumbent governor could not rally the broad support of Colorado unionists.

This split among Democrats reappeared at the state labor political convention held in Pueblo in June. When the majority of labor delegates backed the state federation leadership and endorsed Sweet for governor, opponents accused state labor leaders of "steam-roller, gang-rule" and "double-crossing" tactics. One critic alleged that this "so-called political convention meekly takes orders from this political mountebank [Sweet] and carries out his program, expecting working men to ask no questions but pay in their money and work at the polls."[4] CPPA supporters held out hope that Sweet might be replaced on the Democratic ticket with a candidate committed to a broader reform of economic conditions in the state. The split grew more intense as the summer wore on. A state CPPA member wrote to Ed Costigan in Washington, urging him to return to Colorado to reassemble the fragments of his 1912 coalition.[5]

Amid differences over Sweet's leadership of the state Democratic Party and the possibilities for a third-party ticket, Wisconsin senator Robert La Follette announced his independent candidacy for president in July. La Follette had long championed direct democracy and government intervention to address economic inequalities. His 1924 platform particularly appealed to organized labor, calling for the public ownership of railroads, prohibitions against labor injunctions, and protections for union organizing. La Follette rallied a broad coalition of interest groups, including unions, farmers, activist women, and African Americans.[6]

In July, most state union leaders urged members to back La Follette's independent campaign. State labor leader May Peake and the Denver labor assembly president worked with railroad unionists to organize a labor committee to back La Follette. Leadership of the state La Follette campaign remained uncertain, however, as state Progressive Party members and labor federation leaders each appointed their own directors. These joined former Denver Woman's Club president Mabel Costigan, who sought to rally Colorado women to the La Follette campaign. Costigan projected a plain yet determined style that supporters hoped would appeal to wage-earning and farm women. "There's no 'up-stage' manners about her," enthused a sympathetic newspaper editor. "She wears gingham herself and knows how to talk to her sisters in gingham and calico. And she talks straight from the shoulder. . . . Her eyes and chin are the dominant facial characteristics of this fighting woman Progressive."[7] Appearance and dress typically featured more prominently than Costigan's speech. The American Federation of Labor Executive Committee's endorsement of La Follette in August secured broad union backing for the independent. Labor and women Progressive leaders were hopeful.

In the state and local campaigns, however, divisions emerged. Many union leaders backed the Democratic nominees, beginning with Sweet for governor. Yet as the leading Democratic nominee in the state, Sweet stumped for the Democratic presidential candidate John Davis. As a Wall Street attorney,

Davis was unlikely to generate much excitement among union workers. Still, Sweet insisted that there was "no good reason why any Progressive should vote for La Follette" instead of Davis. When Davis visited Colorado on the eve of the state primaries, Sweet persuaded a few leading labor officials to join him in welcoming the Democratic candidate. State labor leaders struggled to maintain a delicate position: backing Sweet for governor while rejecting Davis for president. Sweet critics quickly cried foul, condemning state labor leaders for their ties to Sweet and potentially to Davis. The anti-Sweet unionists held a second CPPA meeting in early August. Socialists, members of the Non-Partisan League, the Committee of Forty-Eight, the Farmer-Labor Party, the Farmer's Union, the Grange, German voluntary associations, and the Progressive Party assembled to plot a course of action for Colorado. Committed to La Follette but frustrated by Sweet, participants organized an independent Progressive state ticket of left-wing unionists, farmers, and Socialists to challenge state Democrats.[8]

The La Follette campaign encouraged unionists and Progressive party members disappointed in Sweet to abandon the state Democratic Party. State labor leaders, several of whom served appointed positions within the Democratic Party, remained committed to Sweet and his leadership of the party. But the incumbent governor had lost support among a number of workers and farmers disappointed with his performance. In response, Sweet supporters in the state labor federation appealed to Ed Costigan for an endorsement in order to counter the challenge posed by the CPPA faction. Confusion increasingly characterized La Follette's Colorado campaign with rival factions claiming his endorsement.[9]

In September, Costigan did return to Denver in an attempt to sort out competing claims to La Follette. The Wisconsin senator also traveled to Denver to meet with the CPPA and state labor federation factions. Ultimately, La Follette refused to endorse a state ticket in his name, rebuffing CPPA delegates and former Colorado Progressive Party members. La Follette maintained this stand in states across the nation, refusing to back local tickets and insisting on his independence. Nonetheless, Colorado law allowed the recently reconstituted Progressive Party to designate La Follette as its presidential nominee on the November ballot. Additionally, a small farmer-Labor faction presented its own ticket in October and also named La Follette as its presidential choice. Legal challenges by Sweet supporters to separate La Follette from either of these two rival tickets were unsuccessful.[10] La Follette had the endorsement of three labor factions in the fall campaign, each increasingly hostile toward the other.

With left-wing unionists rejecting Governor Sweet and unionists divided about how best to support La Follette, political events in Denver provided another test of labor unity in mid-1924. Democratic mayor Ben Stapleton faced a recall election on August 12 because of his ties to the Ku Klux Klan. Workers appeared increasingly split over the Hooded Order.

DENVER WORKERS AND MAYOR STAPLETON

Stapleton's successful campaign for mayor the previous year had rested significantly on support from the Denver Klan and organized labor in the city. Long a loyal operative within the Denver Democratic Party, Stapleton had emerged as the mayoral candidate in 1923 to challenge Republican incumbent Dewey Bailey. Promising to fight crime, reduce taxes, and administer city government more efficiently, Stapleton secured the support of the city's Democratic organization, Italian clubs, and Governor Sweet. Although Stapleton insisted that attempts to "stir up racial or religious prejudices" were un-American, rumors of his ties to an emerging Klan organization dogged him in spring 1923. Ex-governor George Carlson also entered the mayoral race that spring, receiving the endorsements of many protestant church organizations for his commitment to prohibition enforcement. Denver labor leaders, however, endorsed the former postmaster, Stapleton, and campaigned actively on his behalf. Carlson and Bailey both shared an anti-union legacy that offended most workers. Stapleton narrowly bested his seven rivals in the May 1923 election.[11]

In his first year as mayor, Stapleton struggled to keep hidden his connections with the Klan. Although he was member number 1128 and a friend of Klan leader John Galen Locke, Stapleton did not openly acknowledge the Klan during the campaign or in his first year as mayor. He did, however, grant the Klan access to the Municipal Auditorium and appointed numerous Klansmen to the police department, including William Candlish as chief. The attorney, former state representative, and part-time prospector lacked any law-enforcement experience but had emerged as a leading Klan organizer in his home community of Leadville.[12] The Klan's growing dominance over city law enforcement generated new criticism of the mayor.

In spring and summer 1924, Klan opponents exposed Stapleton's connections to the organization, hoping to turn the city's voters against the mayor. Critics like Jewish attorney Philip Hornbein demanded that Mayor Stapleton acknowledge his Klan ties. In late March, opponents submitted more than 25,000 signatures on a recall petition. The outcome of the August recall election revealed both the growing strength of the Colorado Klan and the reluctance of labor leaders to address its growing influence among Denver's working-class residents.

From 1923 to 1925, the Colorado Klan mobilized some 35,000 members statewide. Not unlike its counterparts in other states outside the South, the Colorado Klan stressed nativistic patriotism, law and order, anti-Catholicism, anti-Semitism, and xenophobia. Historians Robert Goldberg and Phil Goodstein have found that law-and-order appeals proved especially effective in luring Denver residents into the organization, especially those that blamed immigrant Italian and Jewish communities for violations of prohibition. Denver remained the center of Colorado Klan activities with the greatest membership totals statewide. Catholics made up 15 percent of the city's population, but they came in for regular Klan attacks given fantasies of papal intrigue and priestly dominance. Black Denver accounted for about 2.5 percent of city residents, and African Americans too suffered discrimination and intimidation by the Klan.[13]

By summer 1924, Klan opponents in Denver focused their concern on Stapleton. Those leading the recall drive against the mayor were numerous city officials and newspaper editors. Judge Ben Lindsey, District Attorney Philip Van Cise, and *Denver Express* editor Sidney Whipple denounced Stapleton for surrendering control of city government "to a secret outside organization." Just four days before the recall election, Whipple printed a spy report from a recent Klan meeting at which Stapleton had appeared. The mayor had pledged to "work with the Klan and for the Klan in the coming election, heart and soul." If reelected in August, Stapleton had promised to give the Klan the kind of administration it wanted.[14]

Recall supporters appealed to the city's working-class and Progressive voters in hopes of unseating Stapleton. Ben Lindsey invoked the specter of a hidden conspiracy among Stapleton, the Klan, and the city's corporate elite "to deliver the people of Denver gagged, bound, and enslaved through unjust and exorbitant fares and rates, to the Denver Tramway company, the Denver Gas and Electric company . . . and such other public service corporations as care to deal with them in the looting and robbery of the people of this city." Lindsey noted that city attorney Rice Means, also a Klansman, had approved an excessively high valuation of tramway property in the city's ongoing court proceedings to determine an appropriate fare for streetcar service. Comparing them to his earlier political encounters with Mayor Speer and "the Beast," Lindsey insisted that Stapleton and his Klan allies were creating a far worse "debauchery of our politics." Thus former Progressive voters especially should reject Stapleton and the "white-hooded menace" he represented.[15]

The recall movement unfortunately tapped former mayor Dewey Bailey to challenge Stapleton. Bailey remained unpopular with both Protestant Progressives and urban workers. Protestant activists, the Anti-Saloon League, and other moral Progressives had abandoned Bailey for other candidates in spring 1923. Unionists cited a list of problems with Bailey. They protested his decision to ban dancing in public parks on Sundays. Catholic May Peake invoked the language of women Progressives to condemn Bailey for tolerating miserable conditions in the maternity ward at the county hospital. Expectant mothers "were crowded together in a disgraceful manner," Peake alleged. Under Stapleton's watchful eye, the county hospital now offered new mothers "tender and sanitary care," she wrote. Bailey had also refused to enforce the minimum-wage law for women, while Stapleton initiated some prosecutions. But ultimately, Bailey's willingness to turn over police powers to private strikebreakers during the 1920 tramway strike provoked the greatest hostility. *Labor Advocate* editor Palmer conceded that "Stapleton has one thing to be ashamed of—he appointed Rice Means city attorney . . . but he has made up for that in a hundred ways and *he has no blood on his hands!*"[16] Denver labor leaders consistently argued that Bailey, Lindsey, and Whipple had merely created a "smokescreen of corporation baiting and religious controversy" to obscure the economic issues at stake in the recall campaign. The rhetoric of moral Progressivism was losing its persuasive power.

Labor newspapers in the city largely ignored the growing influence of the Klan and its possible appeal to workers. The city's union leaders again backed Stapleton for reelection. Catholic leaders remained largely silent during the recall campaign. Prohibition supporters and other Protestant leaders backed the standing mayor as did the Colored Citizens League.

When a record number of Denver voters went to the polls on August 12, they overwhelmingly rejected the Stapleton recall. Labor editor Palmer enthused that working-class districts had given Stapleton huge majorities, although Jewish West Colfax precincts recorded significant opposition to the mayor. The Klan had contributed $15,000 and many election workers to the Stapleton campaign. The mayor's victory led the *Denver Post* to conclude "that the Ku Klux Klan is the largest, most cohesive and most efficiently organized political force in the state of Colorado today."[17] The recall campaign particularly raises questions about worker participation in the Klan. Did the union leadership or Klan membership exert the greater influence over union voters?

THE COLORADO KLAN AND THE WORKING CLASS

Denver's largely white working class was not immune to the Klan's narrow vision of fraternal and racist Americanism. The Invisible Empire divided the city's workers in ways that union leaders struggled to acknowledge. Efforts to curb the influence of the Klan on the state's unions achieved some success. But in 1924 particularly, the Klan challenged union heads for the political leadership of the city's workers.

Colorado's native-born white workers, like those in other Western states, had long discriminated against Asian laborers who migrated into the region. In the 1910s and 1920s, the state Bureau of Labor Statistics kept a careful count of the few Japanese residents in Colorado—only 2,500 had settled in the state by 1920. State labor statistician Otto Thum argued nonetheless that this small minority presented "a race problem affecting . . . the ownership and occupancy of our most fertile lands by a non-assimilable people, thereby completely crowding out our pioneer white settlers and their posterity." Colorado labor leaders backed the lobbying campaign of the American Federation of Labor to secure immigration restrictions in 1924 that particularly excluded Asians.[18]

Other immigrant workers also came under attack. Throughout much of the 1920s, Denver labor leaders backed efforts to keep Mexican immigrants out of the city's labor market. Southern European immigrants also faced criticism. In the early 1920s, Denver union workers complained of a "Greek menace" in the restaurant business. Greek proprietors employed "cheap labor," including members of their own families, at "starvation wages," alleged Denver unionists. Native-born restaurant managers who conducted their business "according to American standards" claimed they could not compete with some forty-two immigrant Greek restaurant owners who drove wages relentlessly downward. Labor editors also protested the exploitive contracts that padrones negotiated with their immigrant workforce.[19] But nativist attacks on immigrants rarely took center stage in the union's political campaigns.

Concerns about prohibition violations and crime may have generated some worker interest in the Colorado Klan. Debates over prohibition in the early 1920s among Denver unionists revealed significant support for continuing the ban on alcohol. Some city labor assembly leaders claimed there were fewer drunken workers at union meetings since prohibition took effect.[20] Sensational reports of juvenile larceny, assault, bootlegging, and drug experimentation in city newspapers during Mayor Bailey's administration likely contributed to a sense that the police force had failed to contain crime. The *Denver Post* encouraged public perceptions of police incompetence and brazen defiance of the law. A 1923 editorial vowed that the "reign of outlawry that has existed during the past two or three years cannot continue. . . . The government cannot continue to function when its laws are . . . belittled and insulted by law violators everywhere." The Klan was quick to promise an urban cleanup.[21]

Denver's significant Catholic working-class population, however, offered important resistance to Klan expansion. Religion had rarely divided the city's working class in the preceding years. During the 1921 national American Federation of Labor convention in Denver, a number of the city's Protestant workers had joined Catholics to attend a special labor mass at the Denver Cathedral. In 1919, national Catholic leader Reverend John Ryan had argued before a largely working-class audience at the Protestant Grace Community Church in Denver that "Christianity, socialism, and democracy are one and same thing when they are viewed in their proper light." Ryan had earned the

THE COLORADO KLAN AND THE DECLINE OF PROGRESSIVISM

respect of Denver workers for his defense of tramway employees and his calls for a living wage. Many Catholic residents of Denver had made peace with the state prohibition law, given its exception for sacramental wine. *Denver Catholic Register* editor Reverend Matthew Smith voiced his appreciation that Catholic clergy and state Anti-Saloon League leaders maintained a working relationship. Catholic leaders were "consulted regularly regarding every proposed change in the dry laws" during its early years.[22] With few visible differences over prohibition, Catholic and Protestant workers in Denver did not openly clash over this moral reform in the early 1920s.

Still a number of Protestant churches recruited workers into the Hooded Order. Klan organizers made public "love offerings," which amounted to significant financial gifts to congregations in hopes of enticing new members. In central Denver, the People's Tabernacle and Pillar of Fire Church welcomed the Klan. More affluent churches like Highland Christian, All Saints Episcopal, Beth Eden Baptist, and Grant Avenue Methodist churches had extensive Klan ties.[23]

Additionally, the Klan's economic pressure may have had a significant impact on workers. Klan members threatened Denver's Protestant small-business owners and skilled laborers with boycotts in order to boost membership. Reciting its growing list of Klan-friendly businesses became a regular ritual at meetings. Klansmen would approach small-business owners with a list of recent bankruptcies from the newspapers, claiming that they reflected a choice of businessmen not to join. Some Denver employees were also threatened with dismissal if they refused to pledge their membership to the order. Klan-friendly businesses would then post an American flag in their windows to alert Klan customers. Drivers would even plant a flag picture in their car windows to avoid a parking ticket from the Klan-dominated police.[24]

There were thus a number of reasons, both voluntary and coercive, why Colorado workers might have chosen to join the Klan. While Klan secrecy meant that few organizational records have survived, some enduring lists of leaders and members of the Denver Klan allow for socioeconomic analysis. In his study, Goldberg compared several membership lists for the Denver Klan from 1924 through 1926 with the city directory and found very few working-class members among the Klan leadership. The leaders and early joiners were economically middle-class with multiple fraternal associations. Few of Denver's elite belonged to the Klan. Late joiners did include a representative portion of the city's skilled working class but relatively few semi-skilled and unskilled laborers. Goldberg did not find any geographic pattern of Klan settlement, as members were dispersed throughout much of the city. Members tended to be older men with families who hailed from Colorado or the Midwest. Few Spanish-American or Great War veterans belonged to the Denver Klan, although Klan leader John Locke was a notable exception.[25]

Colorado Klansman thus shared important similarities with members in other states. Klansmen in Georgia and Oregon were likewise concentrated in the middling social ranks. This petit bourgeois feared growing concentrations of power in elite hands as well as disruptive threats from unskilled and itinerant workers below. Colorado Klansman displayed much less of the anti-union hostility that historian Nancy MacLean uncovered in the ranks of Georgia Klansmen. Additionally, economic critiques, whether informed by an exclusive vision of republicanism or reactionary populism, did not play as prominent a role in mobilizing Colorado's petit bourgeois membership as in Oregon, for example.[26]

While a number of Protestant churches steered members into the Colorado Klan, one in particular offered workers a site to resist and condemn the Invisible Empire. The Grace Community Church, led by English immigrant George Lackland, infused a sense of class consciousness into its religious program. Lackland organized a regular speaker series called the Open Forum, inviting Margaret Sanger, Charlotte Perkins Gilman, Clarence Darrow, and John Ryan to address social and cultural issues of importance to the working class. In 1921 the city labor assembly began organizing a march to Grace Church the Sunday before Labor Day in order to hear Lackland speak. The minister regularly attacked the open shop, defended striking workers, and appealed to wage-earning listeners to vote their class rather than party loyalties. In 1924, Lackland joined the Klan opposition and openly condemned the group. Yet the minister still endorsed Stapleton during the recall campaign.[27]

State labor leaders also attempted to dissuade unionists from joining the Hooded Order. The growing influence of the United Mine Workers of America within the state labor federation likely shaped the latter's response to the Klan. Committed to interracial industrial unionism, the miners' union had elsewhere attempted to close ranks against the Klan. At the summer 1924 convention, labor delegates approved a mine worker resolution that condemned the Klan for exacerbating "racial and religious prejudices" and threatening workers with economic intimidation. Labor leaders regularly feared that Klan loyalties would dilute class protests. At the summer 1925 labor convention, critiques of the Klan grew more aggressive. After a speech by union organizer Paul Smith that compared the Klan to a pestilence, labor convention delegates denounced union participation in the Klan. Colorado Klan leaders had recently launched their own union, the American Union Workmen, which included some state labor federation members. Delegates likened this Klan union to the "divide and destroy" tactics of employers who developed company unions. While most state and city labor leaders condemned the Klan, some rank-and-file unionists did enlist in the Invisible Empire.[28]

In fall 1924 the Klan relied in part on labor support to launch its campaign for broader political influence. The anti-Asian sentiments of many white workers in Colorado, fears about crime and urban disorder, promises of fraternalism, and economic pressures likely contributed to the decision of some workers to join the Klan. While the state labor federation and some religious leaders with working-class constituencies condemned the Klan, some Denver workers responded to Klan calls for political action in the fall of 1924. Labor leaders thus faced a double challenge that campaign season: smoothing over differences about La Follette and the Democratic Party while countering the nativist and racist appeals of the Klan.

THE COLORADO KLAN BUILDS A MASCULINE PARTY MACHINE

During the primary election campaign in September 1924, the Klan adroitly focused its membership on the task of capturing the state Republican Party. The 1924 campaign particularly revealed that Klan leaders were not simply organizing a social movement but were bent on securing control over state government. By manipulating loopholes in the direct primary system and civil service, the Klan also rallied members into a religiously intolerant political machine of significant influence. Leaders cynically deployed the Protestant Progressive style to appeal especially to male members in an effort to renegotiate the political implications of Protestant manhood.

The leader of the Colorado Klan, Grand Dragon John Galen Locke, was a quirky, insecure, professionally marginal man determined to project an image of aggressive masculinity. As a Denver homeopathic physician, Locke never met the requirements to join the city or state medical societies. Short and heavy in appearance, he had a high, thin voice and maintained an ascetic lifestyle. Brief service in the Spanish-American War had allowed Locke to amass an extensive collection of guns and knives from the Philippines, China, and Japan, which he displayed in his home in an effort to create a museum dedicated to hunting and martial virtue. He also hung mounted heads of moose and elk and nurtured a reputation as an expert marksman. Locke's basement served as the Klan's ultimate and secret headquarters, decorated with elaborate and eclectic mystical regalia.[29] As an unmarried man, the Grand Dragon represented a marginal masculinity outside the domestic sphere.

Locke viewed the Klan and its political potential more in terms of aggressive masculinity than the restrained, respectable manhood of Ben Lindsey or Ed Costigan. Consider, for example, reports of Klan initiation rituals. District Attorney Van Cise had assigned deputies to infiltrate the Denver Klan and report on its activities. At one Klan meeting, a Van Cise spy observed that Locke explained the secret Klan handshakes to new male members in "vulgar" terms. When an initiate asked Locke why the mask was worn, Locke "explained that it was worn for the same reason that one buttoned his pants in the front." Locke demonstrated little regard for the moral conception of manliness that had animated earlier Protestant Progressives. He asserted a more aggressive masculinity and physicality.[30]

Locke helped to construct Klan masculinity in clearly performative terms. At Klan meetings in the summer of 1924, Locke delighted in harassing Democratic mayor Stapleton in front of members, as if to create a shared sense of power among his listeners. The Grand Dragon would send regular messengers to the mayor's home with calls for him to appear before the Klan. Several times the mayor begged off, pleading that he was already in bed or too busy. Ultimately, Locke threatened to bring Stapleton himself, much to the amusement of the largely male audience. When at last Stapleton did appear, just before the recall election in August, Locke insisted it was as a contrite penitent. After the mayor's speech, in which he pledged to work for the Klan, Locke asked members if they "would back Bennie in his desire" for reelection. The vote was unanimous. The Grand Dragon also suspended the Klan membership of Stapleton's manager of public safety, Reuben Hershey, for "pussyfooting" and appointing Jews, blacks, and Catholics to the police force. Locke hoped to convince listeners that he, not Stapleton or any Democratic Party leader, maintained ultimate control over the city's administration. The eager attendance of the chief of police at Klan meetings likely contributed to that impression. Male members relished in the vicarious influence their leader appeared to exercise over city politics.[31]

Eliciting support from a male audience for their theatrical presumptions of power, Klan leaders then worked to rally listeners to political action. Gubernatorial candidate and district judge Clarence Morley, for example, urged every Klansman to get himself registered, "and wife and relatives, in order to do what is expected of them this fall." In the summer of 1924, Klan leaders targeted the Republican machinery for takeover. Exerting its greatest influence in Denver and Canon City, the Klan mobilized members at the state Republican convention to ensure that chosen candidates would appear on the primary ballot. These candidates signed undated resignation letters, which the Grand Dragon kept personally, in exchange for Klan endorsements. Klan leaders also appealed to Denver workers for support at the primaries. At one meeting, Klan candidates for political office professed to be friends of labor, promising that unionists would receive a "square deal" under Klan rule. One senatorial candidate claimed that he only hired union men in his business and never intended to do otherwise.[32] Locke insisted that chosen candidates owed ultimate loyalty not to a party organization or union but to the Klan itself. He worked in numerous ways to control a growing political machine that subsumed party affiliations.

In response to the Klan's activity, a number of male political leaders in both the Democratic and Republican parties offered a limited challenge, one informed by a more respectable conception of manliness. Ben Lindsey had justified the recall against Stapleton by accusing the incumbent mayor and his Klan supporters of debauchery and degrading city politics. The Klan, Lindsey insisted, was linked to corporate Colorado. Once again, corporate-machine corruption threatened honest citizenship and democratic government. As the primaries approached, District Attorney Van Cise led a group of frustrated GOP activists in an effort to avert a Klan capture. Eventually forming the Visible Government League, Van Cise and his supporters gathered enough signatures to field an anti-Klan GOP ticket. The DA contrasted his group's openness with Klan secrecy. Van Cise revived earlier Progressive efforts to make politics transparent. The Klan appeared increasingly like the Speer machine of old: corrupting male loyalties with secret ties of brotherhood. A Great War veteran, Van Cise had earned a law-and-order reputation for his indictments against gamblers and bootleggers in the city. He also opposed boxing and worked diligently to enforce a state law outlawing prize fighting, much to the delight of Denver clubwomen.[33] Lindsey and Van Cise presented a style of Progressive manhood more tied to the domestic sphere. At the state Democratic convention, the social gospel governor Sweet and several candidates openly denounced the Klan, pledging to oppose the Hooded Order throughout the campaign.[34]

During the campaign Van Cise and Lindsey both confronted the Klan machine head on. Their encounters revealed both the breakdown of public discourse and the contest over gender identities that Klan participation sparked. Van Cise organized a meeting at the Municipal Auditorium in early September to expose Klan manipulations within the GOP and city government. The Klan packed the auditorium and did not give the DA the chance to speak. Klan members became, according to *Denver Express* editor Sidney Whipple, "a jeering, howling mob of hoodlums, aflame with passion and hatred," creating a "scene which in its violence and threatened violence carried the mind back to the French Revolution." Whipple's characterization was clearly reminiscent of Ed Keating's earlier description of the Speer machine. Klan opponents contrasted the persistent, restrained Van Cise, who repeatedly attempted to recite a rational analysis of Klan abuses, with disorderly Klan members who shouted him down. The Hooded Order had transformed men into "hoodlums" and undermined femininity among women. One "fat woman in brown" in particular unleashed a "parrot-screeching" and "demoniacal cacophony," shook her fists in rage, and slapped an anti-Klan attorney in the face. A month later Ben Lindsey attempted to denounce the Klan at a Denver church but he too was "insulted, jeered, and hissed down" before Klan listeners turned out the lights.[35] The Klan aroused male and female members alike to menacing public performances bordering on open violence. These frenzied, angry performances reinforced the aggressive character of the Colorado Klan more than its infrequent vigilante actions or cross-burnings

6.1. *The New Driver of the Colorado GOP* (DENVER POST, SEPTEMBER 11, 1925)

conducted under cover of night. By publicly harassing opponents, Klan members created a favorable context for flooding the polls.

At the September 9 primary, Klan voters focused on the Republican ballot. A loophole in the direct primary law allowed voters to select candidates from either party ballot. This meant that even affiliated Democrats could choose to vote in the GOP primary. A record number of voters turned out in Denver to secure victory for the Klan candidates on the GOP ticket and the Van Cise group was easily defeated. Some 40,000 voters cast ballots in the Republican primary while only 7,000 voted in the Democratic one. In cartoons after the voting, *Denver Post* illustrator Wilbur Steele both acknowledged and belittled the new influence of Klan Grand Dragon Locke. On September 11, Steele depicted Locke cracking a whip to drive a "GOP K.K.K." chariot with

6.2. *Waiting to See the Doctor* (DENVER POST, SEPTEMBER 13, 1925)

his chosen Republican candidates eagerly looking over his shoulder to see the road ahead (Figure 6.1). To dispel any doubt, Steele announced in the caption that Locke was clearly boss of the GOP machine now. Yet with his depiction of an overburdened Republican elephant and Klansman Locke as little more than a clown, Steele also undermined the sinister potential of the new political machine.

Two days later, in another cartoon, Steele filled a room full of eager, mostly male candidates "waiting to see the doctor" (Figure 6.2). Locke himself stood on the threshold of his private office to offer his services and guarantee a healthy fall campaign. Prominent among the candidates was Republican nominee for governor Clarence Morley. The KKK doormat made clear the nature of Locke's welcome.[36]

Klan candidates had won primary nominations not only in Denver but even in southern coal counties with large Catholic immigrant populations like Fremont, Huerfano, and Las Animas. Although few of its leaders joined the Klan, the corporate Republican machine that dominated this southern region could not successfully resist Klan candidates in the Republican primary. Additionally, Republican senator Lawrence Phipps had tapped his personal fortune to make a deal with Klan leader Locke. Although not openly allied with Locke or Klan leaders, the former U.S. Steel vice president needed an organization to advance his own senatorial campaign in 1924. Locke agreed to back Phipps, even though the senator had voted against tightening prohibition laws, in exchange for financial support of the Klan organization.[37] The capture of the Republican voting machinery was nearly complete across the state.

After the primaries, GOP candidates sought to avoid mention of the Klan. State Democrats seized on the Invisible Empire as the leading issue. Governor Sweet again promised to work for the repeal of the state Ranger law if reelected. Labor leaders remained focused on the La Follette campaign but divided over Sweet. *Labor Advocate* editor Palmer did not address the Klan issue directly but instead worked to direct attention to class issues. The Republican nominee for Senate, Phipps, was a "double-crossing, steel-trust controlled Pennsylvanian with a weak personality, a weak mind, and no backbone at all," Palmer charged. The GOP gubernatorial candidate, Clarence Morley, came in for critique because of his earlier willingness to jail striking packinghouse workers at the request of the Industrial Commission. Yet his Klan membership did not receive any mention in the union paper. Palmer expressed only suspicion of Van Cise's Visible Government League. The district attorney had led the prosecution of the packing workers in Morley's court. In one October editorial, Palmer did defend the Americanism of German and Jewish immigrants who had served honorably in the recent war.[38] But the editor continued to insist on the primacy of a class protest in a state campaign increasingly dominated by the Klan and its anti-Catholic, anti-Semitic masculine crusade.

The November 1924 election was a major success for the Invisible Empire. Appeals from Progressive reformers such as Van Cise and Lindsey had little impact. Another record turnout in Denver helped elect Klansman Clarence Morley as governor, along with a Klan majority in the state House and several Klan judges. Phipps returned to the US Senate with Klan backing. A few anti-Klan candidates did emerge victorious, including Ben Lindsey, although by narrow margins. The Klan undoubtedly benefited from the national Republican landslide in 1924, but its own mobilizations ensured the success of many local candidates. Labor editor Palmer again ignored the Klan issue in a post-election editorial, commenting only that reaction had swept America. "The effect of money, publicity, and bunk is greater than experts know," mused the editor.[39]

A week after the election, Imperial Wizard Hiram Wesley Evans visited Denver and received a warm welcome from Dr. Locke and governor-elect Morley. Evans addressed a Klan meeting at the Cotton Mills Stadium in South Denver attended by roughly 30,000 in which the leader praised Locke and the new state leadership of Colorado.[40]

THE KLAN'S MASCULINE CRUSADES IN GOVERNMENT

Once the 1925 legislature began its session, Klansmen renewed their effort to advance an aggressive vision of manhood. In late January the order hosted an amateur boxing and wrestling tournament at the Cotton Mills Stadium, which the Klan owned, hoping to defy District Attorney Van Cise. The DA had expressed his frustration with the state's confusing statute on boxing, which banned professional matches but allowed amateur contests. Governor Morley received a standing ovation when he appeared and took a ringside seat. Klan legislators also introduced a boxing bill in the House to legalize prizefighting in the state. Although opposed by Van Cise, clubwomen, and most Protestant leaders, boxing did have the support of Ben Lindsey. The House easily passed the bill in February.[41] Klan legislators in the House also ensured the success of a bill to legalize horseracing and another to reorganize the state fish and game department along with measures to increase the bag limits on fowl and game. One sponsor argued that "Colorado is in a bad way as far as fish and game is concerned." Formerly the "premier game state of the nation," Colorado now lagged behind many other states in aiding hunters to reach their limits.[42] Klan legislators promised Colorado sportsmen a brighter future.

Although working to legitimize boxing and revive hunting, Colorado Klansmen devoted relatively little attention to purity campaigns to protect femininity or promote chastity. In Indiana and Georgia, 1920s Klansmen particularly stressed chivalry, paternal duties, and male breadwinning.[43] Colorado members of the Invisible Empire demonstrated little enthusiasm for these projects. An exception proves the rule in Colorado. In January 1925, Grand Dragon Locke threatened one young Klansman, Keith Boehm, with castration unless he agreed to a forced marriage to his pregnant ex-girlfriend. Klan members posing as police detectives abducted Boehm and drove him to Locke's office late one night. Locke insisted that Boehm should "do the right thing" under the circumstances. But when the mother of the nineteen-year-old East High student later appealed to city authorities for help, District Attorney Van Cise indicted Locke on charges of kidnapping. The Grand Dragon came before Ben Lindsey's juvenile court until the judge reassigned the case. This isolated incident undermined support for Locke and proved an embarrassment to Governor Morley, who personally posted bail for the Grand Dragon. Klan leaders did not otherwise devote significant attention to policing the domestic obligations of Klansmen.[44] Their patriarchal claims of protecting the domestic sphere increasingly appeared as a cynical facade by spring 1925.

Klan chief of police Candlish did pose as a strict foe of bootlegging and drug trafficking. Yet Klan law-and-order campaigns rang remarkably hollow. Publicizing what proved to be largely ineffective raids of bootlegging and narcotics operations near East High School in spring 1925, Candlish ultimately arrested a few boys for vagrancy. The chief actually did little to combat violations of prohibition, although claiming his zeal to protect women and children from urban crime. This did not stop Candlish from bragging in a speech before the Chamber of Commerce about Denver's low crime rate and its eager bootleg squad, which "searched 5,000 places and secured more than 1,000 convictions."[45] Within a few weeks of Candlish's celebration of the Klan police force, Mayor Stapleton would expose it as claptrap.

In April 1925, Stapleton kept secret from Chief Candlish and much of the city police force his plans for a sweeping raid on bootlegging operations across the city. Chafing under Klan control, the mayor sought to demonstrate his independence that spring and embarrass Klan leaders posing as defenders of law and order. Stapleton deputized 125 American Legionnaires and worked with federal agents and his manager of public safety to arrest more than 200 bootleggers, gamblers, and prostitutes in a series of "Good Friday Raids." "Outraged decency rose up in the might of its wrath," reported the *Denver Post*'s Bruce Gustin, and "knocked vice for a goal." Although embarrassing the Klan, Stapleton's agents chose familiar targets. Italian and Greek immigrants made up 75 percent of those arrested. Subsequent investigations exposed the complicity of the Klan bootleg squad in protecting and extorting liquor dealers. The *Denver Catholic Register* happily reported that none of the officers accused of graft was Catholic. Stapleton's raids further undermined the Klan's image as a law-and-order organization. Shortly after the arrests, a *Denver Post* cartoon characterized the roundup in terms of a maternal "housecleaning" in which a broom sweeps a derelict policeman, gambling, vice, and bootlegging from city hall.[46] Given Klan dominance of the police force, the image suggested an effort to clean city government of its aggressively masculine posers. The convictions of twelve police officers for graft later gave Stapleton an excuse to fire Candlish in July 1925.

Stapleton's raids signaled an erosion of Klan influence at city hall. Still, the Invisible Empire had established an elaborate masculine political machine in the preceding months. Stressing loyalty to the Invisible Empire above party, Klansmen had captured the state Republican Party, manipulated the primary election, and secured their favored candidates in state and city offices. To mobilize their machine, Klansmen relied on intimidation, verbal confrontation, a celebration of martial virtues, and theatrical performances of masculine strength and power. For all its aggressive rhetoric, the Colorado Klan engaged in comparatively little direct violence or vigilante action.[47] Yet before Stapleton's raids in the spring of 1925, Klan legislators had set their sights on state government. During the 1925 legislative session they waged a steady offensive against those state agencies associated with women's Progressivism.

KLAN ATTACKS ON THE MATERNAL BUREAUCRACY

In his inaugural address in January 1925, Governor Morley pledged his administration would promote economy in state government. To this end, Morley proposed to abolish a number of state boards that duplicated functions performed by other agencies. Consolidation of various boards might also reduce the cost of state government. "The state should provide generously for the care and comfort of its unfortunates," Morley insisted. "In this we should be intensely humane, but not profligate." The new governor invoked a long-standing theme in politics. Two years earlier Sweet had hoped to reorganize the confusing and diffuse structure of Colorado government. Morley included only two anti-Catholic proposals: a ban on the use of sacramental wine, since this exception to the prohibition law "was flagrantly abused," and the creation of a state woman's reformatory to replace the Catholic Houses of the Good Shepherd.[48]

The claims of reducing government costs masked a more sinister agenda by the Klan governor and legislators. It quickly became clear that the Klan proposed to abolish existing boards in order to dismiss anti-Klan state employees and replace them with a new staff firmly under Klan control. Morley hoped to either eliminate or control the state civil service system. And Klan legislators particularly set their sights on those agencies that implemented the social welfare programs long supported by the state's clubwomen. These attacks at last brought the Klan issue home to clubwomen, whose ranks had also been infiltrated by the Invisible Empire. By threatening the future of the welfare agencies, however, Klan legislators caused a number of female defections from their ranks.

The 1925 General Assembly did include four women legislators in the House, three Denver Republicans and a Pueblo Democrat. All had joined the Klan. In a profile at the start of the legislative session, a *Denver Express* reporter characterized Republican clubwoman Martha Long as a "thrifty housewife" molded of the "same New England clay as thrifty Calvin Coolidge." The new governor's promise of economy resonated strongly with Long. Republican representative Josie Jackson took up her Klan membership with zeal. "She won't hesitate to lift a cudgel in defense of anything that interests her, nor to lay it heavily on anyone who stands in her way," claimed the reporter. Jackson had already earned a public name for herself by leading the heckling of Ben Lindsey when he had attempted to condemn the Klan in a church lecture the previous fall. She did not shrink from assuming the confrontational style of the male Klan leadership.[49]

Dr. Minnie Love, another club member, was a woman "of advanced causes" standing for "the new woman." Love had assumed a leadership position in the Denver women's Klan organization. The *Express* reporter noted that "if the dramatic tinges her bills, as it does her present move to legalize sterilization of the insane and idiots in state institutions, she can be depended on to back her moves by sound arguments." Advancing eugenics, Love also introduced a measure to ban public funding for religious charities that cared for children, an effort to target Catholic orphanages. The Klanswoman had long supported the Women's Christian Temperance Union and served on the Legislative Committee of the Denver Woman's Club. Her agenda, however, would have little influence within the Klan machine. Finally, Louise Patterson, a Democrat from Pueblo, was "motherly, broad bosomed and kindly." An active woman's club member, Patterson proposed a bill to censor movies shown in public schools.[50] Although these women legislators voted with the Klan in the opening weeks, legislative attacks on welfare agencies would reveal key divisions between them.

Among the first state boards the Klan leaders targeted for elimination in the House was the state Nurses Examiners Board. Debate over the bill initially exposed a few squeaky wheels in the Klan's political machine. Representative Josie Jackson agreed to sponsor the bill, likely in exchange for later Klan support of her own measures. After she introduced the bill, Democratic minority leader Elmer Headlee asked for an explanation of its provisions before a vote. Jackson awkwardly denied any responsibility for the measure, claiming simply that it was "a governor's bill and the House can pass it or not as they see fit." Other Klan legislators offered a few brief words in support of the measure before representative Headlee pounced. He explained it in detail and insisted the House reject it. The board had ensured high standards of efficiency and care for nurses and had never been a significant expense to the state. The state's nurses opposed the bill, as did women's club lobbyists. Headlee moved to defeat the bill, but Klan members rallied to keep it alive until the next day before quickly voting to adjourn.[51] Their agenda could not openly withstand rational debate or scrutiny.

After an embarrassing start, Klan leaders in the House caucused to rally member support for their agenda. Martha Long, a nurse, expressed her opposition to the Klan bill. Although most physicians opposed the bill, Dr. Minnie Love supported it, claiming the board was torn by a "fraternal fight." Klan member Gerald Whitney finally spoke on the merits of the bill, alleging vaguely that nurses under the board constituted a state-protected union. This so-called union inflated nursing costs beyond the reach of some poor residents of the state. Louise Patterson was the only House Democrat to vote with the Klan. House Republicans subsequently expressed their support for her bill to make it a felony to operate a still.[52] As a result of long-rolling tactics, Klan leaders in the House secured the complicity of their female legislators for their attack on this maternal bureau.

The Klan effort, however, galvanized the opposition of the Trained Nurses Association of Denver and women's club leaders. The association president feared that Colorado nurses would be without qualifications to practice outside the state should the House succeed in its attempt to abolish the certification board. Ties between the nurses' board and women's clubs remained strong. The Denver Woman's Club had years earlier operated a nurses' training program, which the state board oversaw. In March the Colorado Federation of Women's Clubs' Legislative Committee voiced its opposition to the bill, noting again that the board required only a minimal appropriation from the state to maintain an office and was funded largely by fees. The president of the county medical society also expressed his opposition. The nurses' association and women's club leaders increasingly hoped that the Senate would block the bill. Governor Morley rejected pleas by the nurses' association and women's clubs to denounce the measure, still insisting that the bill was designed to reduce the cost of state government.[53]

After the bill to abolish the nursing board, Klan Republicans in the House introduced a similar measure to eliminate the state Department of Charities and Corrections. This department oversaw the county implementation of the mothers' pension and maternity benefit programs as well as the charitable relief efforts of Protestant and Catholic churches. Directed by Denver social worker Gertrude Vaile, the department also collected valuable statistical data about county compliance with maternal welfare laws. Vaile had earlier collaborated with Klan legislators, who passed a bill to restructure the state's blind benefits program, effectively shifting control from the blind community to a new state bureaucracy appointed by the governor. But when her own department came under Klan attack, Vaile resisted and rallied support among women's club activists and social workers across the state. When the state Senate blocked the move to eliminate Vaile's agency, Governor Morley simply fired her for failing to close it down voluntarily. Unprotected by civil service rules, Vaile became a high-profile victim of the Klan attacks on the social welfare state.[54]

The bill to abolish the Department of Charities and Corrections in fact provoked the first test of Klan strength in the state Senate. Although the Republicans enjoyed a twenty-one-to-fourteen majority in the Senate, only twelve senators were beholden to the Klan. Minority leader William "Billy" Adams of Alamosa rallied the Democrats into a solid opposition. He gradually drew anti-Klan Republicans like Dr. Walter King from Cripple Creek into alliance. State Republican Party chair John Coen had encouraged senate

Republicans to defy the Klan and work with the Democrats. Attempting to persuade other Republicans to join them, Klan senators fatefully ceded control over key committees. Unfortunately for Governor Morley, this allowed Klan opponents to disrupt and ultimately thwart the Klan agenda in the Senate. The Senate vote that defeated the Charities and Corrections bill in late February was twenty to fifteen, with nine Republicans defying the Klan. The Senate next defeated the Klan bill to abolish the nurses' board. One Klan foe noted that House leaders intended to replace that board, along with the state Board of Health, with a new, Klan-controlled Department of Maternity, Child Welfare, and Public Health funded with a $30,000 appropriation. This amount exceeded the existing appropriation for these agencies. Claims of economy masked a broader goal of securing masculine Klan control over an expanded maternal bureaucracy.[55]

The Klan majority in the House nonetheless continued its assault on welfare agencies with a bill to abolish Ben Lindsey's juvenile court. This was not the first effort to oust the controversial kid's judge. In 1915, Speer Democrats and corporate Republicans had passed a bill to eliminate Denver's juvenile court only to have Governor Carlson veto the bill. Women's club opposition to that bill had helped ensure its defeat at that time.[56] Klan hostility to Lindsey in 1925 stemmed from a variety of sources. The judge had been among the first Denver leaders to denounce the Invisible Empire, and he supported the recall campaign against Stapleton. Klan leader Locke had appeared before Lindsey's juvenile court during the Boehm affair. The judge had also expressed growing doubts about prohibition. His articles on adolescent sexuality challenged traditional mores and convention.

Lindsey's broad vision for the juvenile court even appeared to threaten paternal control over children and wives in the domestic sphere. In a 1921 address to the National Education Association titled the "Parenthood of the State," for example, Lindsey had insisted that the state needed to assume more and more responsibility for "the health and morals of the child." In 1925 he expanded on this idea by proposing that the juvenile court operate as a "superparent."[57] In advancing mothers' pensions and maternity benefits, Lindsey had hoped to empower mothers without husbands. Lindsey also sought to project an image of respectable, restrained manliness that competed directly with the Klan's aggressive masculinity.

The House bill to abolish Lindsey's court more immediately grew out of disappointment with the results of the previous election. The judge had narrowly defeated his Klan opponent, Georgetown judge Royal Graham. Backed by the Klan, Graham had contested the election, alleging fraud in a predominantly Jewish district in Denver. A Klan-dominated grand jury had indicted precinct workers in the district for ballot fraud. Overruling the grand jury, Denver judge Julian Moore in April 1925 refused to throw out the entire precinct vote and declared Lindsey the winner of the election. Graham appealed the decision to the Colorado Supreme Court even though he himself faced charges of fraud in connection with his service as a judge in Georgetown.[58]

With the election challenge proving initially unfavorable for the Klan, legislators in the House hoped to eliminate the judge's court and re-create a new one under Klan control. The House bill proposed to restructure the juvenile court, subsuming its operations under the auspices of the criminal courts. This move would have undermined the specific judicial machinery that Lindsey and clubwomen had worked to create in order to treat child and adolescent misconduct with an alternative developmental framework. One critic of the Klan bill noted that it would also eliminate popular election of these judgeships and "result in the selection of judges absolutely untrained and unsuited to the delicate work of handling children."[59] The Klan attack on the juvenile court represented a direct challenge to women's Progressive goals for government protection of children and families.

Protests from women's club leaders were swift and vociferous. The Denver Woman's Club president called the Klan bill a "monstrous error." The state Parent-Teacher Association (PTA) president considered it a "disgraceful" attack on the judge. Women's club activists organized a Denver banquet in Lindsey's honor in early February. The event reminded *Denver Post* reporter Frances Wayne of earlier efforts by Sarah Platt Decker and women's club members to "preserve the court from the destruction ordered by ruthless, selfish, unsocial-minded politicians." Settlement house leader Jane Addams, Ed Costigan, and even AFL president William Green sent telegrams in support of the judge.[60] With its bills to abolish the nurses' board and the Department of Charities and Corrections defeated in the Senate, Klan leaders in the House quietly tabled the bill to abolish Lindsey's court.

Despite its close ties with the PTA, the state Child Welfare Bureau (CWB) did not rise to Lindsey's defense. In fact, bureau officials worked with Governor Morley to create a new maternal network that bypassed Lindsey. When the National Child Welfare League wrote to Governor Morley in February 1925 to request a delegate to attend their national conference on state child-welfare laws, he turned to the Child Welfare Bureau for advice. Bureau director Estelle Mathews offered Morley a list of potential nominees, headed by two long-time foes of Ben Lindsey. Edwin Whitehead, the director of the state Bureau of Child and Animal Protection, who had long challenged Lindsey's court reforms, came in for praise from Mathews for his instrumental part in drafting state laws governing children. Second, Mathews suggested Klansman Royal Graham, Lindsey's election opponent.

Mathews, along with a number of bureau advisers, feared she too might face Klan hostility. The future of the bureau was briefly uncertain, given the House bill to create a new Klan-controlled department of maternity.

Superintendent of education Mary Bradford advised CWB board members to "do as little lobbying as possible" and maintain a low profile during the Klan legislative session. Child Welfare Bureau member Emily Griffith urged colleagues to "work quietly and not give the Bureau too much prominence."[61] Members feared that state matching grants for Shepperd-Towner work might be jeopardized during the Klan-dominated legislative session. Klan legislative attacks on women's welfare agencies put clubwomen and their government allies increasingly on the defensive.

Klan strong-arm tactics ultimately proved too much for Representative Martha Long to bear. In late February the clubwoman exposed the machine rule of Klan legislators in the press and announced her dismissal from the Klan. In addition to opposing the bill to abolish the state nurses' board, Long had opposed the Klan's prizefighting bill. The nurse acknowledged that her decision to join the Invisible Empire the previous fall reflected its patriotic ideals. The representative praised Governor Morley for his moving address at one massive Klan rally on Table Mountain outside Denver. But she resented the discipline that Klan representatives had enforced in the House. When she expressed her desire to vote against the bill to abolish the nursing board, even requesting an excuse from Governor Morley, the Klan whip in the House told her she had to get an excuse from Dr. Locke. Long's protests led to her dismissal from the Klan. Afterward, her bills never emerged from committee. "We must clear the [Republican] party of this control," Long pleaded. "Klan leaders are determined to control or wreck the party."[62] The Klan's male leadership did not tolerate dissent from women members. Klan opponents widely reprinted Long's confession across the state. Her defection particularly exposed Morley's subordinate position within the Klan hierarchy.

Labor protective legislation also became a casualty of the Klan. Proposals to strengthen the women's minimum-wage law and abolish the Industrial Commission, long favored by unionists, increasingly appeared suspect in light of the Klan agenda. Women's club and union leaders had advocated a tougher women's minimum-wage law for more than a decade. A Klan-backed bill introduced by Josie Jackson and Louise Patterson in the House would have established new penalties for violations and transferred responsibility for enforcement of the law from the Industrial Commission to the Bureau of Labor Statistics. Yet the direction of the labor bureau had taken a worrisome turn under Klan rule. Labor commissioner and Klan leader Carl De Lochte had led the heckling of Van Cise the previous fall and approved a recent decision by the Klan-backed secretary of state to rely on convict labor to manufacture auto license plates. The labor commissioner was also a regular speaker before the women's KKK organization. Klan opponents in the legislature claimed that the women's minimum-wage bill would "set up Carl De Lochte as a sub-

THE COLORADO KLAN AND THE DECLINE OF PROGRESSIVISM

limated stepmother of all the employed women and children of the state." Women's club leaders refused to back the bill.[63]

The minimum-wage bill also fit with a larger Klan vision of subsuming the state's labor agencies, charged with enforcing women's labor protections, under its masculine political machine. Although the state labor federation had long called for the elimination of the Industrial Commission, union leaders now urged anti-Klan representatives to defeat the House labor bills. Democrats, taking up the union concerns, expressed their opposition to both bills, arguing that they would create a "labor czar" with more power than the governor. After Democratic legislators hurled "aspersions and recriminations and almost everything but bricks," observed a reporter, Klan Republicans did secure passage of the bill to abolish the Industrial Commission. An anti-Klan majority in the Senate, however, voted to kill the measure before it could reach Governor Morley.[64] Long-standing union hopes to end the coercive power of the Industrial Commission became fatally entangled in the Klan's drive for control over the state bureaucracy.

On one Progressive measure, the direct primary, the Klan affirmed the hopes of clubwomen and trade unionists. Anti-Klan Republican John Holmberg had introduced a bill abolishing the direct primary in the House. Machine Democrats and Klan opponents within the GOP worked together to pass the bill in both houses of the General Assembly. With support for the primary among the Klan rank and file, Governor Morley vetoed the bill and spared the primary system for future elections.[65] That veto offered a moment of relief for clubwoman and unionists.

In Denver too, Klan aldermen had also cynically deployed Progressive tools in hopes of expanding power. After the City Council election of May 1925, six of nine aldermen had Klan connections, including two railroad unionists. Frustrated by Mayor Stapleton's growing independence from the Hooded Order, Klan councilmembers first called for yet another recall of the mayor and then proposed replacing him with a city manager. Denver labor leaders were among the chief opponents of these Klan schemes. Once again, the Klan manipulated the tools of Progressive reform in hopes of building their machine. The recall and city manager proposals met with quick defeat in the courts.[66]

Although labor and women Progressives had largely opposed Klan legislators in the City Council and the General Assembly, the Senate proved the institution of last resistance to the Invisible Empire. The veteran senator Billy Adams emerged as a popular anti-Klan hero by the end of the legislative session. Adams had pledged early on to prevent the elimination of health agencies and "the enactment of freak medical legislation." He led an anti-statist conservative faction in the Senate. When the legislature adjourned, only one of Morley's restructuring proposals awaited his signature—that abolishing the defunct board of horseshoe examiners. Klan Republicans in the House had not even brought the anti–sacramental wine bill out of committee. Nonetheless, Morley slashed funding for the Board of Health and other agencies beyond Klan control.[67]

Klan legislative failure was followed by scandal. Governor Morley's personal secretary and other Klan leaders were indicted for mail fraud in April 1925. In May, Grand Dragon Locke faced charges of tax evasion. When he refused to comply with court orders to submit his financial records for review by tax examiners, Locke was sentenced to ten days in county jail in June. Given rapid defections from the ranks of the Colorado Klan in light of these setbacks, Imperial Wizard Hiram Evans asked Locke to step down on June 30. Locke quickly organized a new organization, the Minute Men of America, and attempted to lure away the state's Klansman. This revolt merely hastened the decline of the Colorado Klan.[68]

THE WOMEN'S KLAN CHALLENGE

With division and dissent undermining the prospects of Colorado Klansmen, women members of the Hooded Order gained new public recognition in the summer and fall of 1925. Led by Denver Woman's Club member Laurena Senter, the women's Klan organization in Colorado had struggled to project a maternal image within an organization dominated by theatrical displays of masculinity. In late 1924, Senter led the effort to create the Women of the Ku Klux Klan, officially devoted to promoting law and order, patriotism, and charitable work. On August 8, 1925, an estimated 10,000 Klanswomen from some thirty local units across the state paraded through Arvada to coincide with the national Klan march in Washington, DC. Although robed and hooded, the women marched unmasked or rode on floats decorated with flags and bunting. Bearing banners that read "Peace," "Spirit of '76," and "Little Red Schoolhouse," the Klanswomen cultivated a less aggressive image than male Klan leaders, one stressing patriotic motherhood (Figure 6.3).[69]

Although the extent of women's club participation in the Klan remains uncertain, there were likely a significant number of wives of Denver's small-business owners and skilled laborers who followed Senter into the organization.[70] Other club members, like Martha Long, may have been drawn to the Klan given its emphasis on law and order and patriotic appeals. The Klan's attack on the welfare agencies of state government undermined any enduring support from women's club members.

Anti-Catholicism continued to define the Klan women's order as it had the men's. Colorado Klanswomen proposed to create a home-school for Protestant orphans and even adopted orphan "Little Richard," who became the "Klan Baby" in order to prevent his adoption by a Catholic family. Baby Richard

6.3. *Ku Klux Klan – Ladies' Auxiliary* (DENVER POST, AUGUST 10, 1925, DENVER PUBLIC LIBRARY, WESTERN HISTORY COLLECTION, X-21548)

appeared in a *Denver Post* montage of the women's Klan activities that fall (Figure 6.4). The photograph showed Klan women preparing Thanksgiving baskets for the deserving Protestant poor in November 1925. Laurena Senter was pictured in the top image on the left, checking off the names of intended recipients.

As with Klanswomen in Indiana, Colorado members focused their energies on Protestant charity efforts and boycotts of Catholic or Jewish businesses. Although Minnie Love would lead a splinter group of Klanswomen into a Minute Women's organization in the fall of 1925, Senter continued to preside over a small group of women followers into the 1940s.[71] Klan women in the summer and fall of 1925 offered a brief foil to the aggressively masculine posturing of Locke and other male leaders. But as a political force, the Colorado Klan was clearly on the wane.

Declining in late 1925 and 1926, the Colorado Klan nonetheless left a distinctive mark on the state's politics. Support for the state's direct primary law, which had allowed the Klan capture of the Republican Party, eroded. More broadly, enthusiasm for political crusades informed by Protestant moralizing faded significantly. Although the Klan threatened to establish a corrupt, masculine political machine in the statehouse, Protestant opponents did not attempt to counter this challenge with new structural innovations in state

6.4. *Ku Klux Klan Montage* (*DENVER POST*, NOVEMBER 26, 1925, DENVER PUBLIC LIBRARY, WESTERN HISTORY COLLECTION, X-21540)

government. Labor and women's club leaders grew increasingly concerned about the coercive power of state government. Anti-statist conservatives, promising to reduce taxes and cut government programs, enjoyed a new legitimacy. The political success of Democratic state senator Billy Adams offers a telling example.

BILLY ADAMS, THE UNLIKELY POLITICAL HERO

After his failures in the legislature and Klan scandals in the summer of 1925, Governor Morley sat out a largely ineffective term in office. When the Republican state convention met in the summer of 1926 with anti-Klan delegates in control, Morley was not even nominated for a second term. The Colorado GOP instead turned to an earlier leader, Colorado Springs businessman Oliver Shoup, to revive the party. Shoup promptly denounced the Klan and pledged to restore order to state government. The Democrats convinced Billy Adams to head their ticket. A rancher from Conejos County, Adams served as mayor of Alamosa, county commissioner, and state representative before his election to the state Senate in 1888. He served continuously in the Senate until his election as governor in 1926. In his many years in the legislature, he introduced only one bill, to establish the Alamosa State Normal School. Although a Democrat, Adams regularly faced criticism for his ties to the coal operators in southern Colorado and their bipartisan political machine. By the early 1900s, he had become a formidable figure in the legislature, regularly leading Senate Democrats as either the minority or majority party.[72] In 1926, his conservative credentials and defiance of the Klan greatly appealed to Colorado voters.

Although labor leaders initially hoped for a different Democratic candidate, they gradually came to embrace Adams as the candidate most likely to defeat Shoup. The campaign turned particularly on Shoup's earlier handling of coal strikes and his support for the state Rangers. Labor editor Palmer acknowledged that Adams was a "thoroughly conservative, machine politician" but Shoup was "even worse." The Republican had brought the "worst days of the Colorado Rangers upon us. . . . Every citizen was subject to insult and even robbery by the gang of armed thugs who intimidated the state." In late August, a state labor political committee endorsed Adams and urged workers to support him. Union leaders also backed former Democratic governor Sweet's bid for a US Senate seat. The *Denver Post* editor Gustin attempted to revive long-standing suspicions that Adams was but a corporate stooge. Union leaders largely rejected the charges. Adams and Sweet at least promised industrial peace, insisted Palmer. Shoup stood for "industrial war" at the hands of the Rangers. By October, Shoup appeared more and more in the labor press as a "militant tyrant." Billy Adams, by contrast, was a "careful, conscientious, square, conservative, against whom no employer in the state can raise the question of 'dangerous' or revolutionary ideas — a man who will give capital and labor just as nearly as impartial, square deal as" possible. Adams's pledge to repeal the state constabulary law generated additional enthusiasm in labor circles.[73]

Although women's club leaders did not openly endorse candidates for governor, they too focused attention on conservative themes of reducing taxes and cutting waste in state government in these years. The *Colorado Club Woman* urged members to support those clubwomen running for the legislature, including ex-Klanswoman Martha Long and women's federation Legislative Council chair Annah Pettee. In their campaign ads in women's magazines, these Republican candidates stressed particularly their commitments to efficiency, economy, and lower taxes. At its annual convention in the fall of 1926, women's federation delegates also affirmed their faith in "the family as the basic unit of society," acknowledging the "physical and financial disabilities voluntarily assumed by women who become wives and mothers" but insisting on "the duty or protection and support also voluntarily assumed by men who become husbands and fathers." The state federation again denounced the ERA. In the late 1920s, debates about economy in government assumed more prominence in Legislative Council meetings than social welfare legislation.[74] Although Frances Wayne had complained nearly a decade earlier about the obstructionist "Adams blight" that thwarted clubwomen's reform agenda in the state Senate, few leaders voiced concerns over his gubernatorial bid in the fall of 1926.[75]

Voters went to the polls on November 2 and elected Adams by a margin of 67,000 votes in an otherwise Republican landslide. Women's club leaders Martha Long and Annah Pettee assumed seats in the state House with the Republican majority. In his inaugural address, Adams pledged to work harmoniously with the legislature in order to reduce tax burdens and curb "extravagance" in state government. Second among his proposals was the repeal of the state Ranger law, followed by a promise to work for "the preservation of industrial peace on terms agreeable and profitable both to employer and employe[e]." His address included little mention of welfare bureaucracies excepting his plea for economy in state government.[76] The consistent advocate of limited government revealed no moral fervor for political change. Adams had set the tone for his administration.

Colorado's economic woes had begun to adversely affect state tax revenues. Agriculture and mining had suffered a steady decline throughout much of the decade in Colorado, as across much of the Mountain West. The early 1920s brought a swift fall in grain and livestock prices. Demands for industrial metals dropped precipitously. Because so much of the state's manufacturing was devoted to processing foodstuffs and minerals, industrial workers also suffered. A number of smelters closed as metal prices fell. State population growth slowed dramatically during the 1920s.[77] Adams offered fiscal conservatism and cautious restraint in response to the declining economic fortunes of the state.

The 1927 legislature initially proved a disappointment for labor and women's club leaders. Pressure to legalize boxing, which the Klan had intensified, at last bore fruit, over union and women's club objections. Despite his opposition to new state spending, Adams signed into law a measure to create a state boxing commission. The new law specified that matches should be supervised and managed by veterans who had received such training during World War I to help reduce riots and fights that might break out in the audience. Bills to ratify the child labor amendment and boost workmen's compensation failed. Labor leaders did praise Governor Adams for appointing a union member, pressman William Young, to the state Industrial Commission. And in late March, the legislature unanimously approved a bill to repeal the hated Ranger law. Adams signed the bill into law surrounded by a host of state labor leaders.[78] The governor's eagerness to trim government costs dovetailed with union demands to limit the coercive power of the state.

ADAMS AND INDUSTRIAL WARFARE

The growing frustration of the state's coal miners undermined Adams's attempt to scale back government and maintain industrial peace. Colorado coal mines were not immune to the depressive conditions that plagued the industry nationwide during the 1920s. Oversupply continued to drive down prices and wages. Throughout the decade, the Colorado Fuel and Iron Company maintained its policy of harassing organizers from the United Mine Workers of America and promoted its company union instead. In 1927, organizers from the Industrial Workers of the World (IWW) began mobilizing ethnically diverse miners in both northern and southern coalfields. IWW leaders notified the Colorado Industrial Commission and then led a statewide strike in October to demand increased wages and improved working conditions.

This move initially embarrassed the commissioners. In September the commission had begun investigations and insisted that there would be no strike. Following the walkout, they urged the governor to uphold a state ban on picketing. Leading the commission was Progressive activist and former Sweet campaign manager Thomas Annear. As the state's leading administrative Progressive, Chairman Annear refused to recognize the IWW, labeling it an "illegal, un-American organization." Fellow commissioner William Young asserted that the IWW-led strike was illegal. Yet after the first month, Chairman Annear declared it "the most peaceful strike the State ever saw." IWW organizers led picketing and protests outside those mines staffed by strikebreakers. Having repealed the state police law just six months before, Governor Adams decided to revive a prohibition "law enforcement" force to stop picketing at Colorado Fuel and Iron Company mines in southern Colorado. This new Law Enforcement Department harassed IWW organizers and mine workers in southern Colorado. Governor Adams used a prohibition enforcement squad to replace the hated Rangers.[79]

Despite peaceful protests and pickets in the northern coalfields, the prohibition police forced a confrontation with strikers on November 21 at the Columbine Mine in the company town of Serene. The presence of industrial commissioner Annear on the scene did little to promote peace. Attempting to disband the picketing strikers assembled at the main gates of the mine, the state police force shot and killed six workers, injuring dozens more. Two months later the state police force shot two more strikers in Walsenburg. After the massacre at Columbine Mine, Adams promptly mobilized the National Guard and declared a state of insurrection, even though the protesters were the victims of state violence. The Industrial Commission continued to hold hearings across the state, exposing the miserable working conditions in coal mines, and eventually supported worker demands for wage increases, which mine operators ignored.[80] Although Adams had officially urged operators to negotiate with the striking workers, he also re-created a state police force under the direction of long-time union foes. Administrative Progressives within the Industrial Commission were once again unable to avert violence against striking workers.

The coal strike of 1927–1928 highlighted the ethnic diversity of the state's working population and the narrowed vision of labor Progressives. Although labor editors gradually conceded that the IWW had adroitly handled the strike, they joined United Mine Worker leaders in insisting that the radical union was "out of sympathy with the public" and not the "bona fide" representative of the coal miners.[81] Their focus on the needs of skilled workers of northwestern European descent, evident also during the recent Klan surge, appeared increasingly marginal in the face of the dynamic and democratic activism of IWW organizers. With the state's workers fragmented and state agencies hostile to most union goals, labor leaders largely abandoned the state's most diverse workers. This decision damaged prospects for challenging Governor Adams and the state's administrative Progressives.

For his part, Governor Adams continued to insist on reducing government costs and cutting taxes. With little in the way of an alternative, union leaders gave him their support. When he again ran for office in 1928, the state labor federation endorsed Adams for his economy, attempts to lower taxes, and "honest application of state affairs." The state federation did not mention his complicity in the Columbine Massacre. Adams faced William Boatright, a Republican attorney general tainted by his declaration as state attorney general that the IWW strike had been illegal. Even Republicans displayed little excitement about Boatright's bid. During the campaign, Adams refused to campaign actively but let Democratic and even some Republican Party leaders promote his two-year record as governor. On the eve of the election, Adams retreated to his ranch near Alamosa. The *Denver Post*, now enthusiastic about Adams, reported that the governor wanted to immerse "himself in the work he loves best" — riding his "cow pony" around his ranch to inspect his cattle. From there Adams awaited news from the polls.[82]

Easily reelected as governor, Adams again renewed calls for fiscal restraint. In his inaugural address, the governor's leading demand was that the legislature "keep its appropriations within the income of the state." During their 1929 session, legislators rejected most women's club proposals, including one to sterilize the mentally ill and another to abolish capital punishment. Bills that would increase state appropriations, like a measure to raise the salary of the state public school superintendent or another to create a small claims court, not surprisingly failed as well. Women's club leaders joined unionists in condemning an anti-syndicalism bill, successfully halting this expansion of the state's coercive powers. Union and women's club members in the state legislature also narrowly defeated a bill to repeal the direct primary law. The primary system, insisted labor and women's club leaders alike, remained the most promising political opportunity for outside challenges to party elites.[83] Yet many Colorado voters had lost faith in the promise of the primary as a tool for challenging corporate influence in politics. The conservative factions in both parties retained a commanding hold over their respective organizations on the eve of the Great Depression.

In 1930, Billy Adams was elected to a record third term as governor. His tenure as state executive signaled a decisive end to hopes for a Progressive reform of politics. Adams led an anti-statist reaction to the Klan and retreated from the heady visions of political reform that had guided women's club and union leaders in the 1900s and 1910s. Although the direct primary survived repeated legislative challenges, the two-party system remained under conservative rule. Calls for efficiency and economy in government replaced demands for state interventions to protect mothers and children and to promote economic justice. Labor leaders hoped to restrain the coercive power of the state by abolishing the state police, limiting the authority of the Industrial Commission, ending injunctions against strikes, and preventing passage of an anti-syndicalism bill. Yet the coal strike of 1927–1928 revealed that workers remained fragmented and state power could easily be mobilized against striking miners. Adams took limited government only so far.

The success of this conservative governor offers a striking contrast to the setbacks endured by Progressive champion Ben Lindsey in the late 1920s. The two had long dominated the state's political landscape. As men of short stature, both sought to project an image of assertive manhood. Adams regularly wore the cowboy hat and boots of the independent western cattleman. Lindsey, by contrast, idolized Theodore Roosevelt and sought to make the battle for social reform a legitimate manly struggle. The two resisted and discredited the Klan, with Lindsey continuing his tradition of exposé to label Klan conspiracies and Adams quietly killing Klan bills in the Senate. Yet in 1927, Lindsey suffered a major defeat. The Colorado Supreme Court finally ruled on Klansman Royal Graham's appeal of Lindsey's 1924 election. The court sided with Graham and ousted Lindsey after nearly thirty years on the bench. Graham had committed suicide in the intervening years, yet his widow pressed his appeal in hopes of claiming the salary he would have received on the bench had he won outright in 1924.[84]

In 1929, the same court disbarred Lindsey for violating a law that prevented judges from advising clients as an attorney. The client in question was a wealthy widow whose estranged husband had disinherited their minor children. Lindsey's intervention in the case had secured the children a fair share of their deceased father's estate. Chief Justice Greeley Whitford, formerly responsible for jailing striking tramway workers, turned the language of moral indignation against Lindsey and ordered his disbarment for corrupt, untrustworthy conduct on the bench.[85] Long a target of Lindsey's condemnations of corporate distortions of state politics, Whitford evened the score. Colorado clubwomen and unionists lost a nationally recognized defender of children's rights and welfare agencies. Adams would frame the political debate about state government largely unchallenged, as union and women's club leaders increasingly adapted to conservative rule.

Epilogue

The Progressive Legacy

Colorado Progressives left a complicated and unfinished legacy: demands that government officials curb prostitution, gambling, and alcohol use while easing burdens on taxpayers; a faith that class conflict could be resolved through scientific investigation despite repeated outbreaks of labor war; and a growing uncertainty about government interventions and concentrated authority in the hands of experts. Protestant reformers and those appealing to church-going voters reified a potent opposition between the vulnerable, respectable citizen and the threatening masculine world of the urban party machine. The link between Protestant morality and reform unexpectedly helped the Ku Klux Klan in Colorado achieve political successes in ways that eastern cities, with their greater ethnic and religious diversity, did not experience. This ambivalent legacy would shape perceptions of the New Deal in Colorado.

With moral crusades largely discredited after the Klan, Progressive reformers had at least convinced Colorado voters of the importance of economy in government. Governor Billy Adams won three elections largely on his efforts to reduce government spending without raising taxes. Confronting a budget deficit upon assuming office in 1927, Adams pressured state agencies to cut expenses. Erasing the deficit in his second term, Adams nurtured a state surplus as he began his third term in 1931. He blamed worsening economic conditions chiefly on "excessive taxes."[1]

After his late 1920s defeats in Colorado, Ben Lindsey moved to California and continued his crusade for juvenile courts. The judge received consoling letters from many, including muckraker Lincoln Steffens. The disbarment, Steffens wrote to Lindsey, "bears out all that you have said of the court itself and of the conditions in Colorado. If you were sincere in your exposures, you cannot be astonished and hurt by the way things are running true to form. . . . The beast has got you."[2]

The Beast had checked Progressive hopes for redefining male citizenship as well. By 1930, Colorado politicians were no longer linking calls for reform with a defense of honorable, restrained manhood. Union men, who with women Progressives had earlier sought state protections for vulnerable miners, now evinced a fear of state power. Strikebreaking guards and state militiamen had paraded their aggressive masculine prowess with the backing of political authorities in bitter labor confrontations over the previous thirty years. With the press, the pulpits, and the unions no longer promoting an alternative manhood grounded in political reform, social responsibility, and honest public service, Lindsey's exodus was a significant loss. Billy Adams, with his stress on individualism and limited government, remained.

Thus, Colorado confronted the Great Depression and Dust Bowl crisis under the leadership of fiscal conservatives concerned mainly with balancing the budget. Democratic governor Edwin "Big Ed" Johnson replaced Billy Adams in 1932, and he maintained his predecessor's zeal for limited government spending. In that year's election, Johnson received 7,000 more votes for governor than Franklin Roosevelt did for president. A successful rancher from Craig, Johnson had served in the state legislature and as lieutenant governor before his run for governor. As a former football player and Mason, Lion, and Elk, Big Ed projected a masculine image not unfamiliar to Colorado voters. Organized labor supported both Adams and Johnson in these years given few alternatives. Workers approved Johnson's efforts to end the use of court injunctions to limit striking. And Johnson was a member of the Telegraphers' Union. The new Colorado governor persuaded the legislature to reorganize the administrative structure of state government, which centralized budgeting authority in the hands of a new executive council. Johnson then ensured that the legislature maintained a balanced budget.[3]

The political successes of Adams and Johnson in the 1930s significantly reflected worker frustrations with administrative Progressivism. Envisioned as a partner to prohibition, the Colorado Industrial Commission had promised to arbitrate class conflicts to secure industrial peace and an uninterrupted supply of consumer goods and services. Over the 1920s it protected consumers at the expense of worker rights. Commissioners had chiefly undermined worker protests but rarely challenged employer prerogatives to determine wage and working conditions. Despite public relations campaigns on behalf of this western experiment, Colorado leaders, like their counterparts in Kansas, could not convince other states to follow suit. Union leaders in the 1920s came to view administrative reforms designed to protect the consuming public as inherently hostile to worker interests.

Worker experiences with state mediation and anti-strike interventions reveal the importance of the West in understanding labor politics in the 1920s. Experiments in compulsory state mediation began in this region on the geographic margins of national struggles in coal mining, meatpacking, and railroads. National trade agreements in coal and meatpacking took only limited hold here. As a result of the coercive movement for state mediation with its narrow definition of the public, workers in these western states developed political tactics less in terms of class-based, independent action than a broad appeal to the public.[4] Labor leaders attempted to convince farmers and the urban middle classes of the dangers of such coercive state interventions in the marketplace. Abandoning proposals to expand state protections for workers, many union workers preferred government retreat in Colorado. Governors Adams and Johnson certainly offered a program of more limited state government.

Still, the New Deal did create some opportunities for labor Progressives in Colorado. Edward Costigan assumed new political influence in these years. After more than a decade as a tariff commissioner in Washington DC, Costigan returned to Colorado in 1928 to challenge the political establishment. Running for the US Senate as a Democrat with broad union and women's club support two years later, Costigan promised to promote labor Progressive goals such as limits to injunctions against striking and the union right to organize. Moral reforms no longer dominated his agenda. Easily elected to office, Costigan introduced an anti-lynching bill and one for unemployment relief. He became a champion of New Deal initiatives in the state. Costigan soon confronted a hostile Governor Johnson, who remained committed to fiscal conservatism and suspicious of the New Deal. The Costigan-Johnson feud also highlighted another success of Progressive reformers: although both men were Democrats, parties mattered less than candidates. Personalities assumed more importance than platforms or party organization in the 1930s.

Despite his Democratic Party affiliation, Johnson emerged as a consistent New Deal opponent in his two terms as governor. In the spring of 1933 the Democratic majority in the state legislature refused to approve matching funds for federal emergency relief required under the New Deal. Johnson offered legislators little encouragement but continued to focus on limiting spending and keeping taxes low. In 1934 he declared: "We need less of government rather than more . . . and we need a curtailment and not an expansion of public service. At the rate we are going, soon half of our people will be paid to regulate the other half." While Costigan urged Coloradans to support New Deal initiatives, Johnson undermined federal leadership of the Federal Emergency Relief Administration and the National Industrial Recovery Administration. The state official charged with setting price and wage codes for the Industrial Recovery Administration was ex-governor Billy Adams.[5]

Progressives like Costigan struggled to revive the earlier coalition between unionists and clubwomen. The passage of prohibition decades earlier had driven a wedge between the two groups that was not easily removed. Although a moral victory for Protestant activists in 1914, prohibition made economic reform much more difficult. Colorado's experience here confirms that of another western locale. Seattle had witnessed a similar coalition of middle-class clubwomen and working-class activists in the years leading up to World War I. Also securing new labor legislation with their joint lobby, the Seattle coalition unraveled in the face of a bitter prohibition campaign in 1914. The Great War further divided clubwomen and unionists in Seattle.[6] In the West it seems, prohibition did not advance any meaningful challenge of corporate power in politics.

The Colorado labor-women's club alliance had instead invested almost millennial hopes in the promise of direct democracy. Spirits soared in 1912 when labor and women Progressives convinced voters to back a series of long-sought social justice reforms via the initiative. Yet just two years later, a critic of the reform observed that "the Initiative and Referendum [are] a two-edged sword." The "interests" could "avail themselves of their right to refer measures antagonistic to what they considered their best business interests, and would initiate measures which they thought would be advantageous to their organizations. These organizations of wealth d[id] not hesitate to furnish ample means for these propositions."[7] In Oregon, Robert Johnston has noted a similar potential for antidemocratic organizations like the Klan to utilize the initiative for their own ends. The political revolution that Oregon's and Colorado's middling classes assumed would follow the enactment of direct legislation simply did not materialize. The initiative did not offer Colorado Progressives in the 1930s much hope for dramatic reform.

In 1934, Johnson faced another Progressive challenge, this time from Josephine Roche. Following the massacre at the Columbine Mine in 1927, Roche assumed control of Rocky Mountain Fuel. As president of the state's second-largest coal company, Roche hired an impressive board of former Progressives: Ed Costigan, United Mine Workers organizer John Lawson, and attorney Merle Vincent. In August 1928, Rocky Mountain Fuel signed a historic contract with the United Mine Workers. The new contract raised worker wages and committed the company to collective bargaining and cooperative efforts to stabilize employment. Insisting that "capital and labor have equal rights," Roche emerged as a labor champion and sought the Democratic nomination for governor in 1934.[8]

Roche also represented the enduring potential of women's Progressivism. She began her political career as an ally of Judge Ben Lindsey and with broad support from religious Progressives. She, like so many clubwomen, backed his projects to remake male citizenship and protect women and children. Lindsey's court offered a key site for exposing urban dangers to adolescent sexuality and the domestic sphere. He and Roche shared with clubwomen a desire to police urban spaces for women and children. They focused mainly on dangers outside, rather than within, the domestic sphere.[9] Yet ultimately, women Progressives like Roche and their ally Judge Lindsey demanded social justice through limitations on corporate business and the party machine.

As the director of Rocky Mountain Fuel, Roche continued a tradition among women Progressives of forging political coalitions. Activist women in Colorado allied with male Protestant leaders at times and union men at others. In Chicago, by contrast, historian Maureen Flanagan has found that women reformers struggled unsuccessfully and largely in isolation against a patriarchal urban order. By 1930, activist Chicago women, stressing social interdependence, had not reformed a "city organized on a model of masculine individualism and striving."[10] Yet in Denver, the largely middle-class leadership of the women's club networks frequently shared with union men a vision of social interdependence. From 1910 to 1912, women and labor Progressives posed a momentary challenge to corporate dominance. Fifteen years later at Rocky Mountain Fuel, Roche sought to reform her company from the inside to align the goals of profitability with social welfare and economic justice.

Roche differed from many Colorado clubwomen, however, when it came to maternalism. Clubwomen tended to promote social justice under the auspices of motherhood. Appealing to women's club members most often as mothers, leaders did not advocate feminist citizenship. Even upon reaching elected office, clubwomen hoped to represent the maternal in politics. The problems of motherhood, especially among the working poor, received their greatest attention. Most activist women in Denver did not champion a living wage as a right for individual women per se. With only a few women's unions in the state, more radical voices rarely challenged the maternal consensus in Colorado. Roche was a consistent exception among women Progressives.

Running for governor in 1934, Roche faced an uphill battle. The Democratic Party leadership rallied behind Johnson and opposed her bid. Even Billy Adams tossed his hat into the ring, in hopes of securing the nomination. The *Denver Post* aggressively opposed Roche, painting her as a socialist. Her Progressive views aroused greater public criticism than her sex. Roche criticized Johnson for not cooperating with New Deal programs and urged a state income tax to address the desperation of the unemployed. She focused on social welfare programs and government protections for the vulnerable. But the former juvenile court referee had abandoned her earlier efforts to reform personal behavior and curb prostitution. Johnson maintained his pledge to keep taxes and government spending low. In primary balloting Roche carried Denver as well as Boulder and a few Western Slope and mountain counties. She lost to Johnson in the remaining fifty-nine counties. In conceding defeat, Roche insisted that no Progressive "battle so well and courageously fought is ever lost in the long run, and I am happy to have had a part in it."[11] In the short term, Johnson went on to defeat his Republican rival in the general election.

During the depression years the conservative outlook of Ed Johnson framed political debate in Colorado. After her defeat, Roche served in the federal Department of the Treasury and helped draft recommendations for the Social Security Act of 1935. She continued to guide Rocky Mountain Fuel until 1950. Edward Costigan decided against another run for the US Senate in 1936 and was replaced by Johnson himself, who would go on to serve there for the next eighteen years. Johnson received the lukewarm endorsement of organized labor in the fall of 1936. Union leaders backed the conservative governor even as they voted for Franklin Roosevelt. Although organized labor benefited from federal New Deal protections and modestly expanded union membership in the 1930s, Johnson set the tone.

During World War II, Johnson looked back at the New Deal as the "worst fraud ever perpetrated on the American people."[12] Federal interventions in the depression-ridden economy and social life of the state during the 1930s did not bring Colorado within the fold of a New Deal order. Rather, Johnson's popularity suggested the potential in Colorado for the grassroots conservative campaigns of the post–World War II era.

Viewed from the 1930s, it becomes clear that Colorado Progressives did not fully realize their visions. Yet theirs was not simply a story of failure. Protestant Progressives shaped a reform movement that demanded that moral standards guide politics. They linked political innovations such as the direct primary and commission government with an end to corporate manipulations of elections. Labor and women Progressives secured state protections for workers in vulnerable occupations. They sustained the Denver juvenile court, which became a model for other cities and states, along with maternal and infant health initiatives to improve the lives of women and children. Administrative Progressives launched a mediation board that at least called for employer accountability and fairness. Denver Progressives Edward Costigan and Josephine Roche assumed national positions in support of the New Deal and on behalf of the unemployed and dispossessed. Although moral goals remained unfulfilled, the social justice promises of Progressives endured.

EPILOGUE: THE PROGRESSIVE LEGACY

Notes

INTRODUCTION: THE VARIETIES OF COLORADO PROGRESSIVISM

1. Colin B. Goodykoontz, *Papers of Edward P. Costigan Relating to the Progressive Movement in Colorado, 1902–1917* (Boulder: University of Colorado, 1941), 4–7, 15–19.

2. H. B. Waters, "Initiative and Referendum," *The Official Colorado State Labor Directory and Manual* (Denver: Colorado State Federation of Labor, 1906), 36–37, Colorado State Federation of Labor (CSFL) Papers, Box 31, Archives, University of Colorado at Boulder Libraries.

3. Rheta Child Dorr, "The Women Did It in Colorado," *Hampton's Magazine* 26, no. 4 (April 1911): 434–435.

4. Colorado Industrial Commissioner William Reilly, May 1924 Speech before the Association of Government Labor Officials, quoted in the *Denver Labor Bulletin*, May 24, 1924.

5. Rev. David Fouse, First Reformed Church, and Rev. J. F. Clark, Park Hill Methodist, sermons excerpted in the *Rocky Mountain News*, May 20, 1912. George Creel in his *Rebel at Large* (New York: G. P. Putnam's Sons, 1947) and in his *Post* and *News* editorials often cast political crusades in these terms.

6. James Wright, *The Politics of Populism: Dissent in Colorado* (New Haven, CT: Yale University Press, 1974), chapter 6.

7. Harvey Garman, former CSFL president and state legislator, quoted in Carl W. McGuire, "History of the Colorado State Federation of Labor, 1896–1905," (Ph.D. diss., University of Colorado, Boulder, 1935), 63; John P. Enyeart, "'By Laws of Their Own Making': Political Culture and Everyday Politics of the Mountain West Working Class, 1870–1917," (Ph.D. diss., University of Colorado, Boulder, 2002); for an insightful analysis of nineteenth-century antipartyism among Colorado workers, see especially chapter 3.

8. Helen Ring Robinson, "The War in Colorado," *The Independent* 78 (May 11, 1914): 245.

9. Helen Ring Robinson, "On Being a Woman Senator," *The Independent* 78 (April 20, 1914): 131–32. See also the editorial "Women in Politics," *Colorado Club Woman* 2 (December 1922): 5. On maternalism and reform, see especially Molly Ladd-Taylor, *Mother-Work: Women, Child Welfare, and the State, 1890–1930* (Urbana: University of Illinois Press, 1994); Felicia A. Kornbluh, "The New Literature on Gender and the Welfare State: The U.S. Case," *Feminist Studies* 22, no. 1 (Spring 1996): 174; Theda Skocpol, *Protecting Soldiers and Mothers: The Political Origins of Social Policy in the United States* (Cambridge, MA: Harvard University Press, 1993); Lisa D. Brush, "Love, Toil, and Trouble: Motherhood and Feminist Politics," *Signs* 21 (Winter 1996): 430; Seth Koven and Sonya Michel, eds., *Mothers of a New World: Maternalist Politics and the Origins of Welfare States* (New York: Routledge, 1993).

10. Maureen Flanagan, *Seeing with Their Hearts: Chicago Women and the Vision of the Good City, 1871–1933* (Princeton, NJ: Princeton University Press, 2002). Flanagan insists that Chicago women's activism was not "solely based on maternalist impulses" (p. 78). Yet city leaders did make regular appeals in those terms. Flanagan's work illustrates the growing literature on women's Progressive activism that insists on motives beyond maternalism. See also Sarah Deutsch, *Women and the City: Gender, Space, and Power in Boston, 1870–1940* (New York: Oxford University Press, 2000), for an insightful analysis of how women forged cross-class alliances and negotiated urban spaces in this period.

11. Elizabeth Clemens argued that "because women lacked the vote" in non-suffrage states, "they were insulated from cooptation by the 'predatory' system of party politics and thus enjoyed a greater degree of organizational and cultural autonomy needed to develop and deploy a nonpartisan model of political mobilization"; *The People's Lobby: Organizational Innovation and the Rise of Interest Group Politics in the United States, 1890–1925* (Chicago: University of Chicago Press, 1997), 13. Even with the vote, Colorado women continued to operate politically with a significant degree of autonomy from the political parties. On the "organized women of the state," see "Thoughts for Your Consideration," *Colorado Club Woman* (May 1925): 5.

12. Recently Phil Goodstein has examined the influence of religious reformers in his detailed work on this period, *Robert Speer's Denver, 1904–1920* (Denver: New Social Publications, 2004). Carol M. Reese offers a nuanced review of Speer and his urban projects in "The Politician and the City: Urban Form and City Beautiful Rhetoric in Progressive Era Denver," (Ph.D. diss., University of Texas, Austin, 1992). Other important works on Colorado Progressivism include J. Paul Mitchell, "Progressivism in Denver: The Municipal Reform Movement, 1904–1916" (Ph.D. diss., University of Denver, Denver, 1966); ibid., "Boss Speer and the City Functional: Boosters and Businessmen Versus Commission Government in Denver," *Pacific Northwest Quarterly* 63, no. 4 (October 1972): 155–164; Harlan Knautz, "Progressive Harvest in Colorado: 1910–1916,"

(Ph.D. diss., University of Denver, Denver, 1969); E. Kimbark MacColl, "Progressive Legislation in Colorado, 1907–1917," (master's thesis, University of Colorado, Boulder, 1949). Reformer battles against saloons are featured in Elliot W. West, "Dry Crusade: The Prohibition Movement in Colorado, 1858–1933," (Ph.D. diss., University of Colorado, Boulder, 1971), and Thomas J. Noel, *The City and the Saloon: Denver, 1858–1916* (Lincoln: University of Nebraska Press, 1982). For analyses of Colorado labor politics in these years, see John P. Enyeart, "'By Laws of Their Own Making,'" and Harold V. Knight, *Working in Colorado: A Brief History of the Colorado Labor Movement* (Boulder: Center for Labor Education and Research, University of Colorado, 1971). Thomas Andrews, *Killing for Coal: America's Deadliest Labor War* (Cambridge, MA: Harvard University Press, 2008), views the coalfield war of 1913–1914 from an insightful environmental perspective. Recent work on Colorado clubwomen and their reform agenda includes Wendy Keefover-Ring, "Municipal Housekeeping, Domestic Science, Animal Protection, and Conservation: Women's Political Activism and Environmental Activism in Denver, Colorado, 1894–1912," (master's thesis, University of Colorado, Boulder, 2002), and Gail M. Beaton, "The Widening Sphere of Women's Lives: The Literary Study and Philanthropic Work of Six Women's Clubs in Denver, 1881–1945," *Essays in Colorado History* 13 (1992): 1–68.

13. For an overview of scholarship that stresses economic and social changes during the late nineteenth and early twentieth centuries as preconditions for political reform, see Arthur S. Link and Richard L. McCormick, *Progressivism* (Arlington Heights, IL: Harlan Davidson, 1983). Studies stressing an organizational imperative include Robert Weibe, *The Search for Order, 1877–1920* (New York: Hill and Wang, 1967); Samuel Hayes, "The Politics of Reform in Municipal Government in the Progressive Era," *Pacific Northwest Quarterly* 55 (1964): 157–169; Louis Galambos, "The Emerging Organizational Synthesis in Modern American History," *Business History Review* 44 (1970): 270–290; James Weinstein, *The Corporate Ideal in the Liberal State, 1900–1918* (Boston: Beacon Press, 1968). The literature on women's public activism in these years is vast. Representative works, in addition to those already mentioned, include Paula Baker, "The Domestication of Politics: Women and American Political Society, 1780–1920," *American Historical Review* 89 (June 1984): 620–647; Robyn Muncy, *Creating a Female Dominion in American Reform, 1890–1935* (New York: Oxford University Press, 1991); and Nancy F. Cott, *The Grounding of Modern Feminism* (New Haven, CT: Yale University Press, 1987). Finally, Daniel Rodgers has emphasized European borrowing in *Atlantic Crossings: Social Politics in a Progressive Age* (Cambridge, MA: Belknap Press, 1998).

14. Michael McGerr, *A Fierce Discontent: The Rise and Fall of the Progressive Movement in America* (New York: Oxford University Press, 2003), 79–81. See also Henry May, *Protestant Churches and Industrial America* (New York: Harper Brothers, 1949); Robert M. Crunden, *Ministers of Reform: The Progressives' Achievement in American Civilization, 1889–1920* (Urbana: University of Illinois Press, 1984).

15. Robert Johnston, *The Radical Middle Class: Populist Democracy and the Question of Capitalism in Progressive Era Portland, Oregon* (Princeton, NJ: Princeton University Press, 2003); Shelton Stromquist, *Re-Inventing the "The People": The Progressive Movement, the Class Problem, and the Origins of Modern Liberalism* (Urbana: University of Illinois Press, 2006); John P. Enyeart, "'By Laws of Their Own Making'"; Melvin G. Holli, *Reform in Detroit: Hazen Pingree and Urban Politics* (New York: Oxford University Press, 1969); Elisabeth S. Clemens, *The People's Lobby.* Older work on the working-class aspects

of Progressive reform includes John Buenker, *Urban Liberalism and Progressive Reform* (New York: Scribner's Sons, 1973).

16. On languages of reform, see especially Daniel T. Rodgers, "In Search of Progressivism," *Review in American History* 10 (1982): 123, and his *Contested Truths: Keywords in American Politics since Independence* (New York: Basic Books, 1987), 179–182; James Connolly, *The Triumph of Ethnic Progressivism: Urban Political Culture in Boston, 1900–1925* (Cambridge, MA: Harvard University Press, 1998), 8–12. Boston reformers created a new style of public action that ultimately stressed ethnic rather than class divisions. Philip J. Ethington, *The Public City: The Political Construction of Urban Life in San Francisco, 1850–1900* (Cambridge: Cambridge University Press, 1994), chapter 8.

17. Anne Hyde, "Round Pegs in Square Holes: The Rocky Mountains and Extractive Industry," in *Many Wests: Place, Culture, and Regional Identity*, ed. David Wrobel and Michael Steiner (Lawrence: University Press of Kansas, 1997), 105.

18. On business support for reform, see Hays, "The Politics of Reform in Municipal Government," 157–169; Weinstein, *The Corporate Ideal in the Liberal State*; Connolly, *Triumph of Ethnic Progressivism*, 39–47.

19. Other studies of the Klan in the 1920s have also noted its opposition to Progressive reforms. In Georgia the second Klan opposed commission government and city manager plans, given their elite sponsors. The Portland Klan was little more than a corporate tool that challenged the radical populist vision of Oregon Progressives and direct democracy in particular. Nancy MacLean, *Behind the Mask of Chivalry: The Making of the Second Ku Klux Klan* (New York: Oxford University Press, 1994), 87–89; Johnston, *Radical Middle Class*, 234–247.

CHAPTER 1: PROTESTANT PROGRESSIVES
AND THE DENVER PARTY MACHINE

1. *Denver Post*, May 24, 1902 (hereafter *Post*); Charles Larsen, *The Good Fight: The Life and Times of Ben B. Lindsey* (Chicago: Quadrangle Books, 1972), 30–32.

2. Benjamin B. Lindsey and Harvey O'Higgins, *The Beast* (New York: Doubleday, Page and Company, 1910), 8, 273.

3. David Emmons, "Constructed Province: History and the Making of the Last American West," *Western Historical Quarterly* 25 (1994): 445; James Edward Wright, *The Politics of Populism: Dissent in Colorado* (New Haven, CT: Yale University Press, 1974); Anne F. Hyde, "Round Pegs in Square Holes: The Rocky Mountains and Extractive Industry," in *Many Wests: Place, Culture, and Regional Identity*, ed. David M. Wrobel and Michael C. Steiner (Lawrence: University Press of Kansas, 1997), 105.

4. Helen L. Sumner, *Equal Suffrage: The Results of an Investigation in Colorado Made for the Collegiate Equal Suffrage League of New York State* (New York: Harper and Brothers, 1909), 66, 90; Richard White, *"It's Your Misfortune and None of My Own": A New History of the American West* (Norman: University of Oklahoma Press, 1991), 353.

5. George Creel, *Rebel at Large: Recollection of Fifty Crowded Years* (New York: G. P. Putnam's Sons, 1947), 96.

6. Wright, *The Politics of Populism*, 119, 153–157.

7. Clyde L. King, *History of the Government of Denver with Special Reference to Its Relations with Public Service Corporations* (Denver: Fisher, 1911); Phil Goodstein, *Denver from the Bottom Up* (Denver: New Social Publications, 2003), 276–282; Thomas Noel, *The*

City and the Saloon: Denver, 1858–1916 (Lincoln: University of Nebraska Press, 1982), 98–99.

8. *Post*, August 3, 1903; Lyle Dorsett, *The Queen City: A History of Denver* (Boulder: Pruett Publishing, 1977), 130.

9. *Rocky Mountain News*, September 3 and 6, 1903 (hereafter *News*). On the origins of the Christian Citizenship Union, see also Goodstein, *Robert Speer's Denver, 1904–1920: The Mile High City in the Progressive Era* (Denver: New Social Publications, 2004), 118.

10. *News*, September 4 and 18, 1903.

11. *Post*, August 4, 1903.

12. Noel, *City and the Saloon*, 99–104; Dorsett, *Queen City*, 131; Edward Keating, *The Gentleman from Colorado: A Memoir* (Denver: Sage Books, 1964), 79–83; David Brundage, *The Making of Western Labor Radicalism: Denver's Organized Workers, 1878–1905* (Urbana: University of Illinois Press, 1994), 153–154; John P. Enyeart, "'By Laws of Their Own Making': Political Culture and the Everyday Politics of the Mountain West Working Class, 1870–1917," (Ph.D. diss., University of Colorado, Boulder, 2002), chapters 3 and 4. In cities such as St. Louis, San Francisco, and Cleveland, organized labor remained less tied to urban party machines than in Denver; Gary Fink, *Labor's Search for Political Order: The Political Behavior of the Missouri Labor Movement, 1890–1940* (Columbia: University of Missouri Press, 1973); Michael Kazin, *Barons of Labor: The San Francisco Building Trades and Union Power in the Progressive Era* (Urbana: University of Illinois Press, 1987); Shelton Stromquist, "The Crucible of Class: Cleveland Politics and the Origins of Municipal Reform in the Progressive Era," *Journal of Urban History* 23 (1997): 192–220.

13. King, *History of the Government of Denver*, 304–305.

14. *News*, September 23 and 24, 1903.

15. J. Paul Mitchell, "Boss Speer and the City Functional: Boosters and Businessmen Versus Commission Government in Denver," *Pacific Northwest Quarterly* 63, no. 4 (October 1972): 157; Ed Costigan letter to Ben Lindsey, November 5, 1907, in Colin Goodykoontz, *Papers of Edward P. Costigan Relating to the Progressive Movement in Colorado, 1902–1917* (Boulder: University of Colorado, 1941), 72.

16. Keating, *Gentleman from Colorado*, 79–83.

17. Roosevelt, however, immersed himself in the plebian world of Manhattan's Republican clubs with its emphasis on physicality and muscular prowess, only to later distance himself from its traditional rites of camaraderie and loyalty. Lindsey never felt at home in the world and was from the first a harsh critic. On Roosevelt and Progressive reform, see Arnoldo Testi, "Gender of Reform Politics: Theodore Roosevelt and the Culture of Masculinity," *Journal of American History*, 81 (March 1995): 1509–1533. For similar comment about Roosevelt's efforts to reinvigorate politics for middle-class men by cultivating a rough, working-class masculinity, see Gail Bederman, *Manliness and Civilization: A Cultural History of Gender and Race in the United States, 1880–1917* (Chicago: University of Chicago Press, 1995).

18. Lindsey quoted in Larsen, *The Good Fight*, 9.

19. Jane Addams, *Democracy and Social Ethics* (New York: Macmillan, 1905), 268, cited in Testi, "Gender of Reform Politics," 1528.

20. Lindsey and O'Higgins, *The Beast*, 161. Lindsey described one example in which the "savages," as he often referred to them, were cut loose by their "unnatural parents."

In the fall 1904 elections, Lindsey alleged, corporate leaders favored the Republican ticket and instructed Mayor Speer to ensure that his Democratic ward heelers did not stuff the ballot boxes. Yet true to party loyalty, the savages ignored Speer's order and elected the Democratic ticket. The Republicans initiated court action, accusing the Democrats of fraud. Uncharacteristically, the state court found the Democratic ward heelers guilty and sentenced them to brief jail terms. Lindsey's visit to their jail cells found them tearfully indignant. "They were like a family of 'bad' boys," Lindsey wrote, "who had been taught by their father to steal for him and had been handed over to the police by their unnatural parent when they stole for themselves!" (ibid., 163).

21. Lincoln Steffens, *Upbuilders* (Seattle: University of Washington Press, 1968), 125, 98. Newspaper editor and reformer George Creel even accused middle-class men of "prostitution" to machine politics; George Creel, "Denver Triumphant," *Everybody's Magazine* (1912): 315.

22. *News*, May 18, 1904.

23. Brundage, *Making of Western Labor Radicalism*, 53–76, 86.

24. George Graham Suggs Jr., "Colorado Conservatives Versus Organized Labor: A Study of the James Hamilton Peabody Administration, 1903–1095," (Ph.D. diss., University of Colorado, Boulder, 1964); Brundage, *Making of Western Labor Radicalism*, chapter 6.

25. Colorado Labor Council, *Proceedings of mass Convention of Organized Labor in Colorado* (Denver: n.p., 1904) 4, quoted in Wright, *Politics of Populism*, 239.

26. George Suggs, "Religion and Labor in the Rocky Mountain West: Bishop Nichols C. Matz and the Western Federation of Miners," *Labor History* 11 (Spring 1970): 195, 200.

27. Goodstein, *Robert Speer's Denver*, 138, 233–235; Brundage, *Making of Western Labor Radicalism*, 142–148.

28. Brundage, *Making of Western Labor Radicalism*, 144–145. For comparative data on Denver workers in small firms, see Robert Johnston, *The Radical Middle Class: Populist Democracy and the Question of Capitalism in Progressive Era Portland, Oregon* (Princeton, NJ: Princeton University Press, 2003), 286–288. Printer W. H. Montgomery was among the most outspoken opponents of the WFM and also a consistent Speer backer during the 1910s.

29. Wright, *Politics of Populism*, 243–249.

30. Speer, "Address to Councilmen and Businessmen," January 7, 1907, reprinted in the *Post*, January 8 and 9, 1907.

31. Mitchell, "Boss Speer," 160.

32. On the importance of commercial elites for commission government reform in such cities, see Samuel Hays, "The Politics of Reform in Municipal Government in the Progressive Era," *Pacific Northwest Quarterly* 55 (1964): 157–169, and James Weinstein, *The Corporate Ideal in the Liberal State, 1900–1918* (Boston: Beacon Press, 1968), 92–116.

33. *Post*, May 2, 1908.

34. Ibid., April 28 and May 2, 1908.

35. Ibid., May 8 and 11, 1908.

36. Lindsey and O'Higgins, *The Beast*, 307–308.

37. *United Labor Bulletin*, November 3, 1910, CSFL Collection, Colorado Historical Society, Denver; *Convention Proceedings of the Colorado State Federation of Labor, 1907*, 14–15, CSFL Papers, Box 27, Archives, University of Colorado at Boulder Libraries;

Post, April 26, May 3 and 11, 1908. Despite the proposals of the state labor and building trades declarations of political solidarity, some local unions were divided by Speer and his machine. Printers were especially divided. Several, including Otto Thum and James Conkle, had developed ties to the Protestant Progressives, even as others backed Speer. Denver pressmen also challenged the CSFL labor ticket; Denver Typographical Union Minutes (May 3, 1908), Archives, University of Colorado at Boulder Libraries. See also *News*, May 4, 1908; *Post*, May 11, 1908; Noel, *City and the Saloon*, 100–103.

38. Elliot W. West, "Cleansing the Queen City: Prohibition and Urban Reform in Denver," *Arizona and the West* 14 (Winter 1974): 335–336.

39. West, "Cleansing the Queen City," 337–338; Keating, *Gentleman from Colorado*, 109, 387, 392.

40. Rev. Robert Coyle and Rev. David Fouse, quoted in *News*, May 11, 1908.

41. West, "Cleansing the Queen City," 338.

42. *News*, May 12 and 17, 1908.

43. On municipal housekeeping campaigns by Denver clubwomen in these years, see Wendy Keefover-Ring, "Municipal Housekeeping, Domestic Science, Animal Protection, and Conservation: Women's Political Activism and Environmental Activism in Denver, Colorado, 1894–1912" (master's thesis, University of Colorado, Boulder, 2002), 70–73; on settlement house leaders like Jane Addams and their opposition to party machines, see Theda Skocpol, *Protecting Soldiers and Mothers: The Political Origins of Social Policy in the United States* (Cambridge, MA: Harvard University Press, 1993), 355–361.

44. Walter Dixon, quoted in *Post*, May 16, 1908.

45. *News*, April 27 and May 3, 1908.

46. *Post*, May 20, 1908.

47. Editorial on June 2, 1908, quoted in Mitchell, "Boss Speer," 161.

48. *News*, May 20, 1908.

49. Ibid.

50. Ibid., May 1, 1906.

51. J. Paul Mitchell, "Progressivism in Denver: The Municipal Reform Movement, 1904–1916" (Ph.D. diss., University of Denver, Denver, 1966), 87–91.

52. Goodstein, *Robert Speer's Denver*, 42–46, 87–88; *News*, May 8, 1906.

53. *News*, May 20, 1906.

54. Ibid., May 22, 1906.

55. Jeanne Varnell, "Sarah Sophia Chase Platt-Decker," in *Women of Consequence: The Colorado Women's Hall of Fame* (Boulder: Johnson Books, 1999), 58–61. Decker quoted by Mary Bradford in Colorado Federation of Women's Clubs, *Yearbook, 1914–1915*, 41, in Colorado Federation of Women's Club Collection, Box 1, Archives, University of Colorado at Boulder Libraries. For a comparison between Decker and Addams, see Frances Wayne's obituary for Decker, *Post*, July 8, 1912. On settlement house women and their support for civil service, see Skocpol, *Protecting Soldiers and Mothers*, 355–356.

56. *News*, May 23, 1910.

57. For example, Thum organized the visit of Social Gospel minister Charles Stelzle to Denver. A labor advocate of temperance, Thum was among the organizers welcoming the union machinist turned minister, who spoke to the packed Municipal Auditorium in May 1909; *News*, May 24, 1909. See also Denver Typographical Union Minutes (May 2, 1909), Archives, University of Colorado at Boulder Libraries.

58. *United Labor Bulletin*, December 3, 17, and 24, 1910, CSFL Collection, Colorado Historical Society, Denver; Mitchell, *Progressivism*, 181–185.

59. *United Labor Bulletin*, January 21, 1910, CSFL Collection, Colorado Historical Society, Denver; Mitchell, *Progressivism*, 188–191.

60. *United Labor Bulletin*, November 19, December 24, 1909; April 15, May 5 and 12, 1910, CSFL Collection, Colorado Historical Society, Denver.

61. *News*, May 23, 1910.

62. Goodstein, *Robert Speer's Denver*, 164–166, 73.

63. Mitchell, *Progressivism*, 221–222.

64. Goodstein, *Robert Speer's Denver*, 173–74.

65. *News*, December 18, 1911.

66. *Denver Express*, December 16, 1911, quoted in Mitchell, *Progressivism*, 266.

67. Creel, *Rebel at Large*, 100.

68. *News*, December 18 and May 10, 1912.

69. Ibid., May 13 and 20, 1912.

70. Goodstein, *Robert Speer's Denver*, 201–202; Mitchell, *Progressivism*, 277.

71. *Denver Express*, May 9, 1912, quoted in Mitchell, *Progressivism*, 283; *News*, May 10, 1912.

72. Mitchell, *Progressivism*, 284–287; Creel articles in the *News*, May 22 and 23, 1912.

73. *News*, May 22, 1912.

74. Goodstein, *Robert Speer's Denver*, 252–256; Elinor McGinn, *A Wide-Awake Woman: Josephine Roche in the Era of Reform* (Denver: Colorado Historical Society, 2002), 20–23.

75. *News*, April 26 and 30, 1913; McGinn, *A Wide-Awake Woman*, 23–25.

76. *News*, May 22, 1912.

CHAPTER 2: PUBLIC ENEMY: COLORADO FUEL AND IRON OR THE SALOON?

1. "A Kentucky colonel" overheard by Helen Ring Robinson, *Rocky Mountain News* (hereafter *News*), July 9, 1908. See also *News*, October 31, 1908. The charismatic Sarah Platt Decker served as president of both the Woman's Bryan Club and the General Federation of Women's Clubs that year. On Bryan as a "godly insurgent," see Michael Kazin, *A Godly Hero: The Life of William Jennings Bryan* (New York: Knopf, 2006). On AFL support for Bryan, see Julie Greene, *Pure and Simple Politics: The American Federation of Labor and Political Activism, 1881–1917* (Cambridge: Cambridge University Press, 1998), chapter 5.

2. Daniel A Smith and Joseph Lubinski, "Direct Democracy during the Progressive Era: A Crack in the Populist Veneer?" *Journal of Policy History* 14, no. 4 (2002): 353.

3. Historian Gary Fink has found that Missouri State Federation of Labor leaders were similarly inspired by the promise of these reforms; Fink, *Labor's Search for Political Order: The Political Behavior of the Missouri Labor Movement, 1890–1940* (Columbia: University of Missouri Press, 1973), 34.

4. On the worker agitation for hours law in the Rocky Mountain West, see David L. Lonsdale, "The Movement for an Eight-Hour Law in Colorado, 1893–1913," (Ph.D. diss., University of Colorado, Boulder, 1963); John Enyeart, " 'By Laws of Their Own Making': Political Culture and the Everyday Politics of the Mountain West Working

Class, 1870–1917," (Ph.D. diss., University of Colorado, Boulder, 2002). The experience of the Mountain West with protective labor laws thus differs from that in other parts of the country. Several scholars have argued that gender-based legislation posed as a surrogate for class protections for the working poor. See especially Kathryn Kish Sklar, "Historical Foundations of Women's Power in the Creation of the American Welfare State, 1830–1939," in *Mothers of a New World: Maternalist Politics and the Origins of Welfare States*, ed. Seth Koven and Sonya Michel (New York: Routledge, 1993), 43–93, and Julie Novkov, *Constituting Workers, Protecting Women: Gender, Law, and Labor in the Progressive Era and New Deal Years* (Ann Arbor: University of Michigan Press, 2001).

5. *In re Morgan*, 26 Colo. 429, 415 (1899); Novkov, *Constituting Workers*, 108.

6. Clarence E. Wunderlin, *Visions of a New Industrial Order: Social Science and Labor Theory in America's Progressive Era* (New York: Columbia University Press, 1992), 6; Harry N. Scheiber, "Public Economic Policy and the American Legal System: Historical Perspectives," *Wisconsin Law Review* (1980): 1167–1168.

7. Novkov, *Constituting Workers*, 32.

8. For a detailed analysis of labor republicanism in these years, see Andrew E. Neather, "Popular Republicanism, Americanism, and the Roots of Anti-Communism, 1890–1925" (Ph.D. diss., Duke University, Durham, NC, 1994).

9. President Gertrude Hollister in Colorado Federation of Women's Clubs, *Yearbook*, 1910–1911, 16, Colorado Federation of Women's Clubs Collection, Archives, University of Colorado at Boulder Libraries. Hollister also wondered "if a woman is ever justified in holding a salaried position unless absolutely forced to be self-supporting? I believe that women who work without needing to do so are largely responsible for low wages for women" (15).

10. Carl W. McGuire, "History of the Colorado State Federation of Labor, 1896–1905" (Ph.D. diss., University of Colorado, Boulder, 1935), 187; Ray Stannard Baker, "'The Reign of Lawlessness: Anarchy and Despotism in Colorado," *McClures* 23 (May 1904): 52.

11. Lonsdale, "Movement for an Eight-Hour Law," 192–194.

12. In his study of workers in the Rocky Mountain West, John Enyeart argues that the Denver laundry workers' campaign reflected a struggle by unionists to politicize consumption and challenge court and legislative hostility with boycotts and cooperatives; "'By Laws of Their Own Making,'" 85–87. His work does not address the cooperation of unionists and clubwomen nor their combined lobbying efforts at the state legislature.

13. Alice Kessler-Harris, "Law and a Living: The Gendered Content of 'Free Labor,'" in *Gender, Class, Race, and Reform in the Progressive Era*, ed. Noralee Frankel and Nancy S. Dye (Lexington: University of Kentucky Press, 1991), 95; Nancy Woloch, *Muller v. Oregon: A Brief History with Documents* (Boston: Bedford Books, 1996), 4, 71–73; Robert D. Johnston, *The Radical Middle Class: Populist Democracy and the Question of Capitalism in Progressive Era Portland, Oregon* (Princeton, NJ: Princeton University Press, 2003), chapter 2.

14. *Union Label League Bulletin*, September 1906, December 1906, CSFL Collection, Archives, University of Colorado at Boulder Libraries. See also Enyeart, "'By Laws of Their Own Making,'" 86–87.

15. *Union Label League Bulletin*, January 1908, February 1908, CSFL Collection, Archives, University of Colorado at Boulder Libraries; Maureen Flanagan, *Seeing with*

Their Hearts: Chicago Women and the Vision of the Good City, 1871–1933 (Princeton, NJ: Princeton University Press, 2002), 109–114.

16. 41 Colo. 503–504.

17. *Union Label League Bulletin*, January 1908, February 1908, CSFL Collection, Archives, University of Colorado at Boulder Libraries.

18. Rheta Childe Dorr, "The Women Did It in Colorado," *Hamptons* 26, no. 4 (1911): 434.

19. On U'Ren and the Republican vision that inspired the Oregon System, see Johnston, *Radical Middle Class*, esp. 115–176.

20. *United Labor Bulletin*, October 13, 1910, CSFL Collection, Colorado Historical Society, Denver.

21. *News*, January 13, 1909.

22. *News*, March 25 and 26, 1909. See also cartoon on March 26, 1909, in which male voters, "regardless of party," swarm the grandstand where Shafroth holds a banner calling for legislators to redeem their pledges or resign (14).

23. On Williamson, see, for example, a report of her speech at St. Paul's Methodist Episcopal Church in July 1910 in *United Labor Bulletin*, July 21, 1910, CSFL Collection, Colorado Historical Society, Denver; Creel quoted in Smith and Lubinski, "Direct Democracy," 354.

24. Stephen Leonard, Thomas Noel, and Donald Walker Jr., *Honest John Shafroth: A Colorado Reformer* (Denver: Colorado Historical Society, 2003), 57–59.

25. Keating in *News*, January 11, 1911.

26. *United Labor Bulletin*, November 10, 1910, CSFL Collection, Colorado Historical Society, Denver.

27. R. E. Croskey in *United Labor Bulletin*, May 11, 1911, CSFL Collection, Colorado Historical Society, Denver.

28. Leonard, Noel, and Walker Jr., *Honest John*, 70–71.

29. Quoted in *United Labor Bulletin*, March 23, 1911, CSFL Collection, Colorado Historical Society, Denver.

30. Smith and Lubinski, "Direct Democracy," 365–366. Smith and Lubinski observe that several unions joined the Western Federation of Miners in exposing the deceptive and outright fraudulent tactics that the mine operators used in collecting petition signatures for the referendum. Even some clubwomen mistakenly collected signatures for this referendum to repeal the hours law while under the impression they were supporting it.

31. *Proceedings of the Eighteenth Annual Convention of the Colorado State Federation of Labor* (1912), 6, CSFL Papers, Box 27, Archives, University of Colorado at Boulder Libraries.

32. *Biennial Report of the Secretary of State of Colorado*, 1913–1914 (Denver: Secretary of State, 1914), 4. Corporations were also busy mobilizing support for initiatives in 1912; see Smith and Lubinski, "Direct Democracy," 357–367.

33. Smith and Lubinski, "Direct Democracy," 361; Wright, *Politics of Populism*, 257–263.

34. Elliot West, "Cleansing the Queen City: Prohibition and Urban Reform in Denver," *Arizona and the West* 14 (Winter 1974): 342–344.

35. *United Labor Bulletin*, November 7, 1912, CSFL Collection, Colorado Historical Society, Denver.

36. *Eighteenth Annual Convention of the Colorado State Federation of Labor* (1913), 21–22, 41, CSFL Papers, Box 27. Among the women's unions who cooperated with the women's clubs were the garment workers, tobacco strippers, and laundry workers. Democrats held a majority in the legislature in this session, as they had for the third time in six years. And again a Democrat sat in the governor's chair.

37. *United Labor Bulletin*, January 23, 1913, CSFL Collection, Colorado Historical Society, Denver.

38. Ibid.; *Minnesota Union Advocate*, November 22, 1912; *Proceedings of the Nineteenth Annual Convention of the Colorado State Federation of Labor* (1913), CSFL Papers, 42.

39. María E. Montoya, "Creating an American Home: Contest and Accommodation in Rockefeller's Company Towns," in *Memories and Migrations: Mapping Boricua and Chicana Histories*, ed. Vicki L. Ruiz and John R. Chávez (Urbana: University of Illinois Press, 2008), 19; United States Commission on Industrial Relations, *Final Reports and Testimony*, 64th Congress, 1st Session, Senate Documents (Washington, DC: Government Printing Office, 1916), 1: 17.

40. The UMW strike, the massacre at Ludlow, and the exposure of CFI abuses by the US Commission on Industrial Relations have received significant scholarly attention. Thomas Andrews, *Killing for Coal: American's Deadliest Labor War* (Cambridge, MA: Harvard University Press, 2008); Graham Adams, *Age of Industrial Violence, 1910–1915: The Activities and Findings of the United States Commission on Industrial Relations* (New York: Columbia University, 1966); George S. McGovern and Leonard F. Guttridge, *The Great Coalfield War* (Boston: Houghton Mifflin, 1972); H. M. Gitelman, *Legacy of the Ludlow Massacre: A Chapter in American Industrial Relations* (Philadelphia: University of Pennsylvania Press, 1988); Priscilla Long, *Where the Sun Never Shines: A History of America's Bloody Coal Industry* (New York: Paragon House, 1989).

41. Quoted in McGovern and Guttridge, *The Great Coalfield War*, 28.

42. Barron B. Beshoar, *Out of the Depths: The Story of John R. Lawson, a Labor Leader* (Denver: Colorado Labor Historical Committee, 1942), 7.

43. *Post*, February 5, 1913; *News*, January 2, 1909.

44. Commission on Industrial Relations, *Final Reports*, 8: 7216.

45. Andrews, *Killing for Coal*, 229.

46. *New Republic* (December 7, 1914): 7.

47. Ibid. (January 9, 1915): 7.

48. *United Mine Workers Journal* (September 25, 1913; January 1, 1914), quoted in Stephen H. Norwood, *Strikebreaking and Intimidation: Mercenaries and Masculinity in Twentieth-Century America* (Chapel Hill: University of North Carolina Press, 2002), 142.

49. Report quoted in Beshoar, *Out of the Depths*, 113.

50. Norwood, *Strikebreaking and Intimidation*, 144.

51. Andrews, *Killing for Coal*, 1–14, 275–276; Norwood, *Strikebreaking and Intimidation*, 146–148.

52. *News*, April 22, 1914.

53. Commission on Industrial Relations, *Final Report*, 8: 7217; *United Labor Bulletin*, May 9, 1914, CSFL Collection, Colorado Historical Society, Denver.

54. W. T. Davis, "The Strike War in Colorado," *Outlook* 107 (May 9, 1914): 70–73.

55. Elliot W. West, "Dry Crusade: The Prohibition Movement in Colorado, 1858–1933" (Ph.D. diss., University of Colorado, Boulder, 1971), 293–294.

56. *News*, August 26, 1914; West, "Dry Crusade," 298.

57. *United Labor Bulletin*, October 10, 1914, CSFL Collection, Colorado Historical Society, Denver; West, "Dry Crusade," 299.

58. Costigan to R. M. McClintock, March 16, 1914, reprinted in Colin B. Goodykoontz, ed., *Papers of Edward P. Costigan Relating to the Progressive Movement in Colorado, 1902–1917* (Boulder: University of Colorado, 1941), 252–253.

59. R. M. McClintock to E. P. Costigan, March 30, 1914, Costigan Papers, Box 7, Archives, University of Colorado at Boulder, quoted in West, "Dry Crusade," 311.

60. Costigan address given on April 6, 1914, at a Progressive Party banquet in Denver, reprinted in Goodykoontz, *Costigan Papers*, 252.

61. Theodore Roosevelt to E. P. Costigan, August 15, 1914, reprinted in Goodykoontz, *Costigan Papers*, 283–289.

62. West, "Dry Crusade," 290.

63. Ibid., 317. Subsequent testimony for the Commission on Industrial Relations confirmed many of these charges. Yet CFI influence, through its party machines, was clearly not the only factor shaping the election.

64. Fred Greenbaum, *Fighting Progressive: A Biography of Edward P. Costigan* (Washington, DC: Public Affairs Press, 1971), 63–70.

65. *United Labor Bulletin*, October 10; September 26; October 3, 17, and 24, 1914, CSFL Collection, Colorado Historical Society, Denver.

66. *Post*, October 31 and November 2, 1914.

67. *News*, May 23, 1910; Dorr, "Women Did It," 434–435.

68. Phil Goodstein, *Robert Speer's Denver: 1904–1920* (Denver: New Social Publications, 2004), 337–338.

69. *Daily Herald*, November 4, 1914, quoted in West, "Dry Crusade," 332.

70. Clubwoman Mildred Morris, *News*, November 6, 1914.

71. *News*, January 1, 1915.

CHAPTER 3: THE DENVER TRAMWAY CRISIS AND THE STRUGGLE FOR MASCULINE CITIZENSHIP

1. *Denver Express*, August 6 and 7, 1920; see also *Denver Post*, August 6 and 7, 1920.

2. Quoted in Stephen Leonard, "Bloody August: The Denver Tramway Strike of 1920," *Colorado Heritage* (Summer 1995): 29.

3. Edward Devine, John Ryan, and John Lapp, *The Denver Tramway Strike of 1920* (Denver: Denver Commission of Religious Forces, 1921), 56. While the tramway conflict has received previous scholarly attention, researchers have not addressed this struggle in the context of Progressivism. An economic analysis of the conflict can be found in Robert Michael Brown, "The Denver Tramway Strike of 1920" (master's thesis, University of Colorado, Boulder, 1967). For an interpretation of the strike in terms of workers' perceptions of moral economy, see John Enyeart, "The Denver Tramway Strike" (unpublished seminar paper in author's possession, 1996); Stephen Leonard, "Bloody August," 18–31.

4. The classic nineteenth-century case involving railroad regulation was *Munn v. Illinois* (1877). A US Supreme Court majority upheld Illinois's regulation of grain elevator rates because these warehousers were private businesses "affected with a public in-

terest." For an analysis of this case, see Harry Scheiber, "The Road to *Munn*: Eminent Domain and the Concept of Public Purpose in the State Courts," in *Law in American History*, ed. Donald Fleming and Bernard Bailyn (Boston: Little, Brown), 329–402. On streetcar utilities and the public interest, see Morton Keller, *Regulating a New Economy: Public Policy and Economic Change in America, 1900–1933* (Cambridge, MA: Harvard University Press, 1990), 43; Paul Barrett, *The Automobile and Urban Transit: The Formation of Public Policy in Chicago, 1900–1930* (Philadelphia: Temple University Press, 1983); Barbara Fried, *The Progressive Assault on Laissez Faire: Robert Hale and the First Law and Economics Movement* (Cambridge, MA: Harvard University Press, 1998), 5.

5. For comparison, see Barrett, *Automobile and Urban Transit*, 4–6.

6. Clyde L. King, *The History of the Government of Denver with Special Reference to Its Relations with Public Service Corporations* (Denver: Fisher Book Company, 1911), 197, 133, 271–275. See also Sam Lusky, *100 Years Young: The Tramway Saga* (Denver: AB Hirschfeld Press, 1968).

7. Clyde Lyndon King, ed., *The Regulation of Municipal Utilities* (New York: D. Appleton and Company, 1923) 12; Devine, Ryan, and Lapp, *Tramway Strike*, 56.

8. Daniel A. Smith and Joseph Lubinski, "Direct Democracy during the Progressive Era: A Crack in the Populist Veneer?" *Journal of Policy History* 14, no. 4 (2002): 360–364.

9. Mitchell, "Progressivism in Denver: The Municipal Reform Movement, 1904–1916" (Ph.D. diss., University of Denver, Denver, 1966), 347–357; Phil Goodstein, *Robert Speer's Denver, 1904–1920* (Denver: New Social Publications, 2004), 285–290.

10. Goodstein, *Robert Speer's Denver*, 290–302, 308.

11. Mitchell, "Progressivism in Denver," 303–304. On the support of business elites for structural reforms in other cities, see Samuel Hays, "The Politics of Reform in Municipal Government in the Progressive Era," *Pacific Northwest Quarterly* 55 (1964): 157–169; James Weinstein, *The Corporate Ideal in the Liberal State: 1900–1918* (Boston: Beacon Press, 1968), 92–116.

12. J. Paul Mitchell, "Boss Speer and the City Functional: Boosters and Businessmen Versus Commission Government in Denver," *Pacific Northwest Quarterly* 63, no. 4 (October 1972): 162–164.

13. Goodstein, *Robert Speer's Denver*, 391–393; Mitchell, "Progressivism in Denver," 393–399.

14. Mitchell, "Progressivism in Denver," 364–368.

15. *Denver Post* (hereafter *Post*), December 17, 1918; Brown, "Tramway Strike," 27.

16. *Denver Labor Bulletin*, September 21, 1918.

17. *Post*, November 20, 1918; *Denver Labor Bulletin*, November 23, 1918; Devine, Ryan, and Lapp, *Tramway Strike*, 10.

18. F. W. Hild, "Open Letter," *Denver Labor Bulletin*, December 14, 1918.

19. *Post*, December 18, 1918.

20. *Post*, January 3, 1919; *Denver Labor Bulletin*, January 4, 1919; *Rocky Mountain News* (hereafter *News*), July 8, 1919; *Post*, January 4, 1919.

21. *Denver Labor Bulletin*, January 4, 1919; Samuel DeBusk introduced the bill in the Senate, John Rotruck in the House; *Post*, January 3, 5, and 6, 1919.

22. *Post*, January 3, 1919.

23. Brown, "Tramway Strike," 31; Devine, Ryan, and Lapp, *Tramway Strike*, 12. The January decision of the Supreme Court was upheld on appeal in July 1919; see *Post*, July 7, 1919.

24. Jon C. Teaford, *The Rise of the States: Evolution of American State Government* (Baltimore: Johns Hopkins University Press, 2002), 20–25.

25. *Denver Labor Bulletin*, March 1 and 8, 1919.

26. *Municipal Facts* (September–October 1919): 6. The Building Trades representatives on the committee were especially critical. See *Denver Labor Bulletin*, June 7, 1919.

27. *Municipal Facts* (June–July 1923): 13.

28. *Denver Labor Bulletin*, March 22 and 29, 1919; April 26, 1919.

29. *News*, May 9, 1919; July 14 and 15, 1919; *Denver Labor Bulletin*, April 26, 1919.

30. *Post*, May 21, 1919; *News*, May 21, 1919.

31. *Denver Labor Bulletin*, May 24, 1919.

32. Brown, "Tramway Strike," 34.

33. *Post*, July 8, 1919; *News*, July 8, 1919.

34. See also the photo of the "gallant young swain" who biked "his best girl home from the office"; *Denver Post*, July 10, 1919.

35. *Post*, July 9, 1919; *Denver Labor Bulletin*, July 12, 1919.

36. *News*, July 9, 1919; *Post*, July 10, 1919.

37. *Post*, July 9, 1919.

38. Ibid., July 11, 1919.

39. Ibid., July 13, 1919.

40. *Denver Labor Bulletin*, December 7, 1918; August 2 and 9, 1919; September 6, 1919; *Municipal Facts* (June 1919): 17, (September—October 1919): 7.

41. *Post*, August 6, 1919; October 23, 1919.

42. *Denver Labor Bulletin*, October 11 and 18, 1919; *Post*, October 21, 1919.

43. *Municipal Facts* (September—October 1919): 6.

44. *Municipal Facts* (September–October 1919): 2.

45. *Post*, October 23 and 25, 1919.

46. On national anti-radical campaigns during the postwar era, see Robert K. Murray, *Red Scare: A Study in National Hysteria, 1919–1920* (Minneapolis: University of Minnesota Press, 1955), and Kim E. Nielsen, *Un-American Womanhood: Antiradicalism, Antifeminism, and the First Red Scare* (Columbus: Ohio State University Press, 2001). On the postwar "open-shop" movement, see especially David Montgomery, *The Fall of the House of Labor: The Workplace, the State, and American Labor Activism, 1865–1925* (Cambridge: Cambridge University Press, 1987).

47. *Post*, October 24 and 26, 1919; Devine, Ryan, and Lapp, *Tramway Strike*, 46–47.

48. *Denver Labor Bulletin*, March 20, 1920; Devine, Ryan, and Lapp, *Tramway Strike*, 15.

49. Bailey here offers confirmation of a national trend for agents of the state. See David Montgomery, "Thinking about American Workers in the 1920s," *International Labor and Working-Class History* 32 (Fall 1987): 7; Devine, Ryan, and Lapp, *Tramway Strike*, 16–18; *Denver Labor Bulletin*, July 3, 1920.

50. *Post*, July 2, 1920.

51. Devine, Ryan, and Lapp, *Tramway Strike*, 20.

52. *Post*, August 1, 1920.

53. Ibid., August 2, 1920; *News*, August 2, 1920; *Denver Express*, August 2, 1920.

54. *Post*, August 1 and 3, 1920.

55. Ibid., August 4, 1920.

56. Ibid., August 3, 1920; *Denver Express*, August 3, 1920; *Denver Labor Bulletin*, August 7, 1920.

57. *Post*, August 5, 1920.

58. *Tramway Bulletin* 11 (September 1920): 13.

59. Stephen H. Norwood, *Strikebreaking and Intimidation: Mercenaries and Masculinity in Twentieth-Century America* (Chapel Hill: University of North Carolina Press, 2002), 17–27.

60. Local 746 member S. J. Lewis, "Street Railway Workers," *Denver Labor Bulletin*, August 14 and 7, 1920.

61. *Denver Express*, August 2, 1920.

62. Ibid., August 5, 1920; *Denver Labor Bulletin*, August 7, 1920.

63. *Denver Express*, August 5, 1920; *Post*, August 4, 1920; *Denver Labor Bulletin*, August 7, 1920.

64. *Post*, August 5, 1920.

65. *Denver Labor Bulletin*, August 7, 1920; *Post*, August 6, 1920.

66. *Denver Express*, August 6, 1920.

67. Ibid., August 6, 1920; *Post*, August 6, 1920.

68. *Denver Labor Bulletin*, September 4, 1920.

69. *Denver Express*, August 6, 1920; *Post*, August 6, 1920.

70. *Post*, August 6, 1920.

71. *Denver Express*, August 6, 1920; *News*, August 7 and 9, 1920; *Post*, August 6, 1920.

72. *Denver Express*, August 7 and 11, 1920; *Post*, August 6 and 7, 1920.

73. *Denver Labor Bulletin*, August 7 and 14, 1920.

74. *Post*, August 6, 1920; *The Tramway Bulletin* 11 (September 1920): 14.

75. *News*, August 8 and 10, 1920.

76. *Denver Labor Bulletin*, September 4, 1920.

77. *Denver Express*, August 7, 8, and 9, 1920; *Tramway Bulletin* (September 1920): 56.

78. *Denver Express*, August 3 and 6, 1920; *Post*, August 4 and 5, 1920.

79. *Denver Express*, August 11, 1920.

80. *Denver Labor Bulletin*, August 14, 1920.

81. *Denver Labor Bulletin*, August 21, September 4, October 9, 1920; *Denver Express*, September 11, 1920.

82. Shoup quoted in *Denver Labor Bulletin*, August 21, 1920. See also issues from November 6 and 13, 1920.

83. *Denver Labor Bulletin*, November 20, 1920.

84. Karen Orren, *Belated Feudalism: Labor, the Law, and Liberal Development in the United States* (Cambridge: Cambridge University Press, 1991), 8.

85. Ibid., 149.

86. *Denver Labor Bulletin*, November 20, 1920. Whether these contract rights applied to women workers was not directly addressed in this case, yet the question arose in a number of other cases before the Colorado Industrial Commission that appear in Chapter 4.

87. This conception of contract has received important scholarly attention in recent years. Amy Dru Stanley in particular argues that as slavery ended in the nineteenth century, contract emerged as a central concept for interpreting social relations,

especially wage labor. Contract rested on principles of self-ownership, consent, and exchange. The ascendance of a broad theory of contract "transformed labor from a relation of personal dominion and dependence to a commodity exchange in which buyers and sellers were formally equal and free, yet also mutually dependent on one other [sic]." Amy Dru Stanley, *From Bondage to Contract: Wage Labor, Marriage, and the Market in the Age of Slave Emancipation* (Cambridge: Cambridge University Press, 1998), 75.

88. *Post*, September 18, 1920.

89. *Denver Labor Bulletin*, September 18 and 25, November 18, 1920; *Denver Express*, September 20, 1920.

90. Devine, Ryan, and Lapp, *Tramway Strike*, 58–59.

CHAPTER 4: THE CONSUMING PUBLIC AND THE INDUSTRIAL COMMISSION

1. An early version of this chapter appeared as "Struggles for the Public Interest: Organized Labor and State Mediation in Postwar America," *The Journal of the Gilded Age and Progressive Era* 4, no. 1 (January 2005): 69–82, published by the Society for Historians of the Gilded Age and Progressive Era.

2. Theodore Roosevelt, "6th Annual Message, Dec. 3, 1906," in *A Compilation of the Messages and Papers of the Presidents* (Washington, DC: Bureau of National Literature and Art, 1910), 10: 7417. For a consideration of Roosevelt's call in terms of the effort by Carroll Wright at the US Bureau of Labor Statistics to compile cost-of-living statistics, see Eric Rauchway, "The High Cost of Living in the Progressives' Economy," *Journal of American History* 88, no. 3 (December 2001): 904.

3. Voluntary mediation boards were established for the railroads under the 1898 Erdman Act and made permanent under the 1913 Newlands Act. The Department of Labor also oversaw the US Conciliation Service, which sent voluntary mediators to address major disputes. President Roosevelt compelled mediation in the 1902 anthracite strike, but no lasting arbitration machinery resulted. Edwin E. Witte, *The Government in Labor Disputes* (New York: McGraw-Hill, 1932), 238–246; Melvyn Dubofsky, *The State and Labor in Modern American* (Chapel Hill: University of North Carolina Press, 1994), 31–44; Mary O. Furner, "Knowing Capitalism: Public Investigation and the Labor Question in the Long Progressive Era," in *The State and Economic Knowledge: The American and British Experiences*, ed. Mary O. Furner and Barry Supple (Cambridge: Cambridge University Press, 1990), 241–286; Clarence E. Wunderlin, *Visions of a New Industrial Order: Social Science and Labor Theory in America's Progressive Era* (New York: Columbia University Press, 1992). On railroad arbitration, see especially Austin Kerr, *American Railroad Politics, 1914–1920* (Pittsburgh: University of Pittsburgh Press, 1968), and David L. Waterhouse, *The Progressive Movement of 1924 and the Development of Interest Group Liberalism* (New York: Garland Publishing, 1991), 17–23.

4. Although government officials in Kansas sought to give their board the trappings and title of a "court," they actually created an arbitration board under the authority of the governor that did not specifically draw on legal precedent and was not tied to the judicial branch. See John Fitch's critique to this effect in *Survey* (April 3, 1920): 7–8.

5. The Colorado Industrial Commission and Kansas Industrial Court have received significant if rather dated scholarly attention that has not considered these experiments in terms of Progressive debates about the public interest. See Colston E. Warne and

Merrill E. Gaddis, "Eleven Years of Compulsory Investigation of Industrial Disputes in Colorado," *Journal of Political Economy* 35, no. 5 (October 1927): 657–683; Ting Tsz Ko, *Governmental Methods of Adjusting Labor Disputes in North America and Australasia* (New York: Columbia University, 1926); John Hugh Bowers, *The Kansas Court of Industrial Relations: The Philosophy and History of the Court* (Chicago: A. C. McClurg & Co., 1922); Julia E. Johnsen, comp., *Kansas Court of Industrial Relations* (New York: H. W. Wilson Company, 1924); William L. Huggins, *Labor and Democracy* (New York: Macmillan Company, 1922); Herbert Feis, "The Kansas Court of Industrial Relations, Its Spokesmen, Its Record," *The Quarterly Journal of Economics* 37, no. 4 (August 1923): 705–733; Domenico Gagliardo, *The Kansas Industrial Court: An Experiment in Compulsory Arbitration* (Lawrence: University of Kansas Publications, 1941); Witte, *The Government in Labor Disputes*.

6. David Montgomery, "Thinking about American Workers in the 1920s," *International Labor and Working-Class History* 32 (Fall 1987): 7–8.

7. Typical was American Federation of Labor president Samuel Gompers's statement in 1888 that he believed in arbitration but not "between the lion and the lamb. . . . There can only be arbitration between equals. Let us organize." *The Samuel Gompers Papers*, ed. Stuart B. Kaufman, 3 vols. (Urbana: University of Illinois Press, 1986), 2: 87, quoted in Mary O. Furner, "The Republican Tradition and the New Liberalism: Social Investigation, State Building, and Social Learning in the Gilded Age," in *The State and Social Investigation in Britain and the United States*, ed. Michael J. Lacey and Mary O. Furner (Cambridge: Cambridge University Press, 1993), 207 n70.

8. See the testimony of James Brewster and Thomas Patterson before the US Commission on Industrial Relations in US Senate, *Industrial Relations: Final Report and Testimony Submitted to Congress by the Commission on Industrial Relations Created by the Act of August 23, 1912* (hereafter *Industrial Relations: Final Report*), Document No. 415, 64th Congress, 1st Session (1916), 7: 6668, 6503–6504. State senator Helen Ring Robinson made a personal study of Canada's compulsory investigation law in 1912. See her testimony, *Industrial Relations: Final Report*, 7217. Denver unionist and state representative Harvey Garman particularly contested compulsory arbitration proposals during the special legislative session called in May 1914 to respond to the Ludlow massacre. *United Labor Bulletin*, May 23, 1914, CSFL Collection, Colorado Historical Society, Denver.

9. California businessman and CIR commissioner Henry Weinstock noted that "the question of mediation . . . or compulsory arbitration is of keenest and deepest interest to this commission." *Industrial Relations: Final Report*, 6506.

10. Shelton Stromquist, *Reinventing "The People": The Progressive Movement, the Class Problem, and the Origins of Modern Liberalism* (Urbana: University of Illinois Press, 2006), 177–186; Joseph McCartin, *Labor's Great War: The Struggle for Industrial Democracy and the Origins of Modern American Labor Relations, 1912–1921* (Chapel Hill: University of North Carolina Press, 1997), 18–30.

11. Remarks of E. P. Costigan at the meeting of the Denver Progressive Club, June 8, 1914; Theodore Roosevelt to E. P. Costigan, August 15, 1914; Costigan Statement before the US Commission on Industrial Relations, December 16, 1914. All reprinted in Colin B. Goodykoontz, ed., *Papers of Edward P. Costigan Relating to the Progressive Movement in Colorado, 1902–1917* (Boulder: University of Colorado, 1941), 265–267, 289, 308–312.

12. *United Labor Bulletin*, December 12, 1914, and January 9, 1915, CSFL Collection, Colorado Historical Society, Denver; Carlson testimony, *Industrial Relations: Final Report*, 6506; *Rocky Mountain News* (hereafter *News*), January 26, 1915; *Denver Post* (hereafter *Post*), March 3 and April 5, 1915.

13. *Post*, March 30 and 31, April 5 and 6, 1915; *News*, March 30, April 6, 1915.

14. John Shaffer, editorial, *News*, April 6, 1915.

15. *Denver Labor Bulletin*, October 16, 1915.

16. Ibid., July 15, 1916; February 17, 1917.

17. Ibid., July 15, September 2, and August 19, 1916.

18. *Post*, October 22 and 29, 1916; *Denver Labor Bulletin*, October 28, 1916.

19. *Denver Labor Bulletin*, January 13, 1917.

20. Ibid., February 24 and March 10, 1917.

21. Ibid., February 24, 1917; *New York Times*, November 12, 1916.

22. Ibid., March 3, 10, 24, and 31, 1917.

23. Ibid., March 31 and 3, 1917.

24. Warne and Gaddis, "Eleven Years," 664, 676, 680; *Second Report of the Industrial Commission of Colorado* (Denver: Industrial Commission, 1918), 103; *Third Report of the Industrial Commission of Colorado* (Denver: Industrial Commission, 1919), 110–115.

25. Joseph A. McCartin, *Labor's Great War*, 95, 90; Erik John Karolak, "'Work or Fight': Federal Labor Policy and the First World War, 1913–1920" (Ph.D. diss., Ohio State University, Columbus, 1994), 128. See also Melvyn Dubofsky, *The State and Labor*, chapter 3.

26. *Fifteenth Biennial Report of the Bureau of Labor Statistics of the State of Colorado* (Denver: Eames Bros., 1916), 15.

27. *Denver Labor Bulletin*, June 9, July 7, August 25, 1917.

28. Quoted in *Denver Labor Bulletin*, January 5, 1918.

29. *Denver Labor Bulletin*, April 30, 1921; June 9, 1917.

30. Ibid., March 10, 1917.

31. Quoted in *Denver Labor Bulletin*, May 3, 1919.

32. In 1925, Elizabeth Baker was among the first to comment on the hopes of reformers that laws based on gender protections might serve as a surrogate for class. See Elizabeth Faulkner Baker, *Protective Labor Legislation: With Special Reference to Women in the State of New York* (New York: Columbia University, 1925), 438. For a more recent assessment of this trend, see Kathryn Kish Sklar, "Historical Foundations of Women's Power in the Creation of the American Welfare State, 1830–1939," in *Mothers of a New World: Maternalist Politics and the Origins of Welfare States*, ed. Seth Koven and Sonya Michel (New York: Routledge, 1993), 45.

33. McCartin, *Labor's Great War*, 92.

34. *Denver Labor Bulletin*, June 29, 1918; April 9, 1921; *Sixteenth Biennial Report of the Bureau of Labor Statistics* (Denver: Eames Bros., 1918), 68.

35. *Post*, April 4, 1921.

36. The CIC had played only a minor role in the Denver Tramway Strike of 1920, largely deferring to city and court authorities.

37. *New York Times*, June 6, 1920; Morrison quoted in Christopher L. Tomlins, *The State and the Unions: Labor Relations, Law and the Organized Labor Movement in America, 1880–1960* (Cambridge: Cambridge University Press, 1985), 4.

38. Warne and Gaddis, "Eleven Years," 660.

39. Ibid., 672; *Third Report of the Industrial Commission of Colorado*, 107.

40. *Third Report of the Industrial Commission of Colorado*, 108; *Fourth Report of the Industrial Commission of Colorado* (Denver: Industrial Commission, 1920), 112.

41. Colorado Reports, LXX: 269–274; *Post*, April 4, 1921.

42. *Denver Labor Bulletin*, September 10, 1921.

43. Ibid., October 1, 1921.

44. Ibid., November 12, 1921; Warne and Gaddis, "Eleven Years," 672.

45. *Denver Labor Bulletin*, December 3, 1921; Warne and Gaddis, "Eleven Years," 673; Governor Shoup Executive Order, November 16, 1921, in Governor Oliver Shoup Papers, Box 26798, FF "Coal Strike," Colorado State Archives, Denver. On mine owner views, see W. B. Lewis, president of Oakdale Coal Company, to Gov. Oliver Shoup, January 6, 1922, and F. R. Wood, president of Temple Fuel Company, to Gov. Oliver Shoup, December 15, 1921, Shoup Papers, Box 26798, FF "Coal Strike."

46. *Denver Labor Bulletin*, December 10 and 17, 1921; Transcript of John Coss speech before Grace Community Church, December 11, 1921, in Shoup Papers, Box 26798, FF "Coal Strike," Colorado State Archives, Denver.

47. Warne and Gaddis, "Eleven Years," 673; *Sixth Report of the Industrial Commission of Colorado* (Denver: Industrial Commission, 1922), 149.

48. As James Barrett has noted, the national arbitration agreement worked two ways, giving the union valuable recognition in the short term but also limiting strike possibilities and requiring union leaders to discipline workers to maintain production. Union structure, which reinforced skill and ethnic divisions, also contributed to postwar fragmentation and vulnerability. James R. Barrett, *Work and Community in the Jungle: Chicago's Packinghouse Workers, 1894–1922* (Urbana: University of Illinois Press, 1987), 200–201, 230.

49. *Denver Labor Bulletin*, July 9 and December 10, 1921; Warne and Gaddis, "Eleven Years," 674–675.

50. *Denver Labor Bulletin*, December 10, 17, and 24, 1921.

51. Warne and Gaddis, "Eleven Years," 675; *Sixth Report of the Industrial Commission of Colorado*, 152.

52. Morley quoted in *Denver Labor Bulletin*, July 7, 1922.

53. *Denver Labor Bulletin*, January 14, 21; February 4, 1922.

54. *State v. Howat et al.*, 109 Kansas 376 (1921), 198 Pacific Reporter 698; Ann Schofield, "An 'Army of Amazons': The Language of Protest in a Kansas Mining Community, 1921–22," *American Quarterly* 37 (Winter 1985): 692–693.

55. Frank Walsh, "Henry Allen's Industrial Court," *The Nation* (June 5, 1920): 755–757; Allen quoted in the *New York Times*, May 29, 1920; Stephen H. Norwood, *Strikebreaking and Intimidation: Mercenaries and Masculinity in Twentieth-Century America* (Chapel Hill: University of North Carolina Press, 2002).

56. *The Survey* (February 7, 1920): 552.

57. Ibid.; Walsh, "Henry Allen's Industrial Court," 755; *State v. Howat, et al.*, 109 Kansas 377, 198 Pacific Reporter 687.

58. *Current Opinion* 68 (April 1920): 472–478, quoted in Julia E. Johnsen, comp., *Kansas Court of Industrial Relations* (New York: H. W. Wilson Co., 1924), 33, 36.

59. See *New York Times*, May 29, 1920.

60. Walter Weyl, *The New Democracy: An Essay on Certain Political and Economic Tendencies in the United States* (New York: MacMillan, 1912), 250. For comment on Weyl's

position, particularly in comparison to Herbert Croly, who stressed participatory democracy over the needs of consumers, see Christopher Lasch, *The True and Only Heaven: Progress and Its Critics* (New York: W. W. Norton, 1991), 340–344; Rexford G. Tugwell, "The Economic Basis of the Public Interest, (Ph.D. diss., University of Pennsylvania, Philadelphia, 1922), vii.

61. Henry J. Allen, "How Kansas Broke a Strike and Would Solve the Labor Problem," *Current Opinion* 68 (April 1920): 472–478, reprinted in Johnsen, *Kansas Court: The Survey* (April 3, 1920): 7.

62. Harding's proposal reprinted in Bowers, *Kansas Court of Industrial Relations: The Philosophy and History of the Court* (Chicago: A. C. McClurg and Co., 1922), 121–122; Basil Manly, "Arbitration and Industrial Justice," *Survey* (April 8, 1922): 45.

63. Huggins, *Labor and Democracy* (New York: Macmillan, 1922) 8, 27–28; Huggins, "Why Compulsory Arbitration in Kansas," *Survey* (May 29, 1920): 301–302; *Colorado Labor Advocate*, November 29, 1923.

64. *New York Times*, May 29, June 7, 1920. For a similar debate about the public interest in labor disputes, see also the exchange of letters between former secretary of war Newton Baker and Gompers reprinted in the *American Federationist* 30 (February 1923): 156–167.

65. *The Survey* (February 7, 1929): 552; Huggins, *Labor and Democracy*, 93–96; *State v. Howat*, 109 Kansas 376.

66. Walsh, "Henry Allen's Industrial Court," 756.

67. *New York Times*, June 17, 1920; September 14, 1922.

68. Although not directly commenting on the state arbitration movement, American Federation of Labor secretary Frank Morrison made a similar point in 1920. Morrison noted that labor was set apart in discussions of industrial relations from "the community" or "the public." For Morrison, the interests of the community and organized labor were structurally antagonistic. He argued that the "community" and "public" were merely camouflage for the "well-to-do." *New York Times*, July 18, 1920, quoted in Tomlins, *The State and the Unions*, 4.

69. Manly, "Arbitration and Industrial Justice," 46; Warne and Gaddis, "Eleven Years," 678–680; see also Clarence Williams, Letter to the Editor, *Survey* (June 19, 1920): 418.

70. Huggins, *Labor and Democracy*, 10, 93.

71. John A. Fitch, "Industrial Peace by Law — the Kansas Way," *The Survey* (April 3, 1920): 8.

72. *Survey* (May 29, 1920): 303.

73. *14th Census of the United States*, vol. 3 (Washington, DC: Government Printing Office, 1923); Graham Adams, *Age of Industrial Violence, 1910–15: The Activities and Findings of the United States Commission on Industrial Relations* (New York: Columbia University Press, 1966), 157. On the "Little Balkans" region of Kansas, see Schofield, "Army of Amazons," 686–701.

74. Huggins, *Labor and Democracy*, 52–53.

75. Ibid., 195–206; Feis, "Kansas Court," 715, 722. *Court of Industrial Relations v. Chas. Wolff Packing Co.*, 109 Kansas 629, 201 Pacific Reporter 418; *Court of Industrial Relations v. Chas. Wolff Packing Co., Continuation*, 207 Pacific Reporter 806, quoted 809.

76. *Chas. Wolff Packing Company v. Court of Industrial Relations of the State of Kansas*, 262 U.S. 522 (1925), quoted 523. In *Dorchy v. State of Kansas*, 264 U.S. 286 (1924), the US

Supreme Court also held compulsory arbitration illegal in coal-mining disputes. Between the Progressive Era and the New Deal, courts "invoked a dizzying array of tests to determine whether a business was affected with a public interest," argues Barbara Fried. These included "what the importance was to the public welfare of the services provided; whether the company acts as a substitute for the state; whether the industry was monopolistic; whether either side was in a position to administer prices, thereby extracting exorbitant profits; what effect the industry had on commerce; whether the owner 'holds himself out' to serve the public, thereby subjecting his business to the public interest; and whether the public has a legal right to demand and receive the good or service in question." Barbara Fried, *The Progressive Assault on Laissez Faire: Robert Hale and the First Law and Economics Movement* (Cambridge, MA: Harvard University Press, 1998), 169.

77. *The Nation* (June 27, 1923): 737.

78. In recent years historians have begun to analyze postwar labor struggles to develop new political strategies to replace the loose partnership with the Democratic Party. Although Gompers remained committed to what Julie Greene has insightfully termed "pure and simple politics," city and state federations of labor challenged Gompers for political leadership of the American Federation of Labor and increasingly turned to an independent party. Much work remains to be done, however, on cities outside of Chicago, New York, Minneapolis, and Seattle to understand how workers even within the federation sought to mobilize along alternative lines in the political arena. Julie Greene, *Pure and Simple Politics: The American Federation of Labor and Political Activism, 1881–1917* (Cambridge: Cambridge University Press, 1998); Andrew Strouthous, *US Labor and Political Action, 1918–24: A Comparison of Independent Political Action in New York, Chicago and Seattle* (Houndsmills, UK: Macmillian and St. Martin's Press, 2000); Richard M. Valelly, *Radicalism in the States: The Minnesota Farmer-Labor Party and the American Political Economy* (Chicago: University of Chicago Press, 1989); David Montgomery, *The Fall of the House of Labor: The Workplace, the State, and American Labor Activism, 1865–1925* (Cambridge: Cambridge University Press, 1987).

79. Gompers quoted in *Denver Labor Bulletin*, March 27 and May 1, 1920. For a review of American Federation of Labor negotiations with the Democratic Party at the national level, see especially Greene, *Pure and Simple Politics*.

80. Valelly, *Radicalism in the States*, 17–32.

81. Ibid.

82. William Walling quoted in *Denver Labor Bulletin*, April 3 and February 21, 1920.

83. *News*, September 11 and November 1, 1920; *Denver Express*, September 15, 1920.

84. *News*, November 4, 1920.

85. *Denver Labor Bulletin*, June 3, August 26, and September 9, 1922.

86. *Denver Express*, September 14, 1920. For a brief biography, see Phil Goodstein, *In the Shadow of the Klan: When the KKK Ruled Denver, 1920–1926* (Denver: New Social Publications, 2006), 185–189.

87. *News*, November 3 and September 14, 1922.

88. Ibid., November 4, 3, and 6, 1922.

89. For example, the editor of the *Denver Labor Bulletin*, Edward Hines, recanted his initial support for Sweet on such grounds to endorse the Republican Griffith in mid-

October. This move so angered the leadership of the statewide and Denver labor federations that the unions quickly formed a new paper, the *Colorado Labor Advocate*, which closely allied itself with Sweet. The *Bulletin* had led the fight against the Industrial Relations Act from the start, but Hines's defection from the Democratic camp meant a widespread loss of support for his paper from organized labor in Colorado. The *Advocate* quickly received endorsements from the major unions.

90. *Colorado Labor Advocate*, November 9, 1922; *News*, November 9 and 11, 1922.

91. For a recent study which insightful reveals the importance of fiscal politics for workers and employers in this period, see Cecelia Bucki, *Bridgeport's Socialist New Deal, 1915–36* (Urbana: University of Illinois Press, 2001), 45–49.

92. *Legislative Report of the Farmers Educational and Co-Operative Union of Colorado on the Work of the Twenty-Third General Assembly* (1921?), CSFL Papers, Box 4, FF 3, Archives, University of Colorado at Boulder Libraries.

93. *Colorado Labor Advocate*, November 23, 1922; February 21 and January 25, 1923; Jon C. Teaford, *The Rise of the States: Evolution of American State Government* (Baltimore: Johns Hopkins University Press, 2002), 70–75.

94. *Colorado Labor Advocate*, March 15 and January 18, 1923; February 15 and 1, 1923. On the failure of administration reform, even into the 1930s, see James F. Wickens, "Tightening the Colorado Purse Strings," *Colorado Magazine* 46 (Fall 1969): 275–276.

95. An editorial on the 1923 Supreme Court decision suggested that mining was "as essential a public service as railroading and more essential than a packinghouse." *The Nation* (April 29, 1925): 483. In 1921, the Colorado Supreme Court had declared coal mining to be an industry clearly affected with a "public interest," thereby reversing a lower court ruling to the contrary. *Post*, April 4, 1921.

CHAPTER 5: BEN LINDSEY AND WOMEN PROGRESSIVES

1. See, for example, Ben Lindsey to Sarah Platt Decker, March 19, 1906, Box 7, Benjamin Barr Lindsey Collection, Library of Congress, Manuscript Division, Washington, DC.

2. Edward T. Taylor, "Equal Suffrage in Colorado," Speech Delivered in the House of Representatives, April 24, 1912, in Consideration of Bill to Confer Legislative Authority on the Territory of Alaska, *62nd Congress: 2nd Session; Senate Document No. 722* (Washington, DC: Government Printing Office, 1912), 5–12.

3. Colorado Federation of Women's Clubs, *Yearbook* (1913–1914), 14, in Colorado Federation of Women's Club Collection, Box 1, Archives, University of Colorado at Boulder Libraries.

4. Molly Ladd-Taylor has presented a similar vision of maternalist ideology during the Progressive Era in her *Mother Work: Women, Child Welfare, and the State, 1890–1930* (Urbana: University of Illinois Press, 1994), 3. On scientific motherhood, see especially Rima D. Apple, "Constructing Mothers: Scientific Motherhood in the Nineteenth and Twentieth Centuries," in *Mothers and Motherhood: Readings in American History*, ed. Rima D. Apple and Janet Golden (Columbus: Ohio State University Press, 1997), 90–110. A developmental model of childhood and adolescence was central to Mothers' Congress activists and juvenile court judges like Ben Lindsey. On scientific and Progressive efforts to reconstruct childhood in developmental terms, see Steven L. Schlossman, "Before Home Start: Notes toward a History of Parent Education in America,

1897–1929," *Harvard Educational Review* 46 (August 1976): 436–467, and Michael Mc-Gerr, *A Fierce Discontent: The Rise and Fall of the Progressive Movement in America, 1870–1920* (New York: Free Press, 2003), 107–117.

5. Wendy Keefover-Ring, "Municipal Housekeeping, Domestic Science, Animal Protection, and Conservation: Women's Political Activism and Environmental Activism in Denver, Colorado, 1894–1912" (master's thesis, University of Colorado, Boulder, 2002), 34–35.

6. Kathryn Kish Sklar, "Historical Foundations of Women's Power in the Creation of the American Welfare State, 1830–1939," in *Mothers of a New World: Maternalist Politics and the Origins of Welfare States*, ed. Seth Koven and Sonya Michel (New York: Routledge, 1993), 69.

7. Ben B. Lindsey and Harvey J. O'Higgins, *The Beast* (New York: Doubleday, Page & Company, 1909), 306–315.

8. Ladd-Taylor, *Mother Work*, 46–47; Schlossman, "Before Home Start," 441–446. On the long-term political and social hopes that Progressive reformers placed in their projects to "reconstruct childhood" in these terms, see McGerr, *Fierce Discontent*, 107–117.

9. George Creel, "Denver Triumphant," *Everybody's* 27 (September 1912): 314; Paul Colomy and Martin Kretzmann, "Projects and Institution Building: Judge Ben B. Lindsey and the Juvenile Court Movement," *Social Problems* 42 (May 1995): 198–208.

10. Lindsey, "Four Questions and Juvenile Crime," *Charities* 20 (August 15, 1908): 591.

11. Lincoln Steffens, *Upbuilders* (Seattle: University of Washington Press, 1968), 107–131; *Report of Hon. Ben. B. Lindsey, Chairman of Committee on Juvenile Courts before the International Congress of the Welfare of the Child*, Held Under the Auspices of the Mother's Congress at Washington, DC (April 22 to 27, 1914), 3, Benjamin Barr Lindsey Collection, Box 1, Denver Public Library, Western History Collection; Juvenile Court of Denver, *The Problem of the Children and How the State of Colorado Cares for Them* (Denver: Merchants Publishing Company, 1904), 206.

12. Lindsey and O'Higgins, *The Beast*, 88.

13. Benjamin Lindsey, "A Secret Political League: Who and What It Is; Its Anonymous Circulars Exposed and Court Cases Involving the Sex Problem Frankly Discussed" (Denver: n.p., 1913), 35, Box 1, Lindsey Collection, Denver Public Library. Gregory's position became official under Colorado's Master of Discipline Act in 1909. A female appointment was not mandatory under the act, but up to judge's discretion. See *Report of Hon. Ben. B. Lindsey*, 7. Elinor McGinn, *A Wide-Awake Woman: Josephine Roche in the Era of Reform* (Denver: Colorado Historical Society, 2002), 13–21.

14. Ben B. Lindsey, "The Trial of Criminal Cases and Adult Probation in the Chancery Court," Address before the National Probation Association, 1925, pp. 21–22, Ben B. Lindsey Collection, Box 2, Denver Public Library, Western History Collection, Denver.

15. Quoted in *Denver Labor Bulletin*, September 23, 1916. On efforts to provide homes for pregnant working-class women in Denver and the West generally, see Peggy Pascoe, *Relations of Rescue: The Search for Female Moral Authority in the American West, 1874–1939* (New York: Oxford University Press, 1990).

16. Edwin K. Whitehead, "The Juvenile Court," *Child and Animal Protection* 3 (September 1910): 1, Ben Lindsey Collection, Box 1, Denver Public Library, Western History

Collection, Denver. See also Women's Non-Partisan Juvenile Court Association, "Denver's Famous Juvenile Court Was Founded by Ben Lindsey," pamphlet issued by the Denver Christian Citizenship Union (Denver: n.p., 1916), 12.

17. *Post*, February 14, 1917.

18. Ibid., February 24 and 15, 1917.

19. Gail M. Beaton, "The Widening Sphere of Women's Lives: The Literary Study and Philanthropic Work of Six Women's Clubs in Denver, 1881–1945," *Essays in Colorado History* 13 (1992): 31–34; *Denver Times*, May 29, 1919, in Women's Council of Defense scrapbook, Box 8853 D, Governor Julius Gunter Papers, Colorado State Archives, Denver.

20. *Post*, December 28, 1918, and April 15, 1918.

21. Proclamation, n.d., in Colorado Council of Defense Papers, Box 1207, FF 2, Colorado Historical Society, Denver.

22. *Report of the Women's Council of Defense*, 12, Colorado Council of Defense Papers, Box 1207, FF 16, Colorado Historical Society, Denver.

23. Theodoshia Raines, Head of the women's division of the US Employment Service and Denver Woman's Club member, quoted in *Denver Post*, December 29, 1918. On intra-class tensions over women's war work in other states and cities, see Greenwald, *Women, War, and Work*, especially chapter 4.

24. Ladd-Taylor, *Mother Work*, 89–90; Joseph B. Chepaitis, "The First Federal Social Welfare Measure: The Sheppard-Towner Maternity and Infancy Act, 1918–1932" (Ph. D. diss., Georgetown University, Washington, DC, 1968), 13–15.

25. Quoted in Ladd-Taylor, *Mother Work*, 45.

26. Chepaitis, "First Federal Social Welfare," 13–15.

27. *Rocky Mountain News* (hereafter *News*), January 15, 1919, in Child Welfare Scrapbook, Governor Julius Gunter's Papers, Box 8853D, Colorado State Archives, Denver.

28. *Denver Labor Bulletin*, October 21, 1918.

29. *Post*, January 5, 1919.

30. Ibid., September 19, 1920; *News*, September 19, 1920.

31. Exchange of letters quoted in *News*, November 2, 1920.

32. *Colorado Club Woman* (April 1921): 9.

33. Ibid., 1.

34. Ibid. (December 1921): 3.

35. Ibid., 15, 3.

36. Jacobsen, "Report: Department of Legislation" (1921–1922), pamphlet in the Colorado Federation of Women's Club papers of recent CFWC president Helen Johnson, Denver.

37. *Colorado Club Woman* (March 1922): 1.

38. Ibid. (November 1923): 6, (December 1923): 7; emphasis in the original.

39. *News*, September 21, 22, 23, and 24, 1923.

40. One exception was the campaign to allow women to serve on juries, which did generate occasional support among Colorado clubwomen over the course of the decade. In 1927, for example, clubwomen endorsed a jury service bill that never emerged from committee in the General Assembly. *Colorado Club Woman* (September 1927): 12. For resolutions against the Equal Rights Amendment, see *Colorado Club Woman* (February 1923): 7; (January 1924): 8.

41. *Colorado Labor Advocate*, January 24, February 14, November 27, 1924.

42. For an extended analysis of working-class consumer strategies in the 1920s, see Dana Frank, *Purchasing Power: Consumer Organizing, Gender and the Seattle Labor Movement, 1919–1929* (Cambridge: Cambridge University Press, 1994), and Lawrence Glickman, *A Living Wage: American Workers and the Making of Consumer Society* (Ithaca, NY: Cornell University Press, 1997).

43. *News*, November 14 and 13, 1922.

44. *Colorado Club Woman* (February 1924): 14; *Denver Labor Bulletin*, January 28, 1922.

45. *Colorado Club Woman* (April 1923): 2; (February 1924): 9.

46. Unsigned editorial, hand-dated August 1923 (likely John Shaffer of the *Rocky Mountain News*), Governor Oliver Shoup Papers, Box 26959, FF "Child Welfare," Colorado State Archives, Denver.

47. Thomas Krainz, "Implementing Poor Relief: Colorado's Progressive-Era Welfare State" (Ph.D. diss., University of Colorado, Boulder, 2000); *Colorado Club Woman* (May 1923): 10.

48. *Colorado Labor Advocate*, August 30 and 9, 1923.

49. Ibid., November 1, 1923.

50. Ibid., August 23 and December 13, 1923; January 24, 1924.

51. *Adkins v. Children's Hospital*, 261 U.S. 525; *Colorado Labor Advocate*, June 26, 1924.

52. Mildred White Wells, *Unity in Diversity: The History of the General Federation of Women's Clubs* (Washington, DC: General Federation of Women's Clubs, 1953), 91, 189; *Colorado Club Woman* (January 1926): 4.

53. *News*, October 23 and 28, 1923.

54. *Colorado Labor Advocate*, November 8, 1923; *Post*, November 12, 1923; *News*, September 14, 1923.

55. See Larsen, *The Good Fight*, chapter 8, for an extended discussion of Lindsey's proposal and the controversies it generated.

56. *Survey* (May 3, 1919): 169; *News*, May 24, 1919.

57. *Report of the Colorado Child Welfare Bureau Board of Control to the Department of Public Instruction from July 15th, 1919, to December 1st, 1920* (Denver: Bradford Publishing, 1920), 1–3, Child Welfare Bureau Papers, Colorado State Archives, Denver.

58. *Colorado Club Woman* (March 1922): 4–5; *Report of the Colorado Child Welfare Bureau Board of Control*, July 15, 1919, to December 1, 1920, 10, Child Welfare Bureau Papers, Colorado State Archives, Denver.

59. *Report of the Colorado Child Welfare Bureau Board of Control to the Department of Public Instruction, from December 1, 1920, to November 30, 1922* (Denver: Eames Bros., 1922), 5; *Biennial Report of the Colorado Child Welfare Bureau of the Department of Public Instruction*, December 1, 1922, to November 30, 1924 (Denver: Eames Bros., 1924), 5, Child Welfare Bureau Papers, Colorado State Archives, Denver.

60. Historians have largely focused on Shepperd-Towner at the national level, without sufficient attention to state-level bureaucracies like the Colorado Child Welfare Bureau and its varied implementation of the program. For a brief overview of work on Sheppard-Towner, see Ladd-Taylor, *Mother Work*, especially chapter 6; Robyn L. Muncy, *Creating a Female Dominion in American Reform, 1890–1935* (New York: Oxford University Press, 1991), chapter 4; Chepaitis, "The First Federal Social Welfare Measure"; Louis J. Covotsos, "Child Welfare and Social Progress: A History of

the United States Children's Bureau, 1912–1935" (Ph.D. diss., University of Chicago, Chicago, 1976). For an important local study, see Sandra Schackel, *Social Housekeepers: Women Shaping Public Policy in New Mexico, 1920–1940* (Albuquerque: University of New Mexico Press, 1992).

61. *Report of the Colorado Child Welfare Bureau . . . July 15th, 1919, to December 1st, 1920*, 5, Child Welfare Bureau Papers, Colorado State Archives, Denver.

62. Schlossman, "Before Home Start," 458. For a related argument, see McGerr, *Fierce Discontent*, 107–114.

63. "Report of the Executive Secretary on Child Welfare Bureau Activities," June 30, 1928, Colorado Child Welfare Bureau Papers, Board of Control Meeting Minutes, Colorado State Archives, Denver.

64. *Biennial Report of the Colorado Child Welfare Bureau*, December 1, 1922, to November 30, 1924, 3–4; *Biennial Report of the Colorado Child Welfare Bureau*, December 1, 1924, to November 30, 1926 (Denver: Bradford-Robinson, 1926), 28–29, Child Welfare Bureau Papers, Colorado State Archives, Denver.

65. Dr. Roy Forbes, "Summary of Child Welfare Conferences" (October 1923), Minutes of the Meetings of the Board of Control, Child Welfare Bureau Papers, Colorado State Archives, Denver.

66. *Colorado Club Woman* (December 1923): 15.

67. *Colorado Labor Advocate*, January 15, 1925.

68. US Children's Bureau, *Child Labor and the Work of Mothers in the Beet Fields of Colorado and Michigan* (Washington, DC: Government Printing Office, 1923), 37, 42, 52, 54, 58–60, 121–122.

69. *Post*, January 23, 1925; *Denver Express*, March 13, 1925; *Colorado Labor Advocate*, March 26 and April 23, 1925. On the national campaign for the Child Labor Amendment, see Clarke A. Chambers, *Seedtime of Reform: American Social Service and Social Action, 1918–1933* (Minneapolis: University of Minnesota Press, 1963), 34–45. On antifeminist and Catholic challenges, see Kim E. Nielsen, *Un-American Womanhood: Antiradicalism, Antifeminism, and the First Red Scare* (Columbus: Ohio State University Press, 2001), 90–104. The defeat of the Child Labor Amendment also reflected the turbulent conditions in the 1925 legislature created by Ku Klux Klan influence. For a discussion of the Klan agenda and its hostility to women's Progressive agencies, see Chapter 6.

70. The midwife campaigns of the US Children's Bureau have received significant scholarly attention. Robyn Muncy has argued that the Shepperd-Towner program enabled Children's Bureau officials to discipline and rationalize the practice of midwifery in keeping with their bureaucratic and scientific ideals. Ladd-Taylor similarly contended that white, Protestant Children's Bureau investigators often blamed lay midwives who lacked scientific training, especially in black and Mexican American communities, for high mortalities rates. In contrast, Sandra Schackel found that in New Mexico, Shepperd-Towner officials demonstrated more sensitivity to cultural differences and attempted to adjust medical, scientific expectations to accommodate traditional healing and childbirth practices. Muncy, *Female Dominion*, 116; Ladd-Taylor, *Mother Work*, 182–184; Schackel, *Social Housekeepers*, 166.

71. "Report for Week of October 14th–20th" (1923), and Pecover, "Midwives Classes Organized," Board of Control Meeting Minutes, Child Welfare Bureau Papers, Colorado State Archives, Denver.

72. Pecover, "Midwives Classes Organized," Board of Control Meeting Minutes, Child Welfare Bureau Papers, Colorado State Archives, Denver.

73. Schackel, *Social Housekeepers*, 47–55.

74. Board of Control Meeting Minutes, January 26, 1927, and April 20, 1926, Child Welfare Bureau Papers, Colorado State Archives, Denver.

75. Julie Lathrop, "Child Welfare Standards a Test of Democracy," National Conference of Social Work, *Proceedings* (1919): 5–9, quoted in Chambers, *Seedtime of Reform*, 56.

76. Mrs. L. H. Hall, "Summary of Legislation" (1931), pamphlet in private papers of Helen Johnson, Denver. The other states that ratified the amendment were Arkansas, Arizona, California, Wisconsin, and Montana, in that order. Early defeats in Massachusetts and New York proved decisive.

77. *Colorado Club Woman* (March 1932): 14.

78. *Post*, January 4, 1919, emphasis in the original.

79. *Colorado Club Woman* (May 1923): 3.

CHAPTER 6: THE COLORADO KLAN AND THE DECLINE OF PROGRESSIVISM

1. D. C. Burns to E. P. Costigan, November 17, 1923, Edward Costigan Papers, Box 38, FF 4, Archives, University of Colorado at Boulder Libraries. On the CPPA effort, see David L. Waterhouse, *The Progressive Movement of 1924 and the Development of Interest Group Liberalism* (New York: Garland Publishing, 1991), and David Montgomery, *The Fall of the House of Labor: The Workplace, the State, and American Labor Activism, 1865–1925* (Cambridge: Cambridge University Press, 1987).

2. *Colorado Labor Advocate*, February 14 and 28; March 6 and 27; May 15, 1924.

3. Ibid., May 22 and 29, 1924; *Denver Labor Bulletin*, June 14, 1924.

4. *Denver Labor Bulletin*, June 14 and 21, 1924.

5. D. C. Burns to E. P. Costigan, February 16, 1924, and May 12, 1924, Costigan Papers, Box 38, FF 5.

6. While labor support for the La Follette campaign has received extensive treatment from historians, the Colorado experience remains largely neglected. For an overview on the national campaign, see Brett Flehinger, " 'Public Interest': Robert M. La Follette and the Economics of Democratic Progressivism" (Ph.D. diss., Harvard University, Cambridge, MA, 1997), 416–433; David L. Waterhouse, *The Progressive Movement of 1924 and the Development of Interest Group Liberalism* (New York: Garland, 1991); David P. Thelen, *Robert M. La Follette and the Insurgent Spirit* (Boston: Little Brown, 1976); Robert H. Zieger, *Republicans and Labor, 1919–1929* (Lexington: University of Kentucky Press, 1969).

7. *Colorado Labor Advocate*, July 24 and September 18, 1924; *Denver Express*, August 15, 1924.

8. *Denver Labor Bulletin*, September 13 and 20, 1924; August 16, 1924; Vance Monroe et al. to John M. Nelson, LaFollette national campaign manager, July 29, 1924, Costigan Papers, Box 38, FF 5, Archives, University of Colorado at Boulder Libraries.

9. D. C. Burns to E. P. Costigan, July 30, 1924, and letter of November 17, 1923; Earl Hoage et al. to E. P. Costigan, July 31, 1924, Costigan Papers, Box 38, FF 5, Archives, University of Colorado at Boulder Libraries.

10. E. P. Costigan telegram to Robert M. LaFollette Jr., September 9, 1924; C. B. Warner, Colorado Chairman of the Farmer-Labor Party, to E. P. Costigan, September 18, 1924, Costigan Papers, Box 38, FF 5, Archives, University of Colorado at Boulder Libraries; *Denver Labor Bulletin*, October 11 and 18, 1924.

11. Phil Goodstein, *In the Shadow of the Klan: When the KKK Ruled Denver, 1920–1926* (Denver: New Social Publications, 2006), 100–116.

12. Ibid., 133–136. Candlish had sponsored the Industrial Commission bill as a state legislator in 1915.

13. Robert Alan Goldberg, *Hooded Empire: The Ku Klux Klan in Colorado* (Urbana: University of Illinois Press, 1981), 13–29; Goodstein, *In the Shadow of the Klan*, 30–32.

14. "Spy Reports," Philip Van Cise Papers, Box 18, Denver Public Library, Western History Collection, Denver; Goldberg, *Hooded Empire*, 32–34.

15. Quoted in *Denver Express*, August 6, 1924.

16. Goldberg, *Hooded Empire*, 33; *Denver Labor Bulletin*, August 7, 1924; *Colorado Labor Advocate*, August 7 and July 24, 1924, emphasis in the original.

17. *Colorado Labor Advocate*, August 14, 1924; Goldberg, *Hooded Empire*, 34–35; Goodstein, *In the Shadow of the Klan*, 154.

18. *Eighteenth Biennial Report of the Bureau of Labor Statistics of the State of Colorado, 1921–1922* (Denver: Eames Bros., 1922), 32; CSFL, *Proceedings of the 29th Annual Convention* (1924), 60, CSFL Papers, Box 27, Archives, University of Colorado at Boulder Libraries.

19. Harold V. Knight, *Working in Colorado: A Brief History of the Colorado Labor Movement* (Boulder: University of Colorado, Center for Labor Education and Research, 1971), 102; *Denver Labor Bulletin*, July 2 and 16, 1921; May 28, 1921.

20. *Denver Labor Bulletin*, October 22, 1921; February 25, 1922.

21. *Denver Post* (hereafter *Post*), April 7, 1923; Goldberg, *Hooded Empire*, 19–21.

22. *Denver Labor Bulletin*, September 3, 1921, and November 22, 1919; *Denver Catholic Register*, January 23, 1919.

23. Goodstein, *In the Shadow of the Klan*, 32–37, 59, 169.

24. *Denver Post* reporter Forbes Parkhill's interview with James Davis (March 1963), Denver Public Library, Western History and Genealogy, Denver.

25. Goldberg, *Hooded Empire*, 35–47.

26. Nancy MacLean, *Behind the Mask of Chivalry: The Making of the Second Ku Klux Klan* (New York: Oxford University Press, 1994), 14, 79, 81; Robert D. Johnston, *The Radical Middle Class: Populist Democracy and the Question of Capitalism in Progressive Era Portland, Oregon* (Princeton, NJ: Princeton University Press, 2003).

27. Coverage of Lackland's Open Forum speakers was a regular feature of the *Denver Labor Bulletin* and *Colorado Labor Advocate*. For a sample of his pro-labor sermons, see *Denver Labor Bulletin*, September 6, 1919; August 20, 1921; January 7, 1922.

28. CSFL, *Proceedings of the 29th Convention* (1924), 70–71; *Proceedings of the 30th Convention* (1925), 91–93, CSFL Papers, Box 27, Archives, University of Colorado at Boulder Libraries; Phil Goodstein, *In the Shadow of the Klan*, 161–164, 338–343.

29. *Post*, April 4, 1935; Goldberg, *Hooded Empire*, 15–16.

30. Van Cise, "Spy Report," May 26, 1924, in the Philip Van Cise Collection, Western History and Genealogy, Denver Public Library. On the useful distinction between masculinity and manliness in these years, see Gail Bederman, *Manliness and Civilization: A Cultural History of Gender and Race in the United States, 1880–1917* (Chicago: University of Chicago Press, 1995).

31. Van Cise, "Spy Reports," April 28, May 5, May 12, June 30, July 14, 1924, Philip Van Cise Collection, Western History and Genealogy, Denver Public Library. Locke's performances suggest the value of analyzing masculinity as a kind of theatrical spectacle. For an insightful work on the ways in which British authors in the nineteenth century fashioned manhood in theatrical terms, see James Eli Adams, *Dandies and Desert Saints: Styles of Victorian Manhood* (Ithaca, NY: Cornell University Press, 1995).

32. Van Cise "Spy Report," June 30, September 1, 1924, Philip Van Cise Collection, Western History and Genealogy, Denver Public Library; James Davis interview with state senator Francis Knauss (February 18, 1963), Denver Public Library, Western History Collection, Denver.

33. *Rocky Mountain News* (hereafter *News*), September 5 and October 4, 1923.

34. Goldberg, *Hooded Empire*, 68–73.

35. *Denver Express*, September 5 and October 30, 1924; *Post*, September 5, 1924.

36. *Post*, September 9, 10, 11, and 12, 1924.

37. Goldberg, *Hooded Empire*, 71.

38. *Post*, September 23, 1924; *Colorado Labor Advocate*, August 14 and October 2, 1924; *Denver Labor Bulletin*, February 4, 1922.

39. *Post*, November 4, 1924; *Colorado Labor Advocate*, November 6, 1924.

40. Goldberg, *Hooded Empire*, 81–82.

41. *Post*, January 22 and February 9, 1925. For earlier debates over prizefighting in Denver, see *News*, September 16, 1923.

42. *Post*, March 14, 1925; *News*, March 14, 1925; Goodstein, *In the Shadow of the Klan*, 261–263.

43. Kathleen M. Blee, *Women of the Klan: Racism and Gender in the 1920s* (Berkeley: University of California Press, 1991); MacLean, *Behind the Mask*.

44. *Post*, January 8 and 9, 1925; Goodstein, *In the Shadow of the Klan*, 412–416. See also Locke's mild handling of a recently divorced Klansman and the disappointment of the Klan audience in Van Cise, "Spy Report," July 14, 1924.

45. *Post*, February 24 and March 14, 1925.

46. Ibid., April 11, 1925; *Denver Catholic Register*, April 16, 1925; *Post*, April 17, 1925.

47. Goldberg notes that Colorado Klansman threatened several black residents of Denver with violence in 1922, including the president of the National Association for the Advancement of Colored People. The homes of several black families that attempted to move into predominantly white neighborhoods were bombed in 1921, but the Klan did not claim responsibility for the attacks. *Hooded Empire*, 17, 26.

48. Quoted in the *Post*, January 13, 1925.

49. *Denver Express*, January 16, 1925.

50. *Denver Express*, January 16, 1925; *Post*, January 14, 1925; Goodstein, *In the Shadow of the Klan*, 248–252.

51. *Post*, January 31, 1925.

52. Ibid., February 2, 1925; Goodstein, *In the Shadow of the Klan*, 260.

53. Report of the Trained Nurses Association of Denver Annual Meeting (1925) and Morley letter to Katharine DeWitt, March 11, 1925, in Governor Morley Papers, Box 27211, FF 1, Colorado State Archives, Denver; *Colorado Club Woman* (March 1925): 9.

54. *Colorado Club Woman* (May 1925): 12; *Denver Express*, February 27 and March 13, 1925; Thomas A. Krainz, "Implementing Poor Relief: Colorado's Progressive-Era Welfare State" (Ph.D. diss., University of Colorado, Boulder, 2000), 360–361. On the

unusual coalition of social workers, Klan legislators, and national blind advocates who cooperated to wrest control of a benefits program from the Colorado blind community, see Thomas A. Kranz, "Transforming the Progressive Era Welfare State: Activists for the Blind and Blind Benefits," *Journal of Policy History* 15, no. 2 (2003): 223–264.

55. Goldberg, *Hooded Empire,* 87–91; *Post,* February 23, 1925; Goodstein, *In the Shadow of the Klan,* 263–266.

56. Goodstein, *In the Shadow of the Klan,* 398–399.

57. *Child Welfare Magazine* 15 (August 1921): 251; Ben Lindsey, "The Juvenile Court of the Future," in Ben B. Lindsey Collection, Box 2, FF 2, Denver Public Library, Western History and Genealogy, Denver.

58. Charles Larsen, *The Good Fight: The Life and Times of Ben. B. Lindsey* (Chicago: Quadrangle Books, 1972), 192–196.

59. *Colorado Club Woman* (March 1925): 9.

60. *Denver Express,* January 15, 1925; *Colorado Club Woman* (January–February 1925): 8; *Post,* January 23; February 3 and 4, 1925.

61. Minutes of the Meeting of Board of Control (February 6, 1925), Child Welfare Bureau Papers, Colorado State Archives, Denver.

62. *Post,* February 26, 1925.

63. *Colorado Club Woman* (February 1923): 7; (March 1925): 14; (May 1925): 12; *Post,* February 5 and 27, 1925.

64. *Post,* February 10, April 3, 1925; *Colorado Labor Advocate,* April 16, 1925.

65. Goodstein, *In the Shadow of the Klan,* 271–272.

66. *Colorado Labor Advocate,* May 13 and 20, 1926; Goodstein, *In the Shadow of the Klan,* 304–310, 334–338.

67. *Post,* January 28; February 5; April 17, 1925.

68. Goldberg, *Hooded Empire,* 103–108.

69. *Post,* August 10, 1925.

70. Gail M. Beaton, "The Widening Sphere of Women's Lives: The Literary Study and Philanthropic Work of Six Women's Clubs in Denver, 1881–1945," *Essays in Colorado History* 13 (1992): 38–39.

71. Meeting Minutes of the Women's Ku Klux Klan (1926–1927), Gano and Laurena Senter Manuscript Collection, Box 36, FF 10, Denver Public Library, Western History Collection, Denver; Blee, *Women of the Klan,* chapter 5.

72. James F. Wickens, "Tightening the Colorado Purse Strings," *Colorado Magazine* 46, no. 4 (Fall 1969): 271–272; *News,* February 5, 1954.

73. *Colorado Labor Advocate,* August 12 and 26; September 23; October 7, 1926; *Post,* November 1, 1926.

74. *Colorado Club Woman* (September 1926): 6–9, 15; "Resolutions Adopted by the Colorado Federation of Women's Clubs at Greeley, September 17, 1926," reported in *Colorado Club Woman* (October 1926): 13 and (May 1929): 7.

75. *Post,* February 26, 1917.

76. Ibid., January 11, 1927.

77. Carl Abbott, *Colorado: A History of the Centennial State* (Boulder: Colorado Associated University Press, 1976), 215–218.

78. *Session Laws, 26th General Assembly* (Denver: Eames Bros., 1927); *Colorado Labor Advocate,* March 10, 1927; *Colorado Club Woman* (March 1927): 9; *Colorado Labor Advocate,* March 17 and 31, April 11, 1927.

79. Frank Palmer, "War in Colorado," *The Nation* (December 7, 1927): 623–624; *Colorado Labor Advocate*, November 10, October 24, 1927; Phil Goodstein, "Colorado's First Columbine Massacre," in *Slaughter in Serene: The Columbine Coal Strike Reader*, ed. Lowell May and Richard Myers (Denver: Bread and Roses Cultural Center, 2005), 114–116.

80. Goodstein, "Colorado's First Columbine Massacre," 117–119.

81. *Colorado Labor Advocate*, November 24, December 1 and 8, 1927.

82. Ibid., October 25, November 1, 1928; *Post*, November 4, 1928.

83. *Post*, January 8, 1929; *Colorado Labor Advocate*, March 14, 1929; *Colorado Club Woman* (May 1929): 7 and (September 1929): 13–14.

84. Larsen, *The Good Fight*, 194–197.

85. Ibid., 204–213.

EPILOGUE: THE PROGRESSIVE LEGACY

1. James F. Wickens, "Tightening the Colorado Purse Strings," *Colorado Magazine* 46 (Fall 1969): 271–272.

2. Quoted in Charles Larsen, *The Good Fight: The Life and Times of Ben. B. Lindsey* (Chicago: Quadrangle Books, 1972), 216.

3. Stephen J. Leonard, *Trials and Triumphs: A Colorado Portrait of the Great Depression* (Niwot: University Press of Colorado, 1993), 43–44; Ellen Slatkin, "A History of the Response of the Colorado State Federation of Labor and the Great Depression, 1929–1940" (master's thesis, University of Denver, Denver, 1984), 46–49, 78; Wickens, "Tightening the Colorado Purse Strings," 275–278.

4. On the impact of the Conference for Progressive Political Action program in the West generally, see David Montgomery, *The Fall of the House of Labor: The Workplace, the State, and American Labor Activism, 1865–1925* (Cambridge: Cambridge University Press, 1987), 436.

5. Speech given in Greeley, July 23, 1934, quoted in Wickens, "Tightening the Colorado Purse Strings," 273–274.

6. John Putnam, "A 'Test of Chiffon Politics': Gender Politics in Seattle, 1897–1917," *Pacific Historical Review* 69, no. 4 (2000): 608–611.

7. *Biennial Report of the Secretary of State of Colorado, 1913–1914* (Denver: Secretary of State, 1914), 4. For an analysis of corporate manipulations of the initiative system in 1912, see Daniel A. Smith and Joseph Lubinski, "Direct Democracy during the Progressive Era: A Crack in the Populist Veneer?" *Journal of Policy History* 14 (2002): 357–367.

8. Elinor McGinn, *A Wide Awake Woman: Josephine Roche in the Age of Reform* (Denver: Colorado Historical Society, 2002), 63–68; Marjorie Hornbein, "Josephine Roche: Social Worker and Coal Operator," *The Colorado Magazine* 53 (Summer 1976): 243.

9. Sarah Deutsch has noted that contemporary reports found more prostitutes came out of domestic service than any other occupation. Middle-class matrons labeled public and working-class spaces as dangerous, when statistics indicated that their own domestic space posed the greater threat to working-class women. Sarah Deutsch, *Women and the City: Gender, Space, and Power in Boston, 1870–1940*. (New York: Oxford University Press, 2000), 76. Lindsey and Roche rarely commented on these domestic dangers. Because the judge destroyed many court records after his unsuccessful battle with the Klan, we lack a full picture of his handling of these cases.

10. Maureen Flanagan, *Seeing with their Hearts: Chicago Women and the Vision of the Good City, 1871–1933* (Princeton, NJ: Princeton University Press 2002), 201.

11. McGinn, *Wide Awake Woman*, 82–95; Roche quoted on page 96.

12. *Rocky Mountain News*, October 23, 1944, quoted in James F. Wickens, "The New Deal in Colorado," *Pacific Historical Review* 38, no. 3 (August 1969): 291.

Index

Adams, William ("Billy"), 173, 177, 181–183, 184, 185, 186
Addams, Jane, 4, 20, 33, 175
Adkins v. Children's Hospital, 141
African Americans, 9, 25, 31, 155, 158, 164, 218n70, 221n47. *See also* Colored Citizens League
Alamosa State Normal School, 181
All Saints Episcopal Church, 161
Allen, Henry, 112, 113, 114, 115
Amalgamated Meat Cutters and Butcher Workmen's Union, 109–111
American Association for Labor Legislation, 134
American Federation of Labor (AFL), 23, 41, 44, 99, 106, 114, 115, 116, 118, 120, 155
American Legion, 87–88, 170
American Union Workmen, 162
Ammons, Elias, 52, 54–56, 63
Annear, Thomas, 123, 183, 184
Anti-Coercion Act, 49, 105

Anti-Prohibition Association, 59
Anti-Saloon League, 14, 26, 30, 57–59, 75
Appeal to Reason, 112
Armour and Company, 110
Arnold, Henry, 35–37, 39, 68, 69
Asian immigration, 159, 160, 162
Auman, Orrin, 37

"Baby Richard," 178, 180
Baby saving campaigns, 130, 133
Bailey, Adelia, 137
Bailey, Dewey, 75, 76, 77, 81, 86, 90, 157, 158, 159, 160
Baker, Newton, 212n64
Baker, Ray Stannard, 44
Bakery and Confectionery Workers Union, 99
Baldwin-Felts detectives, 54
Ballou, C. C., 89, 90
Barela, Casimiro, 53–54
Belgian immigrants, 117

225

Bell, Joseph, 98
Belmont, Mrs. O.H.P., 137
Berry, Joseph, 53
Beth Eden Baptist Church, 161
Bigelow, May, 134, 148
Birth control, 142, 143, 150, 151
Board of Charities and Corrections (Colorado), 5, 173, 174, 175
Board of Public Works (Denver), 17
Boatright, William, 184, 185
Boehm, Keith, 169, 174
Boettcher, Charles, 77
Boxing, 59, 165, 169, 176, 183
Bradford, Mary, 25, 33, 135, 136, 139, 144, 176
Brake, Edwin, 46, 48, 49, 61–62
Bryan, William Jennings, 33, 41–42, 47, 63–64
Building Trades Council (Denver), 25, 32, 34
Bull Moose Party, 51. *See also* Progressive Party
Burcher, Frank, 46
Bureau of Child and Animal Protection, 175
Bureau of Labor Statistics (Colorado), 5, 46, 98, 102, 103, 104, 105, 123, 132, 140, 159, 176
Burt, Allan, 82

Candlish, William, 98, 100, 101, 157, 170, 220n12
Canon City, 164
Carlson, George, 57, 59–61, 63, 97, 98, 100, 102, 122, 157, 174
Carlton, Newcomb, 104–105
Cathedral of the Immaculate Conception, 87, 160
Catholic Daughters of America, 138
Central Coal and Coke, 112
Central Presbyterian Church, 26, 39, 70
CFWC. *See* Colorado Federation of Women's Clubs
Chamber of Commerce (Denver) 24, 35, 69, 70, 170. *See also* Civic and Commercial Association
Chase, Edward, 17
Cheeseman, Walter, 18
Child labor, 50, 117, 126, 127, 134, 135, 138, 139, 140, 147, 148, 150, 183
Child Study Movement, 127
Child Welfare Bureau (CWB), 5, 133, 143–150, 151, 175, 176; Board of Control, 144
Child Welfare Committee, 133, 135, 138, 139

Christian Citizenship Union, 15–17, 31, 34–38, 69–70, 121, 127, 130, 197n9
Chucovitch, Vaso, 17
CIC. *See* Colorado Industrial Commission
Citizens' Alliance, 22–23, 25, 34, 46, 49
Citizens' Party, 32, 34, 36–37, 62
City Beautiful, 12, 18, 24, 25, 26, 27, 28, 35, 37
City Council (Denver), 20, 25, 26, 29, 31, 32, 36, 67, 68, 70, 71, 74, 76, 77, 80, 142, 143, 177
Civic and Commercial Association (Denver), 70, 74, 98, 114. *See also* Chamber of Commerce
Civic Federation (Denver), 14, 31, 126
Clean Denver Men's Committee, 69
Cline, Foster, 130
Coal mine inspection, 52
Coal Operators Association (Kansas), 112, 115
Coen, John, 173
Colorado Federation of Women's Clubs (CFWC), 25, 42, 44, 126, 136, 138, 139, 141, 143, 145, 151, 173; Child Welfare Department, 144; Division of Mothercraft, 150; Legislative Committee and Legislative Council, 49, 126, 135–136, 137–139, 141, 172–173, 182
Colorado Fuel and Iron Company (CFI), 4, 5, 9, 50, 53–54, 55, 57, 58, 59, 62, 70, 91, 97, 98, 106, 107, 108, 109, 116, 183, 184
Colorado Industrial Commission (CIC), 9, 92; creation of, 97–98; and electoral politics, 118–123; 176, 177; investigations of meat packing strike, 109–111; investigations of mine strikes, 106–109, 183–185; labor protests against, 99–102
Colorado State Federation of Labor (CSFL), 4, 22, 25, 28, 42, 43–46, 49, 52, 55, 59, 69, 99, 101, 111, 119, 147, 154, 155, 156, 162, 163, 177, 184; Legislative Committee, 100
Colorado Towel and Supply Company, 46
Colorado Visiting Nurses Association, 149
Colored Citizens League, 159
Columbine Massacre, 184–185
Commercial Telegraphers Union of America, 104, 188
Commission government (Denver), 35, 36, 37, 39, 66, 68–71, 192
Committee of Fifty-Five, 74, 79, 80
Committee on Public Information, 70
Committee on Social Legislation, 134
Commons, John, 4, 96, 97, 98, 101, 109

Companionate Marriage, 143
Conference for Progressive Political Action (CPPA), 154–156
Conkle, James, 34, 49
Cooper, Ryley, 84
Corse, May, 140, 142
Coss, John, 109
Costigan, Edward, 1–3, 6, 12, 26–27, 31, 34–36, 39, 45, 69, 70, 97, 121; campaign for governor in 1912, 50–52; campaign for governor in 1914, 57–60, 63–64; and 1924 Progressive Party campaign, 155, 156; 163, 175; as U.S. Senator, 189, 190, 192
Costigan, Mabel, 45, 155
Council of Jewish Women, 138
Coyle, Robert, 26, 70
Craig, Katherine, 144, 188
Creel, George, 13, 36, 38–39, 49, 70, 127
Cripple Creek Mining Strike, 2, 4, 14, 22
CSFL. *See* Colorado State Federation of Labor
Cudahy Meatpacking, 110
CWB. *See* Child Welfare Bureau

Darrow, Clarence, 162
David, Mrs. Ray S., 66
Davis, John, 155, 156
DeBusk, Samuel, 100, 205n21
Decker, Sarah Platt, 27, 33, 42, 126, 136, 137, 175
De Lochte, Carl, 176
Democratic Party National Convention, 41
Densmore, George, 98
Denver Business Men's League, 24; Women's Auxiliary, 24
Denver Commission of Religious Forces, 66, 93
Denver District Court, 46, 81, 90
Denver Evangelical Association, 62
Denver Law Enforcement League, 26
Denver Rock Drill Company, 73
Denver Trades and Labor Assembly (DTLA), 21, 23, 25, 32, 34, 44, 45, 47, 69, 78, 82, 99, 110, 111, 140, 141
Denver Tramway Company, 13, 18, 31, 68, 70; and government regulations, 71–75; and the strike of 1919, 75–81; and the strike of 1920, 65–67, 81–89
Denver Union Water Company, 18, 32, 58
Denver Voters Federation, 69
Denver Woman's Club, 15, 25, 27, 45, 62, 126, 132, 148, 155, 172, 173, 175, 178, 216n23

Department of Charities and Corrections (Colorado), 5, 173, 174, 175
Department of Maternity, Child Welfare, and Public Health (proposed), 174
Department of the Treasury (Colorado), 192
Devine, Edward, 66
Dick, Florence, 144
Direct Democracy League, 42, 51
Direct Legislation League, 33, 38, 47
Direct primary reform, 3, 9, 47, 137, 153, 177, 179, 185, 192
DTLA. *See* Denver Trades and Labor Assembly

Easley, Ralph, 101
East Side Woman's Club (Denver), 101
Eastwood, Sidney, 33
Eaton, William, 98
Eight Hour Bill (Miners'), 43, 49
Eisler, George, 33–34
Employers' Liability Bill, 50
English immigrants, 117, 162
Equal Rights Amendment (ERA), 137
Erdman Act, 208n3
Evans, Hiram Wesley, 169, 178
Evans, William Gray, 18, 31, 67, 68

False Advertising Bill, 49–50
Farmer-Labor Party, 156
Farmers Alliance, 14
Farr, Jefferson, 53
Federal Emergency Relief Administration, 189, 190
Federation of Kansas Industries, 118
Fire and Police Board (Denver) 12, 17
First Reformed Church, 26
Fisher, Harry, 15, 37. *See also* Christian Citizenship Union
Fitch, John, 116–117
"Five-cents or nothing" clubs, 73, 75
Forbes, Dr. Roy, 146, 147
Forster, Elizabeth, 149
Fouse, David, 26
Frankfurter, Felix, 102, 103
French immigrants, 117

Gabriel, John, 31, 34–35
Garman, Harvey, 46, 50
General Federation of Women's Clubs, 133, 141, 147
German immigrants, 117, 147, 168
Gilman, Charlotte Perkins, 162

Giron, Florenda, 148
Gompers, Samuel, 115, 116, 119
Good Friday Raids, 170
Grace Community Church, 143, 160, 162
Graham, Royal, 174, 175, 186
Grant Avenue Methodist Church, 37, 161
Greek immigrants, 160, 170
Gregory, Ida, 128
Griffith, Ben, 121, 122
Griffith, Emily, 176
Guffy, Ernest, 113
Gunter, Julius, 99, 100, 101, 105, 130, 131
Gustin, Bruce, 73, 77, 79, 86, 170, 181

Hall, G. Stanley, 127
Hamilton, Grant, 99–101
Hamrock, Patrick, 55
Headlee, Elmer, 172
Herrington, Cass, 75
Hershey, Reuben, 164
Highlands Christian Church, 161
Hild, Frederic, 71, 77, 89
Hill, May, 141, 143
Hilts, Hiram, 98
Holmberg, John, 177
Home Rule Charter (Denver), 14–17, 67, 74
Honest Elections League, 14, 15, 23, 38
Hoover, Herbert, 142
Hornbein, Philip, 157
Houston, Clint, 99, 101, 103
Howat, Alexander, 112, 115, 118
Huggins, William, 113, 114, 115, 116
Hunter, John, 37, 69

Industrial Commission. See Colorado Industrial Commission
Industrial League, 44
Industrial Relations Act, 98, 108, 121, 117, 122
Industrial Workers of the World (IWW), 88, 183, 184, 185
Initiative reform, 2–4, 32, 33, 34, 42, 47, 137, 190
Italian immigrants, 117, 157, 158, 170

Jackson, Josie, 171, 172, 176
Jacobsen, Nettie, 136
Japanese immigration, 159, 160, 162
Jerome, John ("Black Jack"), 83, 84, 85, 89, 90, 91
Jews, 15, 66, 138, 157, 158, 159, 164, 168, 174, 179
Johnson, Belle, 46

Johnson, Edwin ("Big Ed"), 188, 189, 190, 191, 192
Jones, Mary ("Mother"), 55

Kansas Industrial Court, 96, 111–116
Keating, Edward, 15, 18, 21, 26, 28, 31, 32, 34, 36, 47, 49, 53, 70, 147, 165
Keating-Owen Act, 147
Kellogg, Paul, 4, 96
Kerr, Lillian, 137
Kindel, George, 23, 34
King, Clyde, 18
King, MacKenzie, 101
King, Walter, 173
Kiwanis Club, 80, 149
Knights of Labor, 21
Ku Klux Klan (Klan), 9, 10, 138, 153; attacks on women's Progressivism, 171–178; and Ben Stapleton, 157–159; in Colorado government, 169–178; and the Republican party, 163–169; and the working class, 159–163. See also Women of the Ku Klux Klan

Lackland, George, 162
Lafferty, Alma, 33, 56, 137
La Follette, Robert, 153, 154, 155, 156, 163, 168
Lapp, John A., 66
Lathrop, Julia, 132, 144, 150
Laundryman's Association, 46
Laundry Trust, 46
Laundry Workers Local no. 22 (Denver), 45
Lawson, John, 190
League of Women Voters, 136
Lee, Frances, 52
Le Roy, George, 32
Lewis, George, 98, 100, 101
Lewis, Inez Johnson, 138
Linderfeldt, Karl, 55
Lindsey, Benjamin (Ben) Barr, 6, 11–13, 15, 20–21, 25, 26, 27, 31, 34, 36, 38, 39, 151, 186, 188, 191, 197n20; and alliances with women's clubs, 125–130, 133–136; and birth control, 140, 142, 143, 145; and direct democracy, 42, 47, 50, 51; 62, 69, 97, 120; and the Klan, 158–159, 163, 164–165, 168, 169, 171, 174
Lions' Club, 80
Lochner v. New York, 43
Locke, John Galen, 157, 161, 163, 164, 166, 167, 168, 169, 173, 174, 176, 178
Long, Martha, 171, 172, 176, 178, 182

Love, Minnie T., 27, 172, 179
Ludlow massacre, 5, 54–56, 65, 96, 106

maternalism, 5–7, 17, 30, 44, 126, 128, 133, 143–150, 194n10, 214n4
Maternity Benefit legislation, 130, 134, 135, 139, 140, 143, 174
Mathews, Estelle, 144, 175
Matz, Nichols, 22
McHugh, Lerah, 126
McLachlan, George, 25, 49
McLennan, John, 50
McMurray, Thomas, 14
Means, Rice, 141, 158, 159
Meredith, Ellis, 15, 27, 33, 46
Mexican Americans, 9, 117, 147, 148, 149, 160, 218n70
Meyer, Arthur, 100
Mine Owners Association, 22
Minimum wage legislation, 52, 99, 102, 103, 106, 117, 118, 132, 141, 159, 176, 177
Ministerial Alliance (Denver), 3, 14, 69
Minute Men of America, 88, 178
Minute Women, 179
Mitchell, James, 104
Moffat, David, 18
Montgomery, W. H., 198n28
Moore, Julian, 174
Morley, Clarence, 110, 111, 164, 167, 168, 169, 171, 173, 174, 175, 176, 177, 178, 181
Morrissey, William, 103–105, 132, 134
Moser, Ralph, 76, 77, 78, 93, 119
Mothers' Congress, 38, 127, 129, 130, 133, 134, 135
Mothers' Pensions, 126, 129, 134, 139, 151, 173, 174
Mullen, John K., 15
Muller, Curt, 45
Muller v. Oregon, 45, 46
Municipal Ownership League, 31, 32, 34, 69
Munn v. Illinois, 204n4
Munroe, Jessie, 132, 134, 135, 137

Napier, Barney, 130
National Association for the Advancement of Colored People (NAACP), 221n47
National Child Welfare League, 175
National Civic Federation, 101
National Coal Mining Board, 114
National Education Association, 174
National Industrial Recovery Administration, 190

National War Labor Board (NWLB), 71, 102, 105
National Women's Party, 137
New Deal, 150, 187, 189, 190, 191, 192
Noland, James, 102
Non-Partisan Charter League, 35, 36
Non-Partisan League (NPL), 119, 156
Nurses Examiners Board, 172

O'Brien, William, 76, 77, 78, 82, 93
O'Ryan, William, 30, 66

Palmer, Frank, 140, 141, 147, 154, 159, 168, 181
Parent-Teachers' Association (PTA), 133, 138, 139, 144, 145, 146, 175
Park Hill Methodist Church, 37
Patterson, Louise, 139, 148, 172, 176
Patterson, Thomas, 15, 31, 36, 57, 60–61, 63, 70
Paul, Alice, 137
Peabody, James, 22, 23, 27
Peake, May, 137, 139, 148, 155, 158, 159
Pecover, Lena, 148, 149
People's Sunday Alliance, 31
Pillar of Fire Church, 161
Pettee, Annah, 139, 140, 147, 151, 182
Phelps, Horace, 27–28
Phipps, Lawrence, 168
Plumb, Glenn E., 78
Poindexter, Miles, 106
Popular republicanism, 7, 42, 44, 54, 57, 58, 162
Populism, 2, 4, 6, 14, 23, 30, 43, 51, 162
Progressive Mothers Club (Colorado Springs), 144
Progressive Party, 2, 6, 50–52, 57–60, 63, 97, 121, 153, 154, 155, 156
Prohibition, 3, 5, 7, 21, 26, 32, 51, 52, 56, 57, 58, 59, 62, 63, 64, 66, 75, 97, 121, 157, 158, 159, 160, 161, 168, 170, 171, 174, 184, 188, 190
Prohibition Party, 21
Public Service League, 33, 38, 126
Public Utilities Commission (PUC), 68, 71, 73, 74
Public Welfare Department (Colorado), 150
Public Works Board (Denver), 17

Railroad Labor Board, 106
Ranger law, 120, 121, 168, 182, 183
Real Estate Exchange, 70
Red Scare, 70, 88

Reed, Clyde, 113
Referendum reform, 2–4, 42, 47, 49, 137, 190
Reisner, Christian, 42
Revolt of Modern Youth, 143
Riddle, Agnes, 130
Robinson, Helen Ring, 5, 27, 39, 52, 53, 54, 56, 131
Roche, Josephine, 38, 39, 51, 57, 68, 69, 128, 129, 190, 191, 192
Rockefeller, John D., Jr., 53, 57, 59, 63, 91, 98, 108
Rocky Mountain Fuel, 190, 191, 192
Rodgers, Platt, 14
Roosevelt, Franklin, 188, 192
Roosevelt, Theodore, 20, 47, 58–59, 95, 96, 97, 186, 197n17
Rush, John, 14, 15, 31, 34, 35
Rush Act, 14
Ryan, John (reverend), 66, 94, 160, 162

Sanger, Margaret, 143, 162
Saunders, Maude, 130, 139, 144
Schoff, Hannah, 133
Senter, Laurena, 178, 179
"Service-at-Cost" plan, 79
Shaffer, John, 70, 77, 88, 89, 98, 120, 121, 122, 144
Shafroth, John, 47, 48, 49, 50, 62
Shaw, Anna Howard, 131, 132
Shepperd-Towner program, 130, 144, 145, 146, 148, 149, 150, 176
Sherman, Mary, 142
Shoup, Oliver, 90, 108, 109, 120, 122, 123, 133, 134, 138, 144, 145, 181
Silberg, Harry, 82
Smith, Paul, 162
Smith, Matthew (reverend), 161
Social Gospel, 7, 41, 42, 121, 165, 199n57
Social Security, 150
South Broadway Christian Church, 1, 2
Speer, Robert Walter, 12, 13, 21, 39, 98, 158, 165, 174; building the Democratic machine, 17–20; and commission government, 66, 67, 68, 69, 70, 71; first term as mayor, 23–25; and Henry Arnold, 35–37; second term as mayor, 26–30; and state Democrats, 42, 48, 49, 50, 51, 64; and the Tramway, 74, 76, 77, 78, 93; and utility franchises, 30–35; and women Progressives, 126, 153
Stapleton, Ben, 141, 153, 156, 162, 164, 165, 170, 171, 174, 177; recall election of 1923, 157–159

State Voters' League, 1, 26, 31
Steele, Robert, 46
Steele, Wilbur, 27, 28, 29, 60, 61, 71, 72, 73, 79, 80, 166, 167
Steffens, Lincoln, 19, 21, 188
Stelzle, Charles, 199n57
Stocker, Allison, 35
Sunday, Billy, 62–63, 64
Sweet, William, 121, 122, 123, 138, 139, 154, 155, 156, 157, 165, 168, 171, 181, 183
Swift and Company, 110

Taft, William, 51, 71, 118
Taxpayers League, 70
Taxpayers' Reform Association, 14
Taylor, Edward, 125, 126
Temple, James, 23
Ten Days' War, 56, 65, 97, 109
Thornton, William, 81, 82, 93
Thum, Otto, 33, 34, 69, 160, 198n37, 199n57
Tikas, Louis, 55
Trained Nurses Association of Denver, 173
Tramway Adjustment Committee. *See* Committee of Fifty-Five
Tugwell, Rexford, 114

United Mine Workers of America (UMW), 53–55, 97, 106, 107–109, 112, 115, 118, 162, 183, 190
U'Ren, William, 47
United States Census Bureau, 142
United States Children's Bureau, 132, 133, 134, 144, 146, 147
United States Commission on Industrial Relations, 100, 113
United States Conciliation Service, 91

Vaile, Gertrude, 133, 173
Van Cise, Philip, 158, 163, 165, 166, 168, 169, 176
Vincent, Merle, 190
Visible Government League, 165, 168

Waite, Davis, 4, 14
Walsh, Frank, 71, 97, 100, 102, 113
Ward Water Users' Clubs, 33
War Labor Policies Board, 102, 103
Waters, H. B., 2
Wayne, Frances, 62, 150, 151, 175, 182
Welborn, Jesse, 57, 131
Welles, Julia, 17

Western Federation of Miners (WFM), 22, 23, 31, 43, 198n28
Western Union, 104, 105
Weyl, Walter, 114
WFM. *See* Western Federation of Miners
Whipple, Sidney, 158, 159, 165
White, William Allen, 113
Whitehead, Edwin, 175
Whitford, Greeley, 81, 89, 90, 91, 92, 120, 186
Whitney, Gerald, 172
Williams, Wayne, 81, 91, 92
Williamson, Kathryn, 49
Wilson, Woodrow, 56, 70, 100, 102, 105, 130
Wixon, Helen, 27
Wolff Packing Company, 117, 118, 123
Woman's Bryan Club, 42
Women and Children Act, 45, 46, 49, 62
Women of the Ku Klux Klan, 178–181. *See also* Ku Klux Klan

Women's Christian Temperance Union (WCTU), 15, 26, 51, 59, 62, 133
Women's Council of Defense (WCOD), 130–134; Committee on Women in Industry, 132, 141
Women's Eight-Hour legislation, 62, 104, 140, 141
Women's Nonpartisan Association, 27, 33
Women's Non-Partisan Juvenile Court Association, 129
Women's Peace Association, 56
Women's Union Labor Political League, 138, 147
Wood, Leonard, 90
Working People's Political League, 119

Young, William, 183

Zott, L. K., 140, 141
Zott Laundry, 140, 141, 142